The Racism of Psychology

The Racism of Psychology
Time for change

Dennis Howitt
and
J. Owusu-Bempah

HARVESTER
WHEATSHEAF

New York London Toronto Sydney Tokyo Singapore

First published 1994 by
Harvester Wheatsheaf
Campus 400, Maylands Avenue
Hemel Hempstead
Hertfordshire HP2 7EZ
A division of
Simon & Schuster International Group

© 1994 Dennis Howitt and J. Owusu-Bempah

Typeset in 10/12 pt Times
by The Midlands Book Typesetting Company, Loughborough

Printed and bound in Great Britain
by BPC Wheatons Ltd, Exeter

British Library Cataloguing in Publication Data

A catalogue record for this book is available from
the British Library

ISBN 0–7450–1352–X (pbk)

1 2 3 4 5   98 97 96 95 94

Contents

Contents

Chapter 1

Psychologists, racism and society

Being largely a product of technological culture, applied psychology has concerned itself primarily with the needs and institutions of industrial societies. . . . Basic or academic psychology has shown some interest in societies fundamentally different from our own . . . but the primary focus of interest has usually been not the other societies as such but what they might tell us about our psychological theories. (Connolly, 1985, p. 251)

There are remarkable continuities in the racism of psychology which span much of the discipline's history and present. If nothing active and positive is done about it, racism will continue to alienate psychology from much of its subject matter. It is dangerous to believe that racism was a thing of psychology's early years, irrelevant to its present. The parallels with modern race-thinking are so close that only the most foolhardy could claim psychology to be racism-free. Psychology's racism reflects the complex racist society of which it is a part.

The biographies of individual psychologists are affected in various ways by racism. While racism may be a world-wide phenomenon, the contrast between victimiser and victim, exploiter and exploited, oppressor and oppressed is at its starkest between Europe and Africa – black and white. One of us is white, the other black, so our experiences collectively reflect strongly some of the extremes of racism. For Dennis Howitt, born in mid-twentieth-century Britain, black people impinged little on his childhood experiences. Just a few things can be recalled – the Sikh man, with his suitcase, peddling household goods from door to door; a church member being a missionary in Africa; adventure stories held black people to be untrustworthy and treacherous; and the ubiquitous reply to a query about a mother's whereabouts: 'She's run away with a black man.' Perhaps an inculcation of a gentle fear, this was not a traumatic matter. Where were the black

1

men to be run away with? Race had little day-to-day significance, racial hostility was generally acceptable in the community, but black people represented nothing other than distant, abstract generalised target.

The experiences of Owusu-Bempah, born in colonial Ghana, have been radically different. White people did not live in a distant continent but impinged on daily life. Instead of being taught to fear foreigners, Ghanaian children learned a different lesson – children's story books told how to be welcoming, kind and helpful to foreigners, especially Europeans, the most foreign of all. Most of the secondary schools were boarding establishments run by European missionaries. His was Catholic, staffed by white priest teachers. In school he sang the British national anthem, *God Save the Queen*. Geography, history, literature and the rest were all European. Little was told about Ghana and virtually nothing about Africa. All subjects, including Greek, Greek mythology, Latin and French, were taught in English and he was encouraged to adopt French as his second language, following English. The language he spoke at home was forbidden; even Asante folk-stories had to be told in English. As with generations before him, he was indoctrinated to serve all things European, to reject Africa and its culture – to talk, worship, dress, dream, think and eat European.

British colonial history is held to be a thing of pride, deserving his gratitude: 'the British character has done . . . so much throughout the world' (Margaret Thatcher, quoted by Barker, 1981, p .15). Even now, he is expected to be thankful to Europeans for the schools, hospitals, roads and railways they built in Africa. However, these things were done for Europe's advantage and Africa's exploitation. In much of Africa, everyone but Africans had servants, it therefore did not surprise him, on coming to Britain, to find black people occupying lowly positions. However, the flagrant racism in British society was a big shock. During a fifteen–year nursing career in Britain, white staff and patients frequently referred to him as 'a monkey'. He was told to accept as a sign of endearment being called 'a black bastard' by a nursing colleague. 'Mentally subnormal patients', as they were then called, relied on him to fulfil their basic needs like feeding and washing but, nevertheless, echoed the abuse. In bars tramps patronise him; he is asked in court whether he is planning to return to the jungle; he is told by those who should know better that he was not appointed to a teaching post in higher education because of his African accent; and the authorship of his publications is questioned.

These may be the experiences of individuals, but they also have parallels in psychology. The history of modern Western psychology (e.g., Boring, 1950; O'Neil, 1968) shows its emergence in the context of European conquest, exploitation and domination. And psychologists, possibly more than members of any other discipline, have sought to impose their own European definition of reality upon the rest of the world.

Race theories and racial policy

Psychology has long played a Byzantine game with racism. The basic ploy is one of scientific detachment, a smoke-screen for psychology's racist work. Usually the question is 'who are the racists in psychology?' But this needs to be reversed: Who is not racist in psychology? Psychology breathes in the air of racism. A misplaced and unfounded trust in the independence of psychologists from racial bias takes its toll in that the profession regards racism as the evil work of a few. Such a view promotes a particular and peculiar conception of racism which pushes the issue to the margins of most psychologists' thinking; by emphasising the biological aspects of racism the problem's full extent is ignored.

The social constructionist view is that scientific knowledge is a social creation serving the purposes of society's dominant institutions (Gergen, 1985). This type of analysis changes the emphasis significantly. Instead of merely asking what psychology says about racism, one should also ask: what does psychology do for racism? Most psychological perspectives on racism have been the work of white academics with, historically, very little input from black psychologists. It is a white view of racism serving white people's purposes. There are exceptions to this rule. The ones which most readily come to mind are Kenneth Clark's work on segregation (Clark, 1965; Clark and Clark, 1939; 1947) and the Jewish theoreticians who evolved the concept of the authoritarian personality. But these people were seeking to do something about the damage done by white racism. Rather, it has been more common for discussions of race to serve the powerful in white societies. In other words, academic discussions of race have frequently been incorporated into sweeping and draconian social policies which serve white people's interests, at the expense of black people. Hume, Malthus, Spencer, Thorndike, Jensen and Eysenck are famous names spanning three centuries of academic endeavour, who have proposed race theories with adverse social policy implications for the well-being of black people. Thus, they are worthy of study as much for their beliefs about social policy as anything else.

Psychologists have tended to bifurcate the issue of racism in the discipline into that of the 'good' liberal and the 'bad' racist bigot. However, in reality there is no stark choice between racism and liberalism. The racism of psychology stretches beyond simple dichotomies. Many psychologists are aware of some racists in psychology's past and present. While these 'great men' or historical figures serve to define aspects of racism in psychology, they may also serve to narrow perspectives on racism within the discipline too much, a danger this book seeks to highlight.

David Hume (1711–76): Between the sixteenth and early twentieth centuries, European scholars and scientists resolutely convinced themselves of the innate inferiority of black people. More than any other, Hume laid down for them the methods of scholarly racism which could justify slavery and domination world-wide. Concerning 'Negroes' he wrote:

> They are characterised by idleness, treachery, revenge, cruelty, impudence, stealing, lying, profanity, debauchery, nastiness and intemperance. They, that is the Negroes, are strangers to every sentiment of compassion, and are an awful example of the corruption of man left to himself. (BBC TV, 1983)

In other words, black people were characterised much as Satan would be. This characterisation helped assuage Christian consciences which might have baulked at slavery's atrocities. Others expanded Hume's inventory so far to claim that African's were black to the core: 'The membrane, the muscles, the tendons and all the fluids and secretions, even the Negro's brain and nerves are tinctured with the shade of pervading darkness' (*Encyclopaedia Britannica*, 1810). Presumably this meant that even the semen of black men was black. It is interesting to note that the 'black baby' myth which has lingered into recent times reflects similar thinking (Pearson, 1973). This myth suggests that long after a sexual encounter between a white woman and a black man, her subsequent children will be black.

Thomas Malthus (1766–1834): Malthus was *the* founding father of scientific racism (Chase, 1977) and provided a blueprint for the extermination of the poor, the sick, the weak and the 'unfit'. These included, amongst others, black people. His *Essay on the Principle of Population* (1798) argued:

> If we dread the too frequent visitation of the horrid of famine, we should sedulously encourage the other form of destruction. . . . Instead of recommending cleanliness to the poor, we should encourage contrary habits. In our towns we should make the streets narrower, crowd more people into the houses, and court the return of the plague. (quoted by Chase, 1977, p. 6)

Malthus regarded it against the laws of God and nature to tamper with poverty. Humankind's ability to produce babies was held to always outstrip the food supply. Global famine, however, was not his primary concern – he wanted to protect the existing social order which favoured his class. Their increased wealth and privilege at the expense of the poor was his pragmatic philosophy.

Nor should it be overlooked the extent to which Malthus represented a stream of thought which culminated in some of the extremes of racism. Adolf Hitler's philosophy was more than reminiscent of Malthus':

> Hitler analysed the prospect facing Germany of a continual increase in population numbers and demand. His fundamental assumption was a world of scarcity. Hitler recognised that continual growth of numbers and levels of demand within, to use the modern term, the limited 'carrying capacity' of the German ecosystem would lead eventually to increasing misery and ultimately starvation. Hitler considered four possible solutions to the population/resource disequilibrium; three would be rejected. (Stein, 1987, p. 254)

Malthus' ideas are alive in the current view that famine in the so-called Third World is caused by over-population. The West's economic, political and cultural invasion and exploitation of these countries is commonly ignored as the major factor in the creation of such catastrophes. In truth, it is Western rapacity, and not the scarcity of essentials, which is responsible for much of the plight of black nations (Clark, 1986). Eckholm (1982) calculated that 2 per cent of the grain fed to animals to provide meat for the Western world would be sufficient to deal with undernutrition. Sterilisation of the poor and similar population control measures may not be necessarily the 'logical' solution that at first they appear. Many of the main objectives of population control could be met by Western countries paying back just a little.

Herbert Spencer (1820–1903): Spencer took Darwin's theory of natural selection and honed it into a powerful tool of social policy. The phrase 'the survival of the fittest' reflects Spencer's disdain for the poor and the weak. Based on powerful Darwinian ideas, it provided 'scientific' justification for his opposition to fundamental social reforms including universal education, minimum standards of health, occupational safety and sanitation (Bulhan, 1985; Chase, 1977; Yeboah, 1988). Spencer claimed that those in poverty were born inferior and therefore deserving of early death. On the basis of the hereditary transmission of many characteristics, he argued for a 'pragmatic eugenics' in his *Principles of Psychology* (1870) – selective breeding was necessary in order to eliminate 'unfit' races. In his hierarchy of the unfit, black people were inferior to the least worthy white person.

Edward Thorndike (1874–1949): The social policies of prominent historical figures in psychology such as Spencer are rarely stressed by psychology's historians (e.g. Boring, 1950; O'Neil, 1968). Nevertheless, Spencer's version of the 'science of eugenics' influenced many psychologists. Thorndike was typical of these (Chase, 1977). His standard textbooks on mental development, the psychology of education and child psychology greatly affected both the psychology and the teaching professions. In terms of the education of the poor and underprivileged, Thorndike's policy recommendations were crystal clear: 'operations seem more beneficent than those of an equal amount of time and skills spent in social education' (quoted by Chase, 1977, p. 354). In other words, he preferred the eugenic solution of compulsory sterilisation to any psychological or educational intervention.

Arthur Jensen (1923–): Nowadays Jensen is probably a better-re-membered name in educational psychology than Thorndike and his contemporaries. Nevertheless, like Thorndike, he proposed a variant of Spencer's ideas. In 1969, in a notorious article, this professor of educational psychology asked: 'How much can we boost IQ and scholastic achievement?' Echoing some earlier writers, Jensen pondered on the 'higher birthrates' among black Americans: 'Is there a danger that current welfare policies, unaided by eugenic foresight, could lead to the genetic enslavement of a substantial segment of our total population?' (Jensen, 1969, p. 95). The mental abilities inherited by the typical black child differed qualitatively from those of white children, according to Jensen. He also believed that much of the education for black children was a waste of resources. He found attempts to compensate for early learning disadvantage amongst black children, caused by social disadvantage and discrimination, particularly wasteful of resources – the problem lay in the inferiority of black genes which could *not* be dealt with by throwing money into their education. Jensen's views caused a major public furore which stretched well beyond the boundaries of his discipline. But Jensen was not alone, and his work attracted a number of important supporters both in North America and Europe.

H.J. Eysenck (1916–): This distinguished European psychologist was a foremost defender and proponent of Jensen's ideas. It is well worth examining Eysenck's argument in some detail since it provides an illustration of the pervasive nature of older ideas in modern psychology, and also in social policies. In an autobiographical account Eysenck (1991) describes how initially he taught that the environment was responsible for differences in intellectual ability between groups of people:

> As the literature grew and grew, so my doubts became more and more definite; I could not in all honesty maintain that environmental pressures

could account for all the differences I found, and yet my hatred of 'racialism' made me most reluctant to entertain the belief that blacks were actually genetically predisposed to lower IQ levels. The publication of Audrey Shuey's great book, *The Testing of Negro Intelligence* (Social Science Press, 1966), brought my doubts to a focus. She reviewed the whole evidence in the most impartial manner possible, and left the reader with little doubt that genetic factors were probably implicated in the observed differences between blacks and whites. (p. 18)

While Eysenck readily points to his antagonism towards Hitler's National Socialism and what he calls racialism, he is adamant that group differences in intelligence are genetically determined to a substantial degree. The notion of the innate superiority and inferiority of racial groups is, of course, a fundamental tenet of biological racism as well as its dictionary definition. Nevertheless, arguments based on 'scientific' evidence are not immune to ideological trappings since it is too easy to confuse interpretations of data with 'facts'. Research on racially inherited differences in intelligence is, at best, highly controversial (Flynn, 1980; Loehlin *et al.*, 1975; Richardson and Spears, 1972); at worst, it is a scientific fraud (Fletcher, 1991). The major argument is *not* about whether there is a universal entity which can be meaningfully designated 'intelligence'. Nor is it a question of the degree of genetic transmission of such a dubious commodity. Both propositions are precarious enough in themselves. A more important argument is whether it is possible to use such dubious suppositions, in conjunction with arbitrary race categories, to explain and justify racially stratified social systems. As we have seen, the genetic argument starts with the present social order and then works backwards to tenuous assertions about genes and biology. Thus, the social disadvantage of black people stems from their biological disadvantage and not *vice versa*. But no one has ever defined intelligence genetically; which are the 'intelligent' genes? (See Mackenzie, 1984, for a description of the fraught problems in genetic explanations of racial differences in IQ test scores.)

Eysenck (1975a) clearly regards socio-politico-economic structures as largely determined by genes when he stresses the distinction between occupations which require 'brawn' and those requiring 'brain'. He reported the average IQ of top civil servants, professors and research scientists to be the highest at 140; school-teachers, accountants and managers averaged 120; machine operators and shopkeepers around 100; and labourers, miners and farmhands around 90. He adds to this his belief that parents tend to transmit to their offspring genes of a similar 'quality' to their own. These two things convince Eysenck of the 'justice' of the social order; nepotism is a myth.

A cursory reading of Eysenck's *Race, Intelligence and Education*

(1971) and other works reveals him to be convinced of the innate disability of black students. Redolent of earlier writers, he has eagerly advocated reactionary social policy on the basis of his 'detached science'. For example, when discussing 'positive action' as a means of reducing the social disadvantage of young black Americans, he writes:

> The outcome of this general quota system has not been documented very extensively, but certain features are already very apparent. Black students are accepted on the basis of much lower entrance requirements than white students; they have a catastrophically high failure rate; and they tend to congregate in separate groups which defy any integration with white students. The high failure rate has led to two interesting developments. Either black students are concentrated on new non-academic courses of the 'black studies' type, or else examinations are specially marked for them at a much lower level. (Eysenck, 1991, p. 48)

Psychology's racism

Psychology hardly takes seriously racism as a central aspect of the modern experience. Instead it stresses that racial bigotry is a thing of the past, a spent force – what remains of 'past' racism is held to be unfair, but curiously benign. The bone-breaking 'sticks and stones' of past racism is claimed by many to have been replaced by mere words which hurt nobody. Worse still, psychology continues to treat racism largely as something apart from itself, something the discipline studies, and not what it does. How can psychology seem so unconcerned about racism and at the same time claim to serve humanity? Few explanations for this lack of concern are appetising. In this regard, the discipline seems best characterised as a cultural artifact, to be understood more or less as any institution in a racist society. Like all professions, it exemplifies a struggle amongst, and for, the vested interests of its members. But, more importantly, it frequently codifies and articulates the concerns and ideologies of dominant groups in society. This may be achieved as much by omission as by commission.

New racism: old racism

Hume's catalogue of the 'natural defects' of black people (described earlier) has been echoed throughout the twentieth century by both psychologists and psychiatrists (e.g. Carothers, 1951; 1972; Jung, 1920; 1930; Parin and Morgenthaler, 1969; McDougall, 1921; Rushton, 1990; and Terman, 1916). No matter how racism is clothed in modern times, in terms of either intelligence or cultural pathology, it remains much the same old stuff; the fundamental sentiment has not changed. Racism draws on stored-up myths which are essential to the *status quo* and may be drawn from psychology or elsewhere (Freire, 1972). Those myths which are particularly pertinent to psychology include the belief that black people are a different species from other human groups, have smaller and consequently less intelligent brains, are driven by their loins rather than their minds, have primitive and deficient cultures, speak less complex language and so forth.

To cut a long debate short, Yeboah (1988) poses an apposite conundrum for those, including some psychologists, who believe that intelligent genes dwell in white skins: why did Europeans, given their wisdom, intelligence and superiority, choose to spend three centuries committing European resources to transporting millions of humanity's laziest, most depraved and good-for-nothing race across vast, hostile oceans to work the mines and plantations upon which European economy and prosperity depended? Similarly, why repeat the exercise by recruiting thousands of black immigrants to work in the industries, transportation systems and medical services of Europe following the Second World War?

Because racism's clothes have changed, because it is now expressed in terms of culture rather than biology, many believe that it is now little more than an embarrassing appendage to psychology. They forget the UNESCO Committee of Experts on Race and Racial Prejudice's (1967) warning that racism finds ever new strategies to justify racial inequality when its biological doctrines are exposed as false. The cloak of culture enables the free expression of racist views disguised as critiques of defects and pathologies in the social organisation of black communities and families. Thus psychologists, along with others, continue to use terms like 'primitive', 'tribal', 'backward', 'undeveloped', 'underdeveloped', 'developing', or simply 'different' when describing black people's cultures. Racism is, perhaps, psychology's most versatile and persistent theory.

Racism flouts natural justice by the creation of edicts on race relations entailing the following beliefs (Nash, 1962):

1. The capacities of races to handle the complexities of civilisation vary.
2. The cultural achievement of different races is determined by relative innate capacities.
3. The inferior races, unless prevented, destroy culture.
4. Racism is a fight for truth in the interest of humanity.
5. Those who favour equality are undesirables.

Each and every one of these propositions has been manifest in psychology.

Some changes within psychology's racism reflect developments in broader society. The prominent British politician of the 1980s, Margaret Thatcher, claimed: 'the whole question of race is not a matter of being superior or inferior, dirty or clean, but of being different' (Gordon and Klug, 1986, p. 21). One implication being that but for cultural differences there would be no racism. This is a fallacy (Rex and Mason, 1986). For example, Cox (1948) compared racism and anti-Semitism in North America. He noted that although the dominant group disliked Jewish people, this did not have to be the case. Jewish people could be liked so long as they ceased to be Jewish by acting 'like the rest of us'. On the other hand, 'Negroes' were liked so long as they stayed contentedly in their allotted place, ready to be exploited. Attempts by 'Negroes' to be 'like the rest of us' elicited hostility. In order to survive, the black person must not matter in the white world (Montagu, 1974); the black person must become a 'non-person', as in the euphemisms 'non-white' and 'non-European'. Thus, racism not only justifies power relations between peoples but also stipulates the detail of the relationship between racial groups.

The emphasis on culture may be the result of a significant historical change in racism's function (Gilroy, 1990). Once, racism fuelled empire-building but now it articulates nationalistic feelings, anti-immigration policies and cultural differentiation linked to 'our customs, traditions, and heritage'. Ideologues of the New Right proclaim that they are not racist since they have no sympathy with notions of white people's innate superiority over black people. Instead, culture conflict is used to raise concerns about the dangers of black communities within white society. Nevertheless, these worries revolve about the selfsame peoples who were previously wrongly categorised as biologically distinct races (Gilroy, 1990).

Amongst racism's more subtle forms is a sort of race-thinking which is linked to a more general conception of human nature than the old biological racism ever was (Barker, 1981). Aspects of this revision can be seen in the following: 'human nature is such that it is natural to form a bounded community, a nation, aware of its differences from other nations. They are not better or worse, but feelings of antagonism will be aroused if outsiders are admitted' (Margaret Thatcher, quoted by Gordon and Klug, 1986, p. 21). Sentiments similar to this are sometimes described as a new form of racism. In fact, it is rather elderly. Barker (1981) has traced it back to David Hume, who claimed that there were 'instincts for national hostilities and racial separation' (p. 76). Given the ingrained nature of this sentiment, it is not surprising that it has been expressed as 'scientific' theory by some academics. So, for example, socio-biologists, and even some contemporary social psychologists, noted for their anti-racist sentiments, have built entire theories of intergroup relations on this suspect premise (Howitt, 1991). We will return to this theme in detail in later chapters.

Others have suggested that black people's cultures are not just different but fundamentally deficient. This lies in the spurious and incorrect assumption of the inseparability of race from culture. However, the number of cultures greatly exceeds the number of distinct 'races' that have been suggested. Furthermore, any two 'black' cultures may differ as much as a 'black' culture and a 'white' one (Levi-Strauss, 1975). In spite of this, race-thinking has promoted the notion of black 'cultural pathology'. 'Defective' family and kinship patterns, marital arrangements, child-rearing practices, diet, religion and other elements of black people's lives are cited as evidence of their inferiority. In short, the focus on the black family has been as if one is 'dissecting the culturally bizarre' (Brittan and Maynard, 1984).

The alleged matriarchal character of black families in Britain, America and elsewhere is claimed by researchers and professionals to be pathogenic and inimical to healthy personal development (Fernando, 1989). In contrast, the Indian family is seen as strong and supportive. Nevertheless, these same families are also held to be oppressive and crippling. Indian families are said to be stress-ridden, notably for the women who are claimed to be isolated, because of their rigid and restrictive cultural practices and anti-Western values and morality (Fernando, 1988; Rack, 1982). Stereotypical assumptions such as these are not commonly made about white families of any class. However, they are frequently used by professionals to deny black people adequate services. For example, it is often claimed that black people, especially Indians, lack the necessary skills and language (spoken English) to avail themselves of, or benefit from, welfare services and facilities. Take note for now of this description of the African-Caribbean family: 'West Indian childbearing patterns are known to be able to cripple a child's development in the curiously cold and unmotherly relationship between West Indian mothers and their children' (Lobo, 1978, p. 34). Such allegations as this have led some to argue that the presumed deficiency of black family structures serves as a ploy for the purpose of social control (e.g. Littlewood and Lipsedge, 1989).

Avoiding the issue of race: colour-blindness

Another perspective which helps eschew racism as a salient issue is known as the 'colour-blind' orientation. One of its main features is a refusal to consider racism to be a special form of social inequity. Attempts to tackle racism independently of other social injustices are resisted. Its particular power lies in its potential to justify inaction. This is usually achieved by invoking the supremacy of individual rights over the needs, disadvantages and rights of black peoples. In this way the *status quo* is protected as well as the personal interests of white people. Holders of the colour-blind perspective typically deny the existence of racism except in the conveniently narrow sense of overt and deliberate discrimination (Ben-Tovim *et al.*, 1986). They even go so far as to assert that raising racism as an issue can incite racial conflict and 'invite a white backlash'. For example, Van den Berghe (1986) expresses a colour-blind view in the following explicit terms:

> My principal reasons for opposing race-based policies is that, whatever their purported intent, such policies heighten racial consciousness, divide minority groups against each other, exacerbate class division within minority groups, and are a fundamentally reactionary ploy to prevent the emergence of class-based solidarity. (p. 252)

In this, Van den Berghe ignores Myrdal's (1944) observation that in a socially stratified society 'the lower groups will, to a great extent, take care of keeping each other subdued, thus relieving, to that extent, the higher classes of the otherwise painful task necessary to the monopolisation of power and advantages' (p.68). So the white working class strive to stay at least one rung above black people. Such an analysis led Myrdal and others (e.g. Rex and Tomlinson, 1979) to classify black people in Western nations as an 'under-class'. Similarly, Montagu (1974) has observed how white down-and-outs see themselves as better than black people. In short, contrary to the colour-blind perspective, and policies based upon it, while black people and the white working class may appear to be in the same boat, they are certainly not on the same deck!

Preventing misunderstandings

We are conscious that discussions of racism risk alienating those who broadly sympathise with the message, and unwittingly playing into the hands of those antagonistic to it. There are numerous reasons why this can happen. What we will not accept is the pseudo-sympathetic message that although the book has a point, 'it goes over the top and does more harm than good'. We have heard this argument made in too many contexts, by too many people, and against too many shades of anti-racist arguments. Usually it is racist code for 'don't rock the boat'. Sometimes it is also code for 'don't wreck our expertise' or, more plainly, 'don't confuse me with facts, I've made up my mind'. Openness to the possibility of racism is the strength of anti-racism. The world is too varied, cultures are too disparate, and institutions too different to allow the problem of racism to be tackled by a few formulae or a list of dos and don'ts. Eliciting such openness of mind has a vital role to play in tackling the racism of psychology.

Read twenty years from now we would expect, and hope, that many of the arguments we make will appear hopelessly old-fashioned and even naive. Some radical positions of the past seem much that way now – time has overtaken them. The choice of language with which to discuss racism is particularly fraught with problems since language and politics are intractably intermingled. Race-related terms are politically loaded and difficult to reach a consensus on. Perhaps this is only fitting. Race has no sustainable biological meaning itself and is socially constructed to serve dominant social groups and institutions. This is readily seen in the use of racially derogatory terms such as 'nigger' (which is vulgarised Latin, *niger* meaning Black) but the slogan 'Black is beautiful' of the 1960s was also an enormously important political act.

In the USA, the current trend is to refer to 'ethnic minority peoples' in terms of their ancestry and nationality. Thus 'African-American' is now a familiar term. One disadvantage is the very crudity with which it acknowledges cultural differences. Africa is no small island but a continent vastly heterogeneous in virtually every aspect of culture. African-American is perhaps more appropriate to the American experience where the precise African geographical and cultural origins of individual black people may be uncertain. In contrast, African people in Britain and Aboriginal people in Australia, for example, are somewhat more likely to have direct knowledge of their cultural identity. Generic descriptions such as African-American go some way to promoting the notion of an underlying micro-cultural identity, but they are so general that their application can be a distortion.

Phrases such as 'people of colour' also occur in the political jargon of race. Again, in the appropriate context, the phrase may be useful, but it can rest uncomfortably on the ears of those not used to hearing racism spoken in overt racist argot. While 'people of colour' may appear politically neutral set against the language of 'nigger', 'coon', and the like, it is very close to 'coloured people', the genteel British way of referring to black people. It is a phrase with connotations of the bumbling, arm's-length racism of Britain in the post-colonial period. Too close to notions such as 'coloured immigration', and all that meant, 'people of colour' may well be a 'politically' correct description to some but it is awkward to us. So, like some other terms, we will confine its use to other people's comments.

The use of 'black' as a generic, politicised description has had a rather chequered history in terms of its general approval. One of its particular problems is its varying acceptability in different communities, usually because of a failure to understand 'black' as a political act of self-labelling and self-unification, as opposed to 'black' as signifying skin-colour or a racial group. Terms like 'black' do have a major problem in some settings, that is they essentially strip the individual of any contextual setting. But, of course, that is exactly what the term is intended to achieve – to identify and unite large groupings of people in terms of their shared experiences of socially disadvantaged status in white socio-politico-economic structures. The possible paradoxes in the use of 'minority' also warrant care. One problem is that the description merely reproduces and fixes in language the disparity in power between the 'haves' and 'have-nots' in terms of majorities and minorities. But this is quite clearly a travesty of the truth world-wide and historically. The victims of colonial racists were the majority just as the victims of apartheid in South Africa are, and will continue to be into the future. Furthermore, when women are also regarded as sharing 'minority' status with other disadvantaged groups, the disadvantaged minorities become the disadvantaged majority in all Western societies.

The choice of appropriate terms depends upon the context. In a book on multi-cultural counselling it would be inappropriate to use the term 'black' routinely since this would mask the crucial aspects of cultural diversity as they impinge on the lives of clients and professionals. In that setting, it would be appropriate to rely very much on the client-group's self-naming rather than to attempt to impose a terminology. In contrast, this book is not primarily about detailed multi-cultural issues in psychology. It is about racism, so that to write generically about racism's victims becomes more appropriate. Also, to repetitively identify and specify victimised cultural groups would be tedious. Inevitably this presents problems; historical and geographical aspects among them. What is appropriate language in a given period, or in one geographical location, may be hopelessly inadequate in other contexts. Dobbins and Skillings (1991) point to the root of the problem:

> most of our current race and cultural labels invite classification into 'haves and have nots' along whatever dimension is salient. They promote hierarchical frames and impede a more egalitarian discussion of differences. . . . [W]e see the progression of race terminology moving from a relatively precise scientific lexicon to one that is quite loose. This shift has come about because the notion of race is inherently invalid and because race

terms have more social and political meaning than biological meaning. (p. 43)

For reasons which include personal preference, compromise and stylistic matters as much as broader historical and political concerns, we have adopted the term 'black people' to denote the victims of racist social systems, and the term 'white people' to signify the primary benefactors. All are afforded the status of humanity. The following should be stressed about the use of the term 'black people':

1. It does not refer to people of African ancestry exclusively – it is being used as a convenient, generic term to indicate the main victims of the Western world's racism.
2. Biological classifications are not assumed to be valid and are not implied by the term.
3. Race has social and political meanings which vary over time and between geographical areas and between people; these have nothing to do with biology but they are very significant social constructs.
4. The term risks riding roughshod over important cultural differences and may well be inappropriate in other contexts such as when dealing with people from a culturally specific group.

Descriptions such as 'non-Western' are also best avoided because of their asymmetric dependency on the concept of 'Western' people. So while we know that the alternative to 'white people' is 'black people', 'non-Eastern' is not a synonym for 'Western'. In other words, racism's victims are defined in terms of being apart from white society, what is white being the norm. This is not tortured academic argument, it is a demonstration of the Eurocentric nature of language, thinking and behaviour. Value-laden language is also common: savage, primitive, underdeveloped and Third World are clear examples of this. Which criteria are to be used in making these judgements? Their identification usually unveils racist assumptions. Thus, when we are forced to use terms like 'Third World', we do so with reservation and apologies.

It is notable that there are few complexities in labelling white people. This is hardly surprising given the access to status and other privileges that being white ensures. Only recently have some preferred a geographical-cum-cultural attribution such as Russian-American, Polish-American and the like. Perhaps this is a sign of solidarity from the offspring of immigrant minorities who not so long ago were the victims of psychology's assault on ethnic minority groups. However, in the end, does it matter what people are called if racism continues? Polite and considerate language on its own is not enough (Dummett, 1984).

Racism and the individual psychologist

Modern psychology's origins in a climate of slavery, of domination and exploitation of black people, notably Africans, ensured that the burgeoning profession was imbued with racism. Similarly, ultimately it is impossible to separate the psychologist as a person from the psychologist as a professional role. Racism is bound to permeate psychology while society remains racist. But this does not mean that psychology as a profession and discipline is helpless to eliminate racism. Acceptance of the nature of the problem may be a first step to genuine resistance; but it is often a difficult and painful process for individuals and organisations to reject racism. Indeed, the elimination of racism as such is an ideal which is fraught with problems. Because of the pervasiveness of racism in our culture, it is more usual to speak of anti-racist strategies than of eliminating racism. This acknowledges racism's permeation throughout society and our limited powers to identify it. Constant vigil and energy are also implied by the term:

> A given society is either racist or it is not. But once racist, none of its members – most of all its best representatives – remain unaffected. Indeed, whether racist or not, every citizen of a racist society is responsible for the crimes committed in the name of his nation. (Fanon, 1967, p. 85)

Long ago, Dollard (1937) identified several gains which white middle-class people, particularly men, derive from their social positions. One of these refers to occupational rewards: for example, black people occupy the lower strata of such professions as medicine, teaching, psychiatry and clinical psychology, thereby enabling their white counterparts to enjoy more power and greater financial rewards (e.g. CRE, 1987c, d; 1988a, b).

Another difficulty for individuals lies in the community's reaction to those wishing to halt racism. Often those who oppose dominant dehumanising views occupy relatively weak positions in their professions and wider society. They may not appear so united in terms of solutions to the problem as the intransigence of those unwilling to change. Some may adopt an easy-going attitude to finding solutions while others may adopt a victim–blame approach despite attributing the problems of the disadvantaged to the structural arrangements of society. A distinctive characteristic of liberal professionals, unlike their tough-minded counterparts, is their frequent pussy-footing and timidity when the chips are down and when practical measures are needed to rectify injustice. This involves the tendency to 'play safe', for example, by moving with the social, economic and/or political tide of the time, seemingly acting fashionably. In so doing they risk mixing action with inaction, and ambivalence with lip-service. As a result, their pronouncements on race issues and proposals for action often have a taint of racism. Hence, they frequently appear as very unreliable allies to black people; they are viewed with suspicion and approached only cautiously or reluctantly.

Changing psychology to rid it of racism and to meet the needs of all humanity, not just those of the privileged, requires much more than mere 'racial tolerance'. Firstly, tolerance defines an attitude of reluctance to change and the necessity to endure something we would prefer not to. It reflects the presence of those (black people) whom we do not like, or would prefer to avoid (Montagu, 1974). Tolerance is putting up with something when you do not like to have it around. Racial tolerance is the hand-washing indifference of the white person who patronisingly condescends to endure black people provided they keep their 'proper' distance. In everyday discourse this kind of attitude is often expressed in statements like 'If they don't bother me, I don't bother them'; 'I'm OK with them so long as they are OK with me'; 'We have no problem with them because there are not many of them around here.' In short, it is the attitude of mind of those who consider themselves not only different but superior. The underlying attitude is not one of understanding and acceptance, but of recognition of differences which one must suffer. It is what Dummett (1984) has aptly termed 'kindness to inferiors attitude'. 'It is an attitude that says "Just so far and no further. I will give you this. I will give you that. But you must not ask for more" . . . the relationship is essentially a colonial one (p. 86).' Psychology cannot afford mere racial tolerance – that is the best that bigots can achieve.

Chapter 2

Fascism and right-wing racist psychology

The ideology of the National Socialists can be put very simply. They claimed that there is a biological basis for the diversity of Mankind. What makes a Jew a Jew, a Gypsy a Gypsy, an asocial individual asocial, and the mentally abnormal mentally abnormal is in their blood, that is to say in their genes. All these individuals, and perhaps others, are inferior. There can be no question of equal rights for inferior and superior individuals. . . . The murder of others is the secret, mystic message. It is an ideology of destruction, of mystery, and of worship of the blood. (Muller-Hill, 1988, p. 22)

This is easily recognised as the fascism of Hitler's Germany; disturbingly, these same beliefs were shared by psychiatrists, psychologists and others. This went far beyond ideology; psychologists and psychiatrists were actively involved in the destruction of the racially despised. Few doubt that the events of this period, especially the holocaust, made biological racism anathema to white people, including psychologists – indeed it had always been rejected by many. However, psychology seems to rest rather too easily with its past complicity with genocide:

To judge from psychology's own history books, the involvement of German psychologists with Nazism has been almost totally forgotten. . . . If the histories of psychology mention Nazism, typically it is in relation to the flight from Nazism by either Freud or Kohler; as a result the misleading impression is conveyed of an opposition between psychology and Nazism. (Billig, 1978, p. 15)

It is an important lesson for psychology that a 'neutral science' can be hijacked to serve causes that most psychologists abhor. The ethical basis of the discipline is not grounded in psychological knowledge as such, but in the actions of practitioners. In other words, the moral debate that must surround psychology is as vital as its knowledge base and simply cannot be left to take care of itself. The role psychology played in Nazi Germany has strong parallels with the experiences of psychologists working in organisations which inadvertently (or sometimes deliberately) perpetrate racism. Does the psychologist have a real choice about what to do? High moral decisions are easily taken in the absence of personal consequences.

Although at first sight the material in this chapter seems history, to dismiss it as irrelevant to modern psychology is profoundly mistaken. For one thing, there has been a return to the racial murders it portrays. But, also, similar race assumptions are to be found in current psychology.

Hitler's practical eugenics

In 1933, a law was passed in Germany which required medical officers to request the sterilisation of people with 'hereditary' diseases. These included schizophrenia, mental defect and manic-depression. Psychiatrists would make the initial diagnosis although it was often left to their medical officers to request the actual sterilisation. Something like a third of a million sterilisations had taken place by the start of the Second World War. The 1935 'law for the protection of German blood' forbade marriage and sexual intercourse between 'Jewish' and 'German' people. Two years later, a group of experts was empowered to decide on the compulsory sterilisation of black children – mainly the offspring of black French soldiers occupying Germany after the First World War. Nearly four hundred black children were sterilised in university clinics under the direction of the Gestapo. More was to come. A euthenasia programme for mental-hospital patients began in September 1939. Some were recommended for killing by a panel of doctors but others were just killed without ceremony. Even after this murderous programme had stopped, tens of thousands of patients were simply starved to death. In occupied France, similar numbers of patients were also killed by starvation although there was no official order to do so. In 1941, the mass execution of Jews, Gypsies and mental patients began, later to be followed by the mass rounding up of victims for the concentration camps.

Psychology prospered remarkably well in Hitler's Nazi Germany. Between 1932 and 1942, the number of professors of psychology practically doubled. In 1930, about half of the thirty state-employed psychologists were in the army. By 1942 there were 450 psychologists employed by the German military forces alone. This was not simply a matter of individual complicity. German psychology's professional body did nothing to oppose the dismissals of Jewish academic psychologists following the 1933 law for the restoration of the professional civil service. Rieffert, a professor of psychology at Berlin, prepared a research proposal with the intention of spying on Jewish people in order to understand how they 'infiltrated' German society (Muller-Hill, 1988). He aimed to carry out his fieldwork in those German regions populated by the pure German 'race':

> The first objective will be to make a psychological study of these communities, and, in addition . . . study the 'tactics' employed by Jews at various times to adapt to the particular characteristics of each community, as well as the ways in which these German communities defend themself against Jewry in their day-to-day affairs. (p. 38)

It says little in psychology's favour that the SS (Nazi party bodyguards) planned to enlist the help of a particular woman psychologist who would decide which Polish children would be removed from their parents for disposal to German families, children's homes or camps on the basis of 'characterlogical' assessment: 'which could mean not only the choice of their future quarters but also between life and death' (Geuter, 1987, pp. 175–6).

None of this was too different from the contribution made by Konrad Lorenz. The state wanted to deal with 'social misfits' using broadly the same murderous methods it applied to mental patients and racial minorities. For Lorenz, this process of detection or recognition of suitable cases for this treatment was surprisingly easy: 'In this, the proper cultivation of our own inborn patterns can help us a great deal. A good man can very easily feel with his deepest instincts whether another is a scoundrel or not' (Lorenz, cited in Muller-Hill, 1988, p. 56). In his discussion of the disturbances to animal behaviour due to the effects of domestication, Lorenz points to the futility of trying to repair degenerate behaviours. He suggests that the treatment of a malignant tumour in the body and that of constitutionally defective asocial individuals in a nation are much the same: 'Fortunately, the elimination of such elements is easier for the public health physician and less dangerous for the supra-individual organism, than such an operation by a surgeon would be for the individual organism' (Lorenz, cited in Muller-Hill, 1988, p. 14).

This was the late Konrad Lorenz, who has had the highest profile in psychology of any animal ethologist. Since the 1960s his work, especially that on aggression (Lorenz, 1966; 1981), has featured heavily in student textbooks and elsewhere. This is the Lorenz who also claimed that one of his life's greatest joys was converting a student to National Socialism (Muller-Hill, 1988). He was apparently also well aware of the deportation of Gypsies to extermination camps. According to Silverman (1987), some of Lorenz's fellow ethologists do not use certain of his concepts because he used them in support of Nazi programmes. This background information suggests a more sinister meaning to Lorenz's work. Take, for example, this passage from a recent introductory psychology textbook:

> Lorenz placed human aggression in the broader context of animal behavior and maintained that aggression enhances survival. Those who successfully aggress against others gain access to water, food, and sex with desirable mates. Thus, according to Lorenz, aggression secures an advantage in the struggle to survive, and natural selection favors the development of an aggressive instinct. (Brehm and Kassin, 1990, pp. 345–6)

Is this any other than National Socialism in code? 'Desirable mates' can only be 'genetically superior' since such matings ensure the survival of the aggressive. In essence the theory claims that aggression prevents mating between the genetically inferior and the genetically superior. The sterilisation of black children, mental defectives and others was intended to assure this under National Socialism. The 1935 'law for the protection of German blood and German honour' did much the same by prohibiting intercourse between Jewish people and German citizens. Modern psychology textbook writers do not knowingly reproduce such despised creeds – that would be far too calculating. However, they incorporate 'commonsense' into their 'science'; the 'law of the jungle' and the 'survival of the fittest' are part and parcel of everyday conversations. That these developed from the bad science which allowed eugenic and fascist ideas to flourish shows how everyday notions can echo disgraced 'science'. The almost 'commensensical' nature of Brehm and Kassin's account should not be too surprising seen in this light.

Eugenics and Social Darwinism

> As it has been observed, next to the blood of Jesus, the Negro blood is the most powerful in the world. One drop makes you whole. (Wilson and Lyles, 1984, p. 139)

The roots of scientific racism go deeper than the evolutionary theory of Charles Darwin. For example, in the 1800s, Dr Cartright 'identified' a disease of slaves, *drapetomania* (Fernando, 1988). Much like a cat's unfortunate habit of straying, drapetomania was characterised as an irrestrainable propensity on the part of slaves to run away to escape from slavery. Quite clearly slavery itself was not seen to be the problem since running away was a mental illness of the slaves themselves! Seen as such, fleeing the plantation was irrational pathology, not a rightful protest. Slaves were insane if they bucked the racist system, deserving to be a victim if they did not. Blaming the victims of racist society remains a common ploy.

While not archetypal in terms of race science, Darwinism provided the bed-rock from which others endlessly assaulted every aspect of the being of black people. Once it is mooted that principles of evolution, such as natural selection, may apply to society the biological justification for a racially hierarchical social order has begun. Bannister (1979) appears very much as Darwin's defence lawyer:

> The Descent of Man reinforced a hierarchical view of human development and the assumption that history was a progression from barbarism to civilization. . . . In this context, Darwin's predictions concerning the extermination of lower races were not prescriptions for racial imperialism but a summary of recent anthropology and the apparently undeniable results of European expansion since the Renaissance. But Darwin also insisted that this process was not to be confused with biological evolution or the process whereby racial differences originally appeared. (pp. 184–5)

We are expected to believe that there was nothing inherently racist in Darwin's view that 'human development' emerges out of 'barbarism'. Since it was held that white society was civilised and black nations were barbarians, essentially this was cultural racism. It may not have been invented by Darwin but he adhered to it. Bannister insists that Darwin and his alumni were model opponents of social programmes which assumed the permanent inferiority of black people. Furthermore, Bannister suggests that Herbert Spencer (the parent of Social Darwinism and the phrase 'survival of the fittest'), together with his American disciples, contributed an intellectual rationale for paternalistic but nevertheless humane philanthropic and educational initiatives. Chase (1977) suggests otherwise: 'He not only proclaimed the moral rights of the Deserving rich to heaven; Spencer also denounced the immorality and impracticality of health, education, safety, and welfare programs that would have materially increased their taxes here on earth' (p. 105). According to Bannister, however, Darwin can only be held to be racist on the basis of 'association and scattered quotations' (p. 183). The problem is not with Darwin but with his critics: 'As with other charges of misapplied Darwinism, this one reflected the sometimes complex psychologies of individuals who were ambivalent towards Darwinism, black equality, or both. Darwinism was a convenient brush with which to tar racists, and vice versa' (p. 186). Whatever else this means, it suggests that the Social Darwinists were blameless. Where does one begin?

Tradition has it that modern psychology came into being when Wundt opened his research laboratories in Leipzig in 1879. The American Psychological Association minted a commemorative gold medallion to celebrate the centenary of this 'momentous' event. For our purposes, though, there is a far better claimant to parenting modern psychology. While Wundt's psychology has long since ceased to be influential, the pernicious psychology laid down by Francis Galton, Darwin's cousin, is still doing its nasty work. Galton most certainly came from a 'good' family. Perhaps this accounts for his interest in hereditary genius and similar matters (Galton, 1869). The theorising was simple: quality breeding stock yields quality offspring. Eminence and brilliance were among such outcomes of good breeding. It appeared to Galton that the lower classes, who lacked these qualities by definition, were rather more fecund than the upper classes, who monopolised constitutional superiority. The danger was obvious – good hereditary stock being swamped by the bad. The solution was also theoretically simple: 'give the more suitable races or strains of blood a better chance of prevailing speedily over the less suitable than they otherwise would have had' (Galton, 1869, p. 25). Clearly there were many ways of doing this. Sterilisation was one suggestion which gained international popularity, as we have seen, and to which Galton gave the name eugenics – the 'science' committed to his bio-social programme.

Eugenicists invented statistical techniques in order to demonstrate associations between measurements. Galton, for example, developed a rudimentary correlation coefficient which was later perfected by Karl Pearson, another eugenicist. This was the eponymous Pearson Correlation Coefficient. What is remarkable is their cavalier approach to the interpretative problem familiar to most psychology students – inferring cause from correlation. Pearson founded a new journal in 1925, *Annals of Eugenics* (now called *Annals of Human Genetics*). Its first issue contains Pearson and Moul's lengthy and extensively tabulated article 'The problem of alien immigration into Great Britain, illustrated by an examination of Russian and Polish Jewish children'. Immigrant Jewish children in London's East End were held to be inferior to the native English child in numerous ways ranging from intelligence to personal hygiene. Jewish children apparently had more tuberculosis, heart disease, ear and eye disease, and displayed a tendency to breathe through their mouths! There are parallels here with accounts of the attitudes of modern health professionals towards black immigrant children (e.g. Lobo, 1978).

Pearson was in no doubt as to the societal consequence of such poor stock: 'They will develop into a parasitic race' (quoted in Kamin, 1981, p. 155). Faced with disparate evidence, he conceded the point but with a sting in the tail: 'Some of the children of these alien Jews from the academic standpoints have done brilliantly', then added: 'No breeder of cattle, however, would purchase an entire herd because he anticipated finding one or two fine specimens included in it' (quoted in Kamin, 1981, pp. 155–6). Recognising that Jewish people had long been the victims of oppression provided Pearson with another justification for victimising them more. Oppression 'does not necessarily leave the best elements of a race surviving. It is likely indeed to weed out the mentally and physically fitter individuals, who alone may have had the courage to resist their oppression' (Kamin, 1981, p. 156). It is curious that Pearson, a staunch bad-gene theorist, chose to believe that good genes were exterminated by oppression. This is tantamount to saying that good genes are bad for you. More curious still is that he ignored the obvious association between the squalid conditions in which these Jewish children lived and their poor physical health. Acknowledging this would have been a heresy in the eugenics movement. Rather than accepting that correlation does not prove cause as is drummed into every psychology student's psyche, Pearson found evidence of bad genes without tearing genes apart. Hayes (1980) specifically identifies what he calls Pearson's 'racially based Social Darwinism' (p. 176) as having a strong and long-lasting influence on the Nazis.

Links between Galton and modern psychology are simple and direct – through Cyril Burt, whose general practitioner father knew Galton personally. As a child, Burt was introduced to Galton, who apparently regarded Burt as his prodigy. Furthermore, Burt had youthful links with other overtly racist psychologists. For instance, while at Oxford University, he was a student of William McDougall, an unremitting propagandist of racism. McDougall's racism is just detectable in his *Introduction to Social Psychology* (1908) in that there is just one sentence in the book which reveals his racism. This speaks of 'deleterious consequences of unrestrained and excessive indulgence of the sexual appetite' (McDougall, 1908, p. 359). McDougall adds: 'It has often been maintained, and not improbably with justice, that the backward condition of so many branches of the negro race is due to this state of affairs' (p. 359).

However, McDougall's racist output was truly prodigious, especially following his migration to the USA: 'I am convinced that a policy of voluntary segregation of the colored people of the United States is the only sound one' (McDougall, quoted in Chase, 1977, p. 448). Or when examining data from psychological tests he found 'scientific' support for the views of 'Englishmen' who have:

> recognized that the natives of India, or very many of them, have much intellectual capacity. . . . [But] as compared with their British rulers, the

natives of India are relatively defective in character or will-power; and they have found the explanation of British ascendency in this fact. (McDougall 1921, quoted in Chase, 1977, p. 231)

Furthermore, he held that Negroes had 'an instinct for submission'.

He was among the most adamant advocating that racial differences in measured intelligence reflected biological facts of inherited racial intelligence. The mental ages of nearly 2 million recruits to the US forces during the Great War had been found to average at just over 13 years. Native white American intelligence was declining rapidly, he held, on the basis of such data. And to this ship of fools was added further cargo – black people, who were even stupider and less capable of handling abstract thought according to these same tests. Little could be done about the decline in intelligence except by preventing 'the reproduction of the least fit, especially of those persons who were indisputably feeble-minded'. For McDougall 'It is needless to argue here the relative advantages of sterilization and institutional segregation. Probably both methods will be used' (McDougall, 1921; p. 194, quoted by Chase, 1977, p. 256). Better schooling, improved preventative medical care, higher standards of housing and the like were no solution, just a waste of taxes and charity. Apart from eugenics, there was no way of reversing the slide. The problem was built into the bad minority and migrant stock. There were no silk purses to be made out of this sow's ear by throwing money around.

Of course, there is nothing in the notion of intelligence measurement which in itself encourages racist assumptions about the superiority of the Western–Anglo-Saxon stock and the inferiority of other races. The origins of the IQ test lay in Binet's attempt to devise a measure which would be helpful in dealing with the intellectually impaired youngsters of Paris. As such, Binet set off on this pragmatic task by measuring a mishmash of abilities. Binet sought to assess a child's potential with a single indicator, not the quality of their biological inheritance. But such motives did not cross the Atlantic well:

American psychologists perverted Binet's intention and invented the heredi-tarian theory of IQ. They reified Binet's scores, and took them as measures of an entity called intelligence. They assumed that intelligence was largely inherited, and developed a series of specious arguments confusing cultural differences with innate properties. They believed that inherited IQ scores marked people and groups for an inevitable station in life. And they assumed that average differences between groups were largely the products of heredity, despite manifest and profound variation in quality of life. (Gould, 1981, p. 157)

It is possible to illustrate the world-view of many of these psychologists with brief quotations from two of the leading figures in the Americanisation of intelligence measurement. Terman suggested of black people: 'No amount of school instruction will ever make them intelligent voters or capable citizens in the true sense of the word' (Terman, 1916, p. 91); and Yerkes was adamant that 'no one of us as citizens can afford to ignore the menace of race deterioration' (Chase, 1977, p. 273).

But bad-gene theorists hardly had things their own way during the early twentieth century. Any number of psychologists railed against the racist interpretations of racial differences in intelligence-test scores and bad-gene theory was gradually pushed from centre stage:

> Changes in the ethnic makeup of the social science community and in the political and social atmosphere constituted a large part of the explanation for the shift in outlook on race, but not the full explanation. . . . Whatever may have brought the change about, a 1939 survey of psychologists certainly documented the shift. The author of the survey remarked that though at one time it had been held that tests 'measured biological differences' among various groups, 'practically no one now believes this'. . . . Along with the Depression, too, came the fateful news from Germany that the Nazis were putting into practice in an increasingly horrible way eugenic ideas about race purity and population improvement. (Degler, 1991, p. 202)

Although he died in 1971, Cyril Burt is still present in the minds of psychologists as their discipline's most famous fraudster. That he 'massaged' his data on mental inheritance in twins is commonly reported in student textbooks. Burt was a convinced hereditarian and a faithful disciple of eugenics long before he commenced his 'scientific' study. As early as 1903, whilst an undergraduate student at Oxford, he is quoted as writing in his notebook: 'The problem of the very poor – chronic poverty: Little prospect of the solution of the problem with the forcible detention of the wreckage of society . . . preventing them from propagating their species' (Kamin, 1981, p. 95). With this firm conviction of the validity of eugenics, Burt set out in search of 'evidence' to 'prove' his belief.

Remarkably, Burt appears to have written virtually nothing overtly racist, but is nevertheless specifically identified with racism by some (e.g. Moore, 1979). Of course, in order to claim that racial differences in intelligence are inherited, one must demonstrate that something called intelligence corresponds to a biological reality which obeys the laws of inheritance. Showing that genetically identical twins have similar measured intelligence levels irrespective of radical differences in upbringing is as close to this as is possible without discovering the biological foundations of intelligence themselves (if this is not to reify the concept of intelligence too much). Naturally, this is predicated on numerous assumptions, including the researcher's honesty. Burt's main contribution to the race and intelligence debate lay in the degree that his twin-studies bolstered the inheritance part of the inherited-racial-differences-in-intelligence thesis, not that he investigated racial differences.

That Burt wrote little that can be construed as directly racist might be explained by his concentration on limited psychological issues. He did not engage in freewheeling discussions of the world-order to which writers such as McDougall had been prone. While Burt was an important educationalist for many years, Britain was anything but a multi-racial society in his day. Black immigration did not reach even modest proportions until late in his career. Thus his pragmatic psychology did not need to deal directly with matters of race. On the rare occasion when he strayed during a discussion of educational backwardness, the agenda was a familiar one:

> exceptionally prevalent in those whose faces are marked by developmental defects, by the round receding forehead, the protruding muzzle, the short and upturned nose, the thickened lips, which combine to give the slum child's profile a negroid or almost simian outline. . . . 'Apes that are hardly anthropoid' was the comment of one headmaster, who liked to sum up his cases in a phrase. (Burt, 1937, p. 186)

Burt did not have to make this connection but the equation is there for all to see. Not only does Burt use the term 'muzzle', language normally reserved for animals, but he links mental 'subnormality' with black facial features. This elides into a linking of black people with gorillas, monkeys and chimpanzees. Quoting the views of the headmaster as if they were genial comments reinforces the routine disparagement of his racial thinking.

Cyril Burt's infamy was a consequence of the uproar surrounding Arthur Jensen's (1969) notorious article which asked whether black achievement could be raised through educational intervention. Jensen's view was that black intellects, due to inferior genes, were a poor match for white people's. Presented as a scientific matter, sand-bagged by seemingly endless data, this was not an issue that began or ended with research. In the barrage of criticisms of Jensen and his supporters, something struck Kamin (1974). A number of things literally did not add up about Burt's data; or they added up much too well. The data seemed to fit his theories consistently despite variations in the data-base as more twin-pairs were researched. This was the core research being used by Jensen and others to help argue that most of the variation in intelligence was due to genetic factors. While Burt's dishonesty remains a controversial matter (Fletcher, 1991; Hearnshaw, 1979; 1990; Jensen, 1992; Joynson, 1989; 1990), his image as fraudster remains in the collective conscience of psychologists. His undoing was his disciples' devotion to his data as crucial to proving the genetic transmission of intelligence. Not surprisingly, as we have seen, Burt's most successful student, H.J. Eysenck, took up the racial differences-in-intelligence theme. In doing so, he provided a focus for the protests of anti-hereditarian and anti-racist factions in Britain, as Jensen had in the USA. Eysenck was no late convert to the cause, he had written two decades earlier on social structure and genetics. His popular psychology books included chapters such as 'Is our national intelligence declining?' which basically reiterated the eugenic obsession that dim genes were breeding faster than intelligent ones (e.g. Eysenck, 1953).

Although a multitude of psychologists rejected Jensen's thesis whole-heartedly, there was an attentive and sympathetic audience. According to Billig, fascist parties made good use of bad-genes theory:

> For the National Front contemporary scientific racism has a crucial signifi-cance. There is no need to turn to the obscurities of [fascist writers], if quotes and misquotes from Shockley, Jensen and Eysenck will do instead. Racialist theories can then be presented in a 'British' manner, without resort to the hidden nazi culture. . . . In the main, knowledge seems to be gained from secondary sources. Eysenck's *The Inequality of Man*, written for a lay readership, is widely quoted and is on the lists of Nationalist Books, the National Front book club. (Billig, 1978, p. 144)

In the words of one prominent far-right political organiser, Martin Webster: 'The most important factor in the build-up of self-confidence amongst 'racists', and the collapse of morale among multi-racialists was the publication in 1969 by Professor Arthur Jensen in the Harvard Educational Review' (quoted in Billig, 1979, p. 9).

Nevertheless, a seemingly mortal blow had struck scientific racism. Psychologists could no longer hide their racism behind reified meas-ures which were nonsense when applied to genetic inheritance of intelligence. The cover had been blown. Tests of intelligence could be seen as nothing other than weapons of subordination when used with society's disadvantaged. Psychologists and the general public had become sensitive to the issues. In Britain, the journalist Oliver Gillie had given national media coverage to Burt's cheating and made Burt's name synonymous with scientific fraud. What had been the totem of scientific racists, the IQ test, became the focus of liberal hatred of racism.

Times were changing in another way. At least some black profes-sionals were in a position to begin to strike back at psychological oppression. For example, in a hard-hitting pamphlet, Coard (1971) launched a devastating attack on the psychology profession. He saw it responsible for making African-Caribbean children appear educationally subnormal within the British education system. The statistics he recruited at the time had alarming implications for black children and their parents. During the late 1960s educationally subnormal schools within the Inner London Educational Authority had disproportionately large numbers of black pupils, who formed around a third of the enrolment. Coard was certain about the reason for this situation – the system, not the child. The difficulties 'revolve around the *manner of assessment* by the authorities. . . . Usually the opinion of the Educational Psychologist is decisive . . . the single most important indicator' (p. 13).

He mentions several sources of bias in the system which disregarded the needs of the black child:

1. *Cultural bias*: for example, differences in the expectations of classroom interaction between Britain and the West Indies create a cultural misunderstanding. According to Coard, in the West Indies, children were not expected to talk or contribute within the classroom as much as in Britain. British teachers see this lack of response as 'indicating either silent hostility or low intelligence' (p. 14).
2. *Emotional disturbance*. Meeting the educational psychologist and others can be a disturbing experience for these children. Coard suggests that some less than honest psychologists claim to take into account a child's upset, distress or disturbance by including this in their report on testing the child. '*There is no assessment or scoring procedure on the IQ test that can add on points to a child's score to take into account any of the disturbance factors*' (pp. 16–17).

Coard's solution lay with the community. Parents of a black child diagnosed as subnormal should 'demand a reassessment' . . . by a Black Educational Psychologist' (p. 40). Whether psychologists agreed with everything Coard wrote matters little. Crucially, a richly deserved antipathy to psychological testing had become widespread.

The use of psychological testing has other important discriminatory outcomes such as in the selection practices of some organisations. There has been growing legal and social scientific opposition to the use of tests in recruitment choices (Burstein and Pitchford, 1990). At first sight, it might appear that measures of abilities such as intelligence could make selection of new employees highly efficient. But such tests do not predict who will be highly productive. Disadvantaged groups, including women, have argued in American courts that their work opportunities are unjustly affected by such tests. Of American equal-opportunities cases related to testing, 7 per cent concerned sexual discrimination but the majority (60 per cent) were about race. There is no need to claim that black people are genetically inferior when they can be excluded from employment using irrelevant criteria which have little or nothing to do with the job. In this way, a black person's failure to gain employment is not immediately discernible as racist. Employers, when challenged in court, have generally failed to show the economic gains of testing in employee output: 'In most cases reaching the appellate level, they did not even try systematically to validate their education and testing requirements; when they tried, the courts usually concluded that they failed' (p. 254).

Back above the parapet

Following the debacle of the unintelligent black genes thesis in the 1970s, more of the same was distinctly ruled out. Animosity to such crude psychological racism had been shown in many confrontations between bad-gene theorists and those persuaded against this familiar scientific racism built on the prejudices of Galton, Pearson, McDougall and others. A vigorous proponent of bad-genes theory, Hans Eysenck had staunchly defended the ideas of Jensen and the rest of them during the early 1970s (1971; 1973). Perhaps this is not surprising remembering that Eysenck's writings had more than a hint of older eugenics themes. For a while, Eysenck vigorously defended Burt against the charges laid against him (1976; 1977), but then relented and became a hostile critic of Burt's character (see Fletcher, 1991). Times were no longer conducive for bad-genes theorists.

Perhaps encouraged by a developing climate of political antipathy towards 'welfare society' in Britain, America and elsewhere during the 1980s, one North American psychologist, Rushton, ventured to go public with a revised version of the bad-genes thesis. He might also have been encouraged by the growing interest in socio-biology during the 1970s (Crawford et al., 1987; Ruse, 1979; Wilson, 1975) which enjoyed a comparatively smooth passage despite dealing with putative evolutionary bases for matters of morality. However, while the socio-biologists explored sex differences, they were less keen to enter the race-differences controversy. The twist in Rushton's bad-genes theory was that genes were deemed to govern morality. Of course, there is nothing new in associating moral turpitude with racial characteristics. After all, as we have seen, McDougall had no difficulty in hypothesising that sexual over-indulgence by black people was responsible for their plight in the world order. The 'degeneracy' of black people has always had this sort of moral dimension – 'traits' like stinking, drug-taking, being oversexed and laziness are scarcely anything other than moral condemnation.

So during the 1980s, J. Philippe Rushton set on his own bad-gene crusade. Much the same in overall effect as any previous version of bad-gene theory, Rushton based his variant on the suggestion that there are different reproductive strategies associated with different races – one has to concentrate more on the 'negroid–mongoloid' contrast than 'negroid–caucasoid'. Despite Rushton's claims to the contrary, the theory puts black people at the bottom of the moral heap, mongoloid people on the top and white people comfortably in the middle. This time it all boils down to the deportment of their private parts by the different races. It is all a bit like the difference between rabbits and kangaroos. Rabbits have sex like – er – rabbits and since they do it so often and have so many offspring, it does not matter too much if a few of the family meet a sticky end between car headlights. This is the 'r' reproductive strategy. Kangaroos, on the other hand, have few offspring and look after each one carefully. This is the 'K' reproductive strategy:

> In studies of dandelions, fish, flies, milkweed bug, and field mice, many of the covariant r/K traits are also found within species and to be genetic in origin. There is no reason why such analyses should not be applied to human differences. One analysis, for example, contrasted within the Caucasoid population, the characteristics of the mothers of dizygotic twins who, because they produce more than one egg at a time can be considered to represent the r-strategy, with the mothers of singletons representing the K-strategy. As expected, the former were found to have a lower age of menarche, a higher rate of coitus, a greater fecundity, more wasted pregnancies, an earlier menopause, and an earlier mortality. (Rushton, 1990, p. 196)

What sort of dandelion are you? Ignoring the jargon, digging deeply into the pot of racist stereotypes, there is little difficulty in guessing which traits are associated with the black – sorry, 'r'– strategy according to Rushton. How about small brains, small IQs, younger age of first intercourse, younger first pregnancies, aggressiveness, low cautiousness, sociability, frequent intercourse, high rates of sexually transmitted disease, unstable marriages, poor mental health – oh – and large genitals? Although much of Rushton's data has been criticised for being faulty or faultily interpreted according to numerous critics (Anderson, 1991; Cunningham and Barbee, 1991; Fairchild, 1991; Lynn, 1989a, b; Mealey, 1990; Roberts and Gabor, 1990; Vanderwolf and Cain, 1991; Weizmann *et al.*, 1990; 1991; Zuckerman and Brody, 1988), the parallels with the old scientific racism are marked even in so far as he uses craniological measurements of brain size. (Gould, 1981, discusses this flawed 'science' of craniology scathingly.) Take, for example, the following passage from Rushton's report which seems to reflect Darwin's *Descent of Man* pretty well but in a less than direct form:

Evidence (a) from molecular biology including DNA sequencing, (b) from the fossil record, and (c) from the mapping of linguistics on genetic trees, suggests that archaic versions of the three races emerged from the ancestral hominid line, out of Africa, in the following order: Negroids about 200,000 years ago, Caucasoids about 110,000 years ago, and Mongoloids about 41,000 years ago. . . . Negroids, the earliest to emerge, were least K selected. (Rushton, 1991, p. 983)

The hostility which views like Rushton's attract is not predicated primarily on the inadequacy of the accompanying 'science'. Such views are seen as reflecting biological racist ideas based on bad science. They appear to be vestiges of eugenic ideas. Rushton explicitly 'disavows' conceptions like superior and inferior since these have no meaning in terms of evolution. However, when applied to races which have clearly been biologically successful, this cuts little ice. Given the 'r' strategy, for example, is associated with criminality (according to Rushton's thesis), it is difficult to avoid the social implication that 'r' is bad, K is good. Granted the impossibility of scientific understanding which exists independently of the community which developed that science, one cannot divorce a morality-free science from moral society just to provide Rushton with a convenient excuse.

The theory is notable for more than the outrage it generated throughout the academic and general community. Rushton chose to incorporate elements which had previously proved difficult to entrain directly into bad-gene theory. One of these is the notion of the pathology of the black family, another the criminality of black people. Previously such views had been largely confined to racist disparagement of black culture although quite clearly they drew on earlier ideas concerning the inheritance of criminality (e.g. Eysenck, 1964).

When Rushton was prevented from giving lectures face to face at his Canadian university, the hostility which is manifested against grass-roots bad-gene racism re-appeared as strongly as it had for Jensen, Eysenck and others in the previous decade. (One should not imagine that Rushton was at all naive about the risks – in Pearson (1991) a photograph is reproduced in which a young Rushton is seen to be defending Eysenck from a physical attack by students in 1973.) But similarly older 'scientific' frauds were redolent of Rushton's theme. Craniometry, for example, was the nineteenth-century science of brain size. But the frauds in this were manifest and manifold, as Gould (1981) demonstrated:

Science is rooted in creative interpretation. Numbers suggest, constrain, and refute; they do not, by themselves, specify the content of scientific theories. Theories are built upon the interpretation of numbers, and interpreters are often trapped by their own rhetoric. They believe in their own objectivity, and fail to discern the prejudice that leads them to one interpretation among many consistent with their numbers. . . . Shall we believe that science is different today simply because we share the cultural context of most practicing scientists and mistake its influence for objective truth? (p. 74)

Our answer is no. But the reasons will begin to take us away from the biological racism of this chapter.

A final example of how far the bad-genes theorists will go involves Jensen's return to the fray in the mid-eighties (Jensen, 1985). Among Jensen's remarkable claims was that speed of reaction to the onset of a stimulus was rather slow in one of the world's greatest ever boxers – Muhammad Ali – during his prime. This is a difficult notion to sustain if one assumes that high-speed reactions are the *sine qua non* of a top-flight athlete. But the issue becomes a little clearer when we remember that reaction time largely involves processing delay by the brain – the physical response taking a fraction of the brain processing time. Thus the 'problem' lies in the brain. It will come as no surprise to find that Jensen was making a general statement of the paucity of black reaction time compared to that of white people. But there was no level playing field involved in the comparison (Kamin and Grant-Henry, 1987). For example, the author of the research failed to adjust the total reaction time appropriately. (The reaction time should exclude the period that the physical punch took since the size of the punch will affect the time it will take to deliver, for example.) When adjustment is made, Muhammad Ali's brain reaction time was faster than white laboratory subjects carrying out a much simpler and less demanding task than throwing a sizeable punch:

> What does it tell us about our innermost selves that psychologists, who watched Muhammad Ali float like a butterfly and sting like a bee, can write and publish and read that his reaction time was 'very average'? These and similar questions, we think, could profitably be pondered by students of race differences in intelligence. (Kamin and Grant-Henry, 1987, p. 304)

It is a salutary lesson to compare Jensen's views of one of the world's boxing greats with a long-term debate in racist psychology. Bache (1895) was an American disciple of Galton, who used electrical apparatus to measure the delays in reaction of white, American Indian and African-American men to vision, touch and sound. The white group was found to have the slowest reactions. Bache saw this as proof that white people were the intellectual superiors. Being a more 'reflective race', quite clearly they should react more slowly as they were not governed by simple reflex action which essentially would by-pass the higher faculties (see Chase, 1977). It was black people who were the automatons. The quickness of their movements made black people inferior!

In Africa, Gerber (1958) found that black children were developmentally superior to white children of the same age. This was true of both physical and intellectual development. Gerber interpreted these findings in sociological terms: differences in child-rearing practices, notably breast-feeding. Ignoring his interpretations, such findings have been twisted to give them a different thrust. For example, in *Race, Intelligence and Education*, Eysenck (1971) wrote:

> These findings are important because of a very general law of biology according to which the more prolonged the infancy, the greater in general are the cognitive or intellectual abilities of the species . . . thus sensory-motor precocity in humans . . . is negatively related with terminal IQ. (p. 84)

This is in stark contrast to Terman and Oden's (1947) finding that precocity is a characteristic of gifted children. Inferiority seems to be the African's allotted place in psychological theory.

A contemporary defence of scientific racism

Pearson (1991) argues that there are left-wing factions opposing all genetic theory and research on human ability. His book is a detailed account of the opposition to bad-gene theorists in psychology. As such it is worthy of attention. However, it also reveals a great deal of the thinking of the bad-gene theorists. His range of 'defences' is wide but nevertheless informative of the underlying ideology. For example, he describes Galton's behaviour on one particular Derby day at Epsom Race Course. Training his binoculars on the crowd of the upper classes, Galton noted that the crowd was pink:

> Here was an observation that demonstrated the genetic distinctiveness of the British upper classes of the nineteenth century, and also demonstrates to us today the genetic changes which have taken place in Britain, where the old land-owning class . . . has been almost totally replaced by a new upper class whose faces by no means 'uniformly suffused with a strong pink tint', and who are to no small degree of non-British descent. (Pearson, 1991, p. 60)

Or when criticising those who insist that poverty is responsible for much of the apparent racial difference eagerly sought by the eugenicists:

> How did a defeated nation like Germany, which suffered years of malnutrition in the wake of the widespread destruction of its cities during World

War II, produce a generation of creative, productive children who rebuilt their country's economy if . . . the control of environment over IQ is valid. (p. 180)

What answer does Pearson expect? That the 'German race' is genetically superior and should be protected from dilution by alien 'bad genes'? Rather than being merely a defence of eugenics, this reflects the ideology which had its most pernicious expression in Hitler's cries of racial pollution. Perhaps none of this is surprising since, according to Billig (1979), Pearson was involved with founding the Northern League in 1958, which sought to promote solidarity among Teutonic nations and has been chair of the World Anti-Communist League.

Racism: psychological violence

The question remains of the relevance of biologically based racism to the activities of most modern psychologists. Overwhelmingly they would publicly repudiate such views, many with a degree of anger and outrage. But that may be part of the problem. If racism is abhorred for its most violent extremes, how do we construe the effects of racism which does not leave corpses? Just what do we think the experience of racism is like for the victim?

The horror of physical extermination and sterilisation of millions carried out throughout the world, in the name of eugenics, should not detract from the *psychological* violence and oppression of racism. However, many have neglected this psychological aspect, especially white European theorists and investigators. They tend to approach the problem from purely academic and detached standpoints. In contrast, oppression and racism have a personal urgency and immediacy for black people. Their daily encounters with racism or oppression do not encourage them to approach the subject with the cold detachment of the white academician. While it might appear somewhat ludicrous to discuss physical and psychological violence together, doing so highlights the question of the nature of the harm done by racism to its victims.

Violence is difficult to define. But irrespective of the fine detail, psychologists have tended to regard it largely as physical – in terms of bodily injury, damage, or harm. It is uncommon for them to conceive of it as psychological; rarely is a distinction made between physical and psychological violence. Indeed, psychological violence to many people, including researchers and theorists, seems not to exist. For example, Newman (1979) defined violence as 'that which leads to physical injury or damage' (p. 2); Gelles and Straus (1979) defined it as 'an act carried out with the intention of, or perceived as having the intention of, physically hurting another person' (p. 4). In these definitions, racism, anti-Semitism, sexism and other forms of oppression, together with their concomitant adverse psychological and social effects, are virtually never seen as violence. Definitions which use 'intent' as the criterion (or a criterion) of violence are particularly inadequate, because racism and sexism, for instance, as forms of violence or oppression are often perpetrated unconsciously. Breakwell (1989) provides a good illustrative case of the inherent inadequacy of definitions based upon physical harm and intent:

> VIOLENCE comprises those acts in which there is a deliberate attempt to inflict physical harm. Thus *accidental* harm does not comprise violence. For example, damage which is a by-product of anger but is not intended does not comprise violence. It may feel the same to the victim but it cannot be explained in the same way as deliberate attempts to harm. This distinction between intended and accidental outcomes is made in our everyday lives and in the legal system. We make it in deciding how we react to the individual causing the damage. (p. 9)

This may be adequate for explaining such incidents as stepping on another person's foot, nevertheless it raises a number of uncomfortable questions: What does it imply for a rapist who believes that women secretly enjoy being raped? If he claims his intention was to cause his victim pleasure rather than physical harm, do we regard the rape as non-violent? Dismissing the victim's feeling or subjective interpretation of her ordeal as more or less irrelevant would appear grotesquely insensitive and arrogant. Or, to take the case of the extreme bigot whose blood boils at the sight of a black person and so attacks a black family. Is this person violent or not? Was there any intention to be violent or was it the accidental consequence of anger? From a psychological point of view, the most flagrantly unsatisfactory aspect of this definition is that it negates and invalidates the victim's definition of what constitutes a violent act.

Definitions of violence based solely upon physical harm and/or intent are not merely narrow but, perhaps more importantly, they signify a lack of understanding of violence and/or oppression. By reducing the essence of violence to a moral issue, for instance, such definitions serve to legitimise state and institutional violence and oppression. An immigration law which, for instance, keeps black families apart solely on the grounds of their colour or ethnic origin and causes the members untold emotional distress, social and economic hardships and anguish is nothing but violent, and ought to be seen as such. In short, to understand violence and oppression better, we need to go beyond the skin, we must transcend the physical and/or moral aspects of violence. Such an approach would enable psychologists to understand better their own racism and its adverse psychological effects on the victims of racism.

Black writers are more likely to take this into account. For example, Bulhan (1985; p. 135) has defined violence as 'any relation, process or condition by which an individual or a group violates the physical, social and/or psychological integrity of another person or group. Likewise, Freire (1972) defined oppression or violence as:

> Any situation in which A objectively exploits B or hinders his pursuit of self-affirmation as a responsible person is one of oppression. Such a situation in itself constitutes violence, even when it is sweetened with man's autological and historical vocation to be more fully human. With the establishment of a relationship of oppression, violence has *already* begun. (p. 31)

Such situations and relationships have been very forcefully and graphically described by Parekh (1974), an Indian professor of political science and former vice-chairman of the British Commission for Racial Equality:

> Racism appears in the way the immigrant is cheated by, say, a shop assistant as if honesty in her view was not to be practised with respect to him; it appears in the way promises given to him are broken as if promises given to a black man are not binding; it appears in the way he is gratuitously insulted as if his feelings deserved no consideration; it is expressed in his social ostracism, in the ways his favours are taken for granted and those by the white man to him considered to require more than equal in return, in the way his social graces and intellectual skills are treated as unusual in 'someone like him', in the perverse glee taken in not being able to spell or pronounce an immigrant's name correctly. . . . Such instances are all individually trivial but can be cumulatively shattering and general enough to make an immigrant's life unbearable. . . . if he reacts to them on each occasion, he is in danger of getting consumed by the fire of his rage. (p. 234)

From the perspectives of its victims, racism inhibits human growth, limits productive living and causes death; and it matters very little, if at all, whether or not the perpetrators are conscious of or intend the psychological harm they inflict upon them (Owusu-Bempah, 1985).

In Hitler's Germany, medicine, including psychology, did not work for the individual's well-being; it had to serve the collective body of the German people, securing its racial health (Hanauske-Abel, 1986). 'Non-Aryan' individuals, foreign to the 'Aryan' constitution of the German people, were deemed to have invaded its collective body and have infected its organs: they had to be dealt with in exactly the same way health professionals cope with living pathogenic agents – isolation and disinfection was the therapeutic imperative. For this task, only 'Aryan' physicians were judged qualified and within five years over 90 per cent of 'non-Aryan' doctors were 'eliminated'. This 'New German Medicine' worked to provide quantifiable criteria for discriminating 'Aryan' from 'non-Aryan'; and in the interest of medical education continually published articles on racial biology and racial hygienics, concerning the differential diagnosis and phenotypic appearance of 'non-Aryan' genetic inferiority. Little has changed and psychologists continue to publish on racial biology and the 'inferiority' of the black 'race'.

Psychology purports to be a science concerned with the well-being of humanity. Psychological ethics shout this message loud. Yet its practitioners continue to racially violate and oppress others. That being a psychologist or a scientist does not in itself inoculate one against racism or oppression is evident in Freire's (1972) observation that 'the oppressors and revolutionary humanism both make use of science'. Acknowledging our role in racism is part of the process of change. However:

> Discovering oneself to be an oppressor may cause considerable anguish, but it does not necessarily lead to solidarity with the oppressed. True solidarity with the oppressed means fighting at their side to transform the objective reality which has made them these 'beings for another'. (Freire, 1972; p. 26)

The danger, of course, lies in disavowing responsibility using whatever defences are available. A White Rose leaflet published in Hitler's Germany makes the point:

> Do not hide your cowardice under the cloak of sophistication. Everyone is in a position to contribute to the fall of this system. What matters now is not to allow oneself any rest until everyone is convinced of the utmost importance of his fight against this order. . . . We see the most horrible crime against the dignity of man, a crime that is unprecedented in all of human history. Why is apathy the reaction of the German nation? Everybody strives to acquit oneself of complicity, everybody does it and then sleeps with a clear and peaceful mind. But no-one can be exonerated, everyone is *guilty, guilty, guilty*! (quoted by Hanauske-Abel, 1986, p. 273)

To assume that the racism of psychology confines itself to the bad-gene theorists is to fall at the first hurdle. It makes the problem too simple, too easy and too distant from ourselves. In short, by defining the problem narrowly, the extent of the problem is ignored.

Chapter 3

The 'liberal' tradition in the psychology of racism

Just as a science of fish must eventually say something about water, social psychology remains woefully deficient as long as it neglects culture and cultural racism. (Jones, 1983, p. 119)

The assumption, largely unstated, that bad-gene theorists just about exhaust racism in psychology is wrong historically and now. The broader stream of psychological racism which systematically attacks black culture rather than black genes is largely ignored (Howitt, 1991). But even psychologists specifically rejecting biological racism have been tempted into cultural disparagement:

Whites in contact with aborigines let down. Certain of the first trans-Alleghany settlers became so Indianized as to wear a buckskin dress, marry a squaw, and let the scalp-lock grow. Realizing this danger of let-down, an isolated white enveloped by savages becomes intensely conservative. The French Canadians of to-day are French of the seventeenth century, and their conservatism has, no doubt, the same root . . . [as] Boer conservatism. (Ross, 1908, p. 150)

This is stark paralogism. How can inferior subhumans like black people exert such an enduring and powerful influence on the superior white race? Such claims are tantamount to warning that domestic pets drag down mentally and morally the families they live among. No matter how absurd such beliefs appear now, they are still current in modified forms; for example, objections to the presence of black families in one's neighbourhood and fears that at school the presence of black children impairs white children educationally.

Ross was no biological racist. However, like that biological racist McDougall, he published an introduction to social psychology in 1908. In his book, Ross virtually rejects the view that national and racial

39

differences are biologically in-built (Howitt, 1991). However, there is no doubt at all that he was a cultural racist; the above quotation shows this. Even the use of a word like 'squaw', a seemingly neutral term, is not what it appears to be. Squaw is not a native American word for woman or wife as might be supposed. It is their word for cunt. In effect the native American woman was described as her sexual organs by European Americans. Further to this disparagement, Ross argues strongly that aboriginal cultures harm white ones. White people may not adopt the aboriginal culture but they do 'let down' or, in other words, abandon their standards. Aboriginal peoples are described as savages, not as nations. Somehow the world-wide atrocities of Europeans makes them expert judges of savagery. Ross also makes a case for 'separate development' when he praises conservatism which prevents white culture from 'sinking' to the aboriginal level. It is virtually impossible to differentiate Ross from McDougall on the desirability of separating white from black cultures. Aboriginal people are not shown to be victims of white conservatism but its cause. Such victim-blaming highlights how racist psychology cannot be understood completely if one concentrates solely on biological racism. Violation of black cultures has been as relentless as the war on black genes.

Recognition of cultural racism has encouraged some black scholars to trace the ancient African roots of significant intellectual achievements. A good example is Nobles (1986), who demonstrates the importance of ancient black African Egyptian scholarship and philosophy in the origins of modern psychology. Of course, if black African thought was an influence on psychology then where is it found in histories of psychology? Nobles supplies evidence that African ideas were hijacked by ancient Greek philosophers. Some, such as Plato, acknowledged the sources of their thinking as African, but Aristotle conspired to obscure the link. He was tutor to the future Alexander the Great, the Macedonian empire builder:

> Clearly Aristotle saw the 'foreign invention' (i.e. philosophy) . . . as a political weapon which would assist Alexander in concretizing his rulership. Through a methodology of revision and modifications, the conspiracy between Aristotle and Alexander . . . was . . . to falsify the African roots of Greek thought and to fabricate Greek's authorship. . . . Until Alexander gave Aristotle the keys to the libraries of the African mystery system, Aristotle . . . had only written books on nine different areas. The books Aristotle is now credited with range from 400 to 1000. . . . [Alexander] could feel more comfortable in representing Greek/Macedonian culture as excelling all 'others in the knowledge of what is excellent'. (p. 26–7)

A profound desire to right a wrong permeates Nobles' account as well as those of others (e.g. Davidson, 1984; James, 1954; Williams,

1976). While, as is commonly accepted, somewhere in ancient Greek philosophy lie the roots of modern psychology, day-to-day, bread-and-butter psychologists are little concerned with the philosophies of long-dead men. However, that these dead white men stole from black dead men graphically highlights white nations' denial of black culture. Aristotle's chicanery had echoed throughout history. The screw has had extra turns. Aristotle merely robbed black culture, others sought to destroy it.

Nobles was rightly concerned to establish black African culture as central to Western psychology. However, the denial of black culture goes deep. The Dogon of Mali in West Africa possessed tremendous knowledge about the universe (Yeboah, 1988). They knew of Jupiter's moons, Saturn's rings and many other things. Remarkably, they were also aware of the tiny star Sirius B. This star is invisible to the naked eye but, nevertheless, they had plotted its trajectory through the milky way. Anthropologists working in Mali between 1931 and 1956 revealed this great knowledge to the Western world. Predictably, a familiar but bizarre denial process was set in train. For example: 'Robert Temple, a member of the Royal Astronomical Society of Great Britain, in his book, "The Sirius Mystery", speculated that "space-beings" from the Sirius star-system must have brought this marvellous knowledge down to the Africans' (Yeboah, 1988, p. 166).

Available historical evidence (e.g., Davidson, 1984; James, 1954; Williams, 1976) indicates that the racist construction of general historical reality is founded on fiction and falsehoods rather than observation and analysis. There has always been a deliberate and persistent effort to distort and falsify. Science has often been replaced by desire and wishful thinking. The full complexity of all branches of humanity has generally been ignored in favour of subtle and crude attempts to arrogate the scientific and cultural achievements of black people to white people; in short, to demonstrate the superiority of white people over black people (Yeboah, 1988). Psychologists' complicity in this shameful enterprise is demonstrated over and over by the 'greats' of psychology and their modern disciples. In recent years, the antagonism to black culture has moved slightly to concentrate on the families of black people as the focus of allegations of deficit and pathology.

The attack on black family culture

We have seen a growth of interest, curiosity and research on the black *family*. A new 'blame the victim' form of explanation has taken hold of the black family as the primary locus of social pathology, the cycle of deprivation and the culture of poverty. A new and widened scope has emerged for explaining racism away by defining resistance to it as a psychological malfunction. . . . They were part of an attempt to delegitimate black politics by re-defining them as psychological reactions to 'prejudice' and deprivation. (Mercer, 1984, p. 25)

The psychiatrist Schoenfeld (1988) sought to explain why in the USA black people commit half of violent crime, substantially disproportionate to their representation in the population. Following a well-laid trail which shifts the blame from white society to the black family, he takes us back to slavery times to find fault:

the fathers of black slave families were often unrecognized or absent, the consciences of their sons would have been, to such an extent, seriously incomplete. (p. 276)

it could hardly have helped the ego to contend with the anger and aggression presumably triggered in the slaves by the unending blows to their self-esteem and sense of self-worth. (p. 275)

The superegos or consciences of the black males who rioted during the late 1960s should not have been expected to be strong enough to enable their egos to control their aggression. (p. 289)

So black people lack conscience because their families fail to develop their superegos. Furthermore, a now familiar political theme can be found to underlie this psycho-history of the black family. In Schoenfeld's 'what is to be done' section he articulates his antipathy to preferential recruitment of black people on job training programmes, education and the like. Rather than a means of righting social inequity, the 'aid' given black people is construed by Schoenfeld as crucial to the problem. Such programmes proclaim the state's message of the incapability of black people of achieving equality in their own right, according to Schoenfeld. This:

cannot help be a blow to their self-esteem and sense of self-worth, and arouse their aggression. 'Affirmative action' as a means of eliminating the consequences of *de jure* and *de facto* discrimination is, in short, dubious psychologically. . . . Similar comments can be made about the welfare system. (pp. 292–3)

Punishments to be given black criminals are similarly reactionary:

To support the superego, punishments should be specific and determinant. The superegos of blacks are far more likely to gain support from a statute that decrees . . . a specific term of imprisonment, or a specific corporal punishment. (p. 226)

Arrest and punishment are *needed* by the black superego:

we must do much more than we are to make sure that violent criminals are apprehended and punished in the manner prescribed by the law. Far from being an antiblack policy, as some civil libertarians would have us believe, it is the *sine qua non* of helping blacks cope with the fires that rage within them as a result of more than 300 years of physical and psychological abuse. (p. 297)

Socially repressive measures are this psychiatrist's medicine for his putative black family pathology. For example, to help black people cope with their abuse, they must suffer more abuse. The way in which racial issues are constructed contributes to this social 'remedy' for the socially 'ill'. Once the cupboard of biological racism has been swept clean, it is easy to uncover the disguised 'liberal' cobwebs. Short on history, it is convenient to consider current race-thinking as progress when it rejects arcane biological racism.

The notion of black family pathology was at the roots of Rushton's thesis concerning reproductive strategies (Chapter 2). Even shed of this biological aspect, the thesis remains offensive to black people. It represents a ubiquitous stereotype which Lyles and Carter (1982) examine with reference to the USA when they discuss some of the strengths and adaptive patterns typical of black families. This requires familiarity with the history of the black family in the USA:

The literature is replete with documentation of the obstacles that black families have encountered in developing and retaining a sense of cohesion, identity, and security in the face of socially condoned racial stigmatizations. . . . With slavery, black families were separated – ergo bonding and the extended family network were discouraged. In post slavery society, the psychological scars that remained were further intensified by continuing personal and institutional racist practices that devalued personal worth and family pride. (p. 1120)

Knowing the mythical nature of much 'knowledge' about black families can be important in understanding them properly (Lyles and Carter, 1982). Among the common myths relevant to therapy are the following:

1. *Family power structure*: It has been commonly accepted that the families follow a matriarchal structure led by domineering females with the men subordinate or missing. Lyle and Carter provide evidence that contrary to this view black families are typically egalitarian.
2. *Black family fragmentation*: Characteristically black families are regarded as fragmented – partly exacerbated by males deserting the family. Despite this view, most black families are intact. The prevalence of one-parent families is, however, relatively greater among the poor.

3. *Difficulties in enculturation*: Fragmented families are held to be incapable of providing proper socialisation and to promote serious psychopathology in their children. However, black youngsters from 'fragmented' families are just as likely to go to college as any other black youngsters. In other words, they are equally well enculturalised.

4. *Family interdependence*: The extended black family brings with it a responsibility to provide reciprocal help when it is needed. Some suggest that this might encourage feelings of guilt in upwardly mobile members of the family. Research provides no support for this view which essentially pathologises the black family with respect of achievement.

According to Lyles and Carter (1982):

> a black family may not readily disclose their feelings about personal issues and in fact may appear overtly suspicious of the therapist. One may neglect the effects of culture and the realities of being black and attribute this behavior to the dynamics of the family system. (p. 1122)

Of course, these myths systematically pathologise and disparage black family culture. Often they fall just short of suggesting that black family culture is a fiction, much as historically black culture has been held to have not existed (Yeboah, 1988).

Social scientists, in the guise of a well-meaning liberalism, can serve black people a poisoned chalice. The social science literature on black families after the Second World War concentrated on the effects of racial discrimination on black people's personalities. A notable study of this kind is by Kardiner and Ovesey (1951) in the book *The Mark of Oppression*. This claimed that the original (African) culture of black people was pulverised under slavery in America. Since no culture could flourish under the repressive conditions of slavery, black people live in a sort of cultureless void. This lack of culture, social cohesion and social belonging, together with racial oppression and discrimination, are assumed to be integral to the lives of all black people. Kardiner and Ovesey even went as far as suggesting that every personality trait of black people could be traced to their difficult circumstances. This pathologisation of black people stimulated much research seeking the problems and weaknesses in black families. This culminated in Moynihan's renowned report of 1965 in which he saw black American families as a 'tangle of pathology'; slavery and its deprivations had forced African-American communities into a matriarchal structure. Consequently, according to Moynihan, black males were 'emasculated'. Disastrously, these ideas were incorporated into American (and to a large extent British) social policy. In addition, they have also had a profound influence on the thinking and research of social scientists, including psychologists.

Other critics have seen this alleged matriarchal character of black families as pathological and detrimental to black children's personality development (e.g. Lobo, 1978). Yet others suggest that the matriarchal family is an outgrowth of the failure of black men to fulfil their paternal roles. Lawrence (1982) provides evidence of the 'pathological' approach of the Moynihan report in British studies (a perverse sort of 'multi-culturalism'). Frequently, such research portrays African-Caribbean families as weak and unstable, lacking in paternal responsibility towards children and inadequately controlling their youngsters (e.g. Cashmore, 1979; Pryce, 1979). Elsewhere, as Littlewood and Lipsedge (1989) have noted, African-Caribbean families are accused of being too religious and exercising strict discipline over their children, including corporal punishment (e.g. Lobo, 1978).

Some suggest that recently the focus on black families has shifted from a pathological/dysfunctional approach to a strength/resilient model. According to Wilson (1992), a number of factors characterise this change, including: (a) an examination of black families within a black cultural context, and (b) an analysis of the presence rather than absence of the father within the family. Studies taking these into account highlight the way in which earlier investigations had overwhelmingly concentrated on deficiencies, weaknesses and problems of the black family (e.g. Hale, 1982; McAdoo, 1981a; Nobles, 1978). Not surprisingly, the long list of black family pathologies from earlier studies included father-absence, poverty and low-income status, fathers' precarious position in the job market and high delinquency rates (e.g. Bernard, 1966; Frazier, 1947).

Problem-based studies of black families are not at fault solely because of their *over*-concentration on the harsh reality faced by many in the black community. The failure of research to describe and analyse how black families survive adversities is more crucial. The strength/resilient approach, now gaining currency, represents a more complete picture. It considers features of black culture which enable coping with difficult life circumstances. For instance, such studies consistently show that the extended family structure acts to preserve black family life (e.g. McAdoo, 1981a, b; Wilson, 1992). In addition, the strength approach demonstrates the effects of the father's presence on the family. The historical neglect of the father in the social science literature has erroneously led to the assumption that black fathers have no interest or role in their children's socialisation (McAdoo, 1981a, b). However, once father-presence is taken into account, both black and white fathers are shown to share similar expectations of child behaviour.

Differences are of degree rather than in kind; black and white fathers may be different to some extent in the detail of their interactions with their children. For instance, white fathers concentrate most on the development of their sons. Black fathers, owing to their experiences of discrimination, socialise both their daughters and their sons to be competent and independent at an earlier age (McAdoo, 1981b). In short, black fathers, like any other group of fathers, are nurturant, warm and loving towards their children (Hill, 1972; Young, 1970). Notwithstanding such research evidence indicating many positive strengths of the black family structure, stereotypes about the black family abound and persist in the social science literature, especially psychology.

Antipathy to alien culture

> one might legitimately applaud the marvellous way the Chinese have richly transformed that important English institution, the fish and chip shop . . . as well as the willingness of Pakistani shopkeepers to work much longer hours than their English counterparts to serve the community better. (Honeyford, 1986, p. 50)

Honeyford is an advocate of the view that antipathy to black culture is not racist. His training was partly in psychology and he has postgraduate qualifications in sociolinguistics and educational psychology which qualify him to be a full member of the British Psychological Society. He came to public attention during the early 1980s while he was Headmaster of Drummond School in Bradford, northern England. During his time there, the school's catchment area became increasingly multi-cultural. He published various articles on racial matters while he was head teacher – most significantly in the right-wing *Salisbury Review*. These boil down to a disparagement of black culture and an attack on anti-racist strategies. He finally took early retirement from his post following the public scrutiny of his beliefs enforced by parents at the school (Gordon and Klug, 1986). Examples of his disparagement of black cultures are easily found:

> 'Cultural enrichment' is the approved term for the West Indian's right to create an ear-splitting cacophony for most of the night . . ., of the Notting Hill Festival whose success or failure is judged at the level of street crime which accompanies it. (Honeyford, 1984, p. 30)

Honeyford described his visit to a 'troubled' parent whom he had previously never met thus:

A figure straight out of Kipling is bearing down on me. . . . He wears white baggy trousers, a long black coat buttoned, military style, up the front, and a 'white' hat, and he sports a beard dyed orange. His English sounds like that of Peter Sellers' Indian doctor on an off day. (Honeyford, 1983b, p. 19)

Or take his views on anti-racism initiatives:

A fundamental of respect for racial minorities is reflected in the notion of 'positive discrimination' in education . . . what an insult to the individual and his origins, and what a cast-iron method of confirming the prejudice of those psychologists who argue that blacks are intellectually inferior! (Honeyford, 1983a, p. 12)

Honeyford has expressed the belief that racism is often alleged in circumstances which do not warrant such a description. Given his very limited and traditional definition of racism, this is inevitably the case. He shares with much of psychology the view that racism is the ideologically based acceptance of racial superiority:

To Honeyford, [racism] refers to 'the odious doctrines of racial superiority'. . . . To define the word in this way is all well and good, so long as one then proceeds to find another word to describe, for example, the often quite unintentional discrimination experienced by ethnic minorities simply because of the way the institutions in our society are structured. . . . Honeyford's statement that 'Britain is not a racist society' . . . may be true on his own definition of racism, but is hardly likely to offer much reassurance to those who are daily on the receiving end of gratuitous insults, violence, bullying, threats and other less direct but more insidious forms of discrimination directed at them for no other reason than the colour of their skin. (Halstead, 1988, pp. 65–6)

Psychology shares much of the thinking which allows Honeyford to reject allegations of racism despite becoming a focus of the anger of the black community and its sympathisers. Significantly, Honeyford received considerable support from the British press, which saw him as the victim not the victimiser (Searle, 1989). He represents a more general view of black people which professes that the problem is that they are not like us – they do not do things our way. Following centuries of colonial oppression in which savage attempts were made to enforce compliance to Western ways, the fear is that 'they' follow 'their' ways in 'our' back yard! The dilemma is only resolved by members of other cultures abandoning their culture to become just like white society. Trying to be 'white' is likely to make white society even more antagonistic towards them (Cox, 1948).

Unfortunately, Honeyford's views are not merely those of an individual on the margins of psychology. One of the major contributions of modern social psychology has been 'social identity' theory. In its basic assumptions, this goes even further than Honeyford in that it provides a rationale for the view that hostility to other groups is 'natural', just as positive regard for one's own group is 'in-built'.

Social identity theory

One watershed for race relations in Britain was the 'rivers of blood' speech in 1968 by Enoch Powell, a government minister at the time. Catalytic in dividing public opinion, Powell's view, in essence, was that cultures do not mix smoothly; that multi-cultural Britain was sliding towards extremely violent ethnic conflict. Powell's argument is illustrated in the following:

> We have an identity of our own . . . and the instinct to preserve that identity is one of the deepest and strongest implanted in mankind. (Powell, cited in Gordon and Klug, 1986, p. 19)

> Physical and violent conflict must sooner or later supervene where an indigenous population sees no end to the progressive occupation of its heartland by aliens with whom they do not identify and who do not identify themselves with them. (Powell, cited in Gordon and Klug, 1986, p. 19)

The history of European occupation of the Americas and Australia, and the imposition of their culture upon Africa and elsewhere, is conveniently forgotten by Powell. By identity Powell does not mean how individuals define their individual self for themselves and others. Rather, he is referring to a 'social identity' which serves to define communities to themselves. But social identity was also a major theme central to much social psychology during the 1970s and beyond. Perhaps a different term should be found to demarcate Powell's concept from that of psychologists. However, this could not completely disguise the intimate parallels between Powell's thinking and social identity theory.

Social identity theory was developed at the University of Bristol in England during the 1970s. Henri Tajfel was the most significant psychologist associated with it. Originally an experimental psychologist, he became attracted to social psychology. This is important since Tajfel's experimental work on cognition had led him to see the process of categorisation as a basic characteristic of human thought (Tajfel, 1969; 1978b; Tajfel *et al.*, 1971). A few years later, coincidentally with Powell's racial doomsday scenario, Tajfel began to explore categorisation as a fundamental process in the perceptions groups of people have of others. His most famous research became known as the 'minimal group paradigm'. Quite simply, this showed that when people have even the most trivial things in common, they categorise themselves as being part of a 'group'. That is, petty similarities are enough to create a 'group' identity. When the opportunity is offered to distribute 'rewards' to others, more would be given to unknown people who had a trivial resemblance to oneself than to others who did not share this minor affinity.

The theory implies that this process is natural and in-built:

> The assumption is that even when there is no explicit or institutionalized conflict or competition between the groups, there is a tendency toward ingroup-favouring behavior. This is determined by the need to preserve or achieve a 'positive group distinctiveness' which in turn serves to protect, enhance, preserve, or achieve a positive social identity for members of the groups. . . . 'Social identity' is defined as 'that *part* of the individuals' self-concept which derives from their knowledge of their membership of a social group (or groups) together with the value and emotional significance of that membership' . . . in a vast majority of cases, only through appropriate inter*group* social comparisons. (Tajfel, 1982, p. 24)

If intergroup hostility is natural and built into our thought processes as a consequence of categorisation, racism, conceived as a form of intergroup hostility (or in-group favouritism), may also be construed as natural. In terms of the distribution of resources, racism is thus justified as the norm – 'charity begins at home'. Some argue that it is wrong to suggest that Tajfel's theories were borrowed broadly from racist ideology and do not give academic credence to these notions:

> my own Professor and intellectual mentor, Henri Tajfel was a lifelong opponent of racism, born both of conviction and his own experience of the Holocaust. . . . [H]e showed that the mere categorisation of people into groups . . . was sufficient to set in motion a chain of events which led them to regard each other as somehow different and to behave towards each other in a discriminatory fashion in order to achieve some measure of superiority and self-esteem. A fascinating finding, but one which, when taken out of context and elevated to the status of a universal human characteristic, is easily *misrepresented* as an explanation and a justification for racism. It would be the most cruelly ironic twist to Henri's life and work if, having lost his family and community to Fascism, his own writing was to be quoted in racist publications. (Milner, 1991, p. 10, emphasis added)

Of course, Tajfel never intended to justify racism. Nevertheless, his theory is fuel to an ideology which regards intergroup hostility as inevitable. We should not pretend that intergroup relations are merely 'charity begins at home' writ large. Racist jokes, nationalistic impulses and cultural disparagement are aspects of racism throughout the world.

This aside, social identity theory reflects ideas which are regarded as directly racist in different contexts.

Cowlishaw (1986) presents a critique of the notion of racism as natural though paying attention to a more obvious target than Tajfel. He concentrates on a book by Van den Berghe (*The Ethnic Phenomenon*) which argues that racism is 'deeply rooted in our biology' and is an extension of 'nepotism between kinsmen' (1981, p. xi). This theory has influenced one eminent British race relations theorist and researcher, John Rex, who accepts a 'primordial tendency to advance the interests of those thought of as one's own' (Rex, 1983, p. xx)'. Van den Berghe's views are a variant of the socio-biologist position which posits species' survival value in current social structures and relationships. The gene pool is most likely to survive if genetically similar organisms co-operate rather than compete. One 'prediction' from this theory is that co-operation is a direct function of the proportion of genes organisms share; the more genetically similar people are, the more they should co-operate. However, there are numerous problems with such a notion. For example, humans share virtually all of their genes irrespective of race, so racism is hardly conducive to the preservation of the gene pool. Also, it is difficult to explain why people of mixed-race parentage are not accepted but treated with hostility by white people. After all, they are closer in their genetic make-up to white people than other races. There is another fundamental fallacy:

> What van den Berghe calls the ethnic phenomenon is known in popular psychology as the fear of strangers, suspicion of the unknown or division into 'us' and 'them'. Such sentiments are widely accepted as being a natural part of social sanctioning. But there are many *us's* and a multitude of *them's* based on place, profession, sex, age, interests as well as kin, and sociobiology does not explain why certain loyalties are extended to certain groups, and why certain group boundaries are continually broken. There are many who show passionate interest in strangers and there is much exploration of unfamiliar cultures. Are we to say that these are mutant genes at work? (Cowlishaw, 1986, p. 10)

The genetic basis of racism is not an important difference between van den Berghe and Tajfel. Both agree that out-group hostility is a basic human characteristic, either for the survival of the close gene pool or because categorisation has a fundamental role in human cognition. They also agree that favouritism towards the in-group is natural. Van den Berghe claims it is genetically programmed for its survival value. On the other hand, Tajfel apparently felt it did not deserve explanation and virtually took it for granted as a basic tenet. Followers of the Tajfel tradition, Hewstone and Giles (1984), illustrate this quite clearly when they write of social identity theory:

Claiming that motivational as well as cognitive factors underlie intergroup differentiation, *the theory holds that positive comparisons (intergroup differences seen to favour the ingroup) provide a satisfactory social identity*, while negative comparisons (differences which favour the outgroup) convey an unsatisfactory identity. . . . Empirical support . . . demonstrated that social *categorization alone can be sufficient to engender intergroup discrimination* in which the ingroup is favoured over the outgroup. (p. 278, emphasis added)

So there is little doubt that social identity theory promotes the view that the disparagement of other groups is crucial in creating a satisfactory social identity and a positive personal self-regard. The argument is not whether people frequently do favour their own group at the expense of others, but with what is meant by the assertion that this is satisfactory and natural.

The process of favouring one's own group is a substantial component of racism. So, for example, objecting to black people's refusal to adopt white cultural patterns is to disapprove of their failure to confirm the dominant culture's superiority. The disparagement of cultures beyond one's national boundaries demonstrates the intrinsic nationalism and racism of the viewpoint. There are difficulties inherent in treating disadvantaged groups as victims of irrational racial prejudice or of their cultural individuality (Cowlishaw, 1986). To accept that hostility towards out-groups is due to their being different, as Tajfel and others implicitly do, excuses the in-group for choosing to regard them as different. There is little difficulty in recognising the attitudes of the woman in Cowlishaw's research who, when faced with the news that there was a loiterer near her car one night, suggested 'I'd like to shoot anything with a bit of colour in it' (p. 17). Nevertheless, in a more reflective mood, she asserts that she is not a racist and it is only the aboriginal people who 'can't live like we do' who would be unwelcome in her home:

theories that reify race or ethnic differences . . . must explain how it is that the biological and cultural convergences, the increased similarity in appearance and life-style that has developed gradually between Europeans and Aborigines over the last 200 years, has not been accompanied by a closing of the racial divide . . . Why is it that Aborigines remain a distinct and clearly defined group although in many cases there is a greater biological and cultural heritage from white ancestry? (Cowlishaw, 1986, pp. 12–13)

The problem is not to justify intergroup hostility but to explain how out-group categories such as 'Aboriginal' or 'Paki' are created and continue despite major changes in the characteristics of the out-group and the dominant 'host' nation. Just how are in-groups and out-groups socially generated and maintained? By taking hostility between groups for granted, psychological theory reinforces its apparent naturalness. It is not surprising to find that psychology transfers ideas wholesale from wider society. Equally expected is the lack of rebellion against such ideas within the discipline. In this light, the replacement of biological racism in psychology by the 'naturalness' thesis may be one consequence of pressures on psychology to appear egalitarian, in line with political developments in wider society.

Anyone seeking to appreciate the influence of Tajfel's ideas on theory would do well to read du Preez (1980), who provides a chilling account of apartheid in South Africa's politics using the basic assumptions of social identity theory:

> It is impossible to eliminate competition between groups, if this theory is correct. Nor would it be desirable, since individuals derive positive identity from group membership. What can be done is to attempt to regulate some of the forms which group competition takes. (p. 23)

It is informative to compare this with a quotation from Dr H. F. Verwoerd, the psychologist architect of South African apartheid:

> The Apartheid policy was described as that which was practicable in the direction of what one looked upon as ideal. Nobody will deny that, for the Natives as well as for the Europeans, total separation would have been the ideal if that had been the course of history. (du Preez, 1980, p. 90)

There would appear to be no argument against this in social identity theory. Verwoerd, for example, could have argued that he was allowing black South Africans to compete and, thus, form a satisfactory social identity in their homelands. The reality was clearly of tremendous damage inflicted by apartheid.

Tajfel's fundamental error lies partly in method. By forcing people to make choices in circumstances in which context was minimalised, it is not surprising that they resort to the sort of hostile treatment of out-group members. Western culture has taught them that this is an appropriate style of response. Furthermore, social identity theory reifies culturally learnt intergroup hostility as being biologically programmed human nature. One can only offer conjecture about why psychologists who are antipathetic to racist ideas can create such fundamentally racist theories. Of course, adopting a critical attitude to one's own theoretical writings during the tenuous process of their development is difficult. Working in a cultural and work context which embraces a similar ideological framework to that contained within the theory does not help critical thinking either. But this does not seem a sufficient explanation of academic failures on matters of racism in general. This becomes abundantly evident when we turn to examining feminism and race.

Schisms in the -isms: the feminist takeover bid

> Martha, a very bright 30-year-old African-American woman, described a situation in which she worked as a babysitter/housekeeper for Carol, a 35-year-old White woman, with two young children. Carol was very involved in feminist causes and taught courses on women's issues at a local university. She had been a major advocate for extended maternity and paternity leaves at her university. Martha had felt a growing friendship with Carol who had encouraged her to go on to college part time. After two years of employment, Martha, who was unmarried but living with her boyfriend, became pregnant. She decided to have her child and to take a three-month maternity leave after the birth of her baby. She discussed this with Carol who panicked at the thought of losing her child care support and became angry. In her anger she said to Martha, 'I thought you people returned to work right after the birth of your children'. (Boyd-Franklin, 1991, pp. 30–1)

Superficially, there is no great divide between racism and sexism. Both are terms used to describe the subjugation of disadvantaged groups, so it is tempting to consider them so similar that in crucial respects they overlap. Certainly in terms of their outcomes they are much the same. However, when it comes to their perpetrators things are not so clear-cut. Reid (1988) points out the considerable imbalance in their meanings. Using Webster's dictionary definitions, she notes that racism is described as 'a belief that race is a primary determinant of human traits and capacities and that racial differences produce an inherent superiority of a particular race.' But sexism is defined as 'prejudice or discrimination against women'. Quite clearly, a belief system is held as central to racism but no such notion is inherent in the definition of sexism. Essentially there is a bigger hurdle to define something as racist than as sexist. Perhaps this is part of the reason why it has been possible for women effectively to challenge sexism in psychology while racism has largely been tackled only at its ideological extreme.

Some feminists have paid lip-service to racism by claiming the authority to address the mistreatment of other minorities. There is some appeal in this. Surely victims of prejudice are on a higher moral ground to speak of prejudice in general than would be the victimisers. One corollary of this would be, of course, that black men could speak just as effectively for white women as white women could for black men.

But this has not emerged in the feminist literature, presumably because it is fallacious.

Some, notably black women (e.g., Davis, 1981; Lewis, 1977), argue that the gains of feminism owe much to black protest which greatly influenced North American politics during the 1960s. The civil rights movement provided the impetus for radical white women to challenge sexist social structures. Cued by concerted black protest, feminism was advanced as an articulation of their common discontents and interests as members of a subjugated group. Like black people, they perceived white men as thwarting their legitimate aspirations to power and resources. In the view of these authors, the women's movement surfaced principally to obtain for women the same access to political and economic power as black people were striving for.

Modern feminism has generated a multitude of theories, especially sociological and psychological ones. These aim to explain female subordination and to provide models to combat sexism. However, these have focused almost exclusively on sexism and gender issues. As a consequence, they have little or no applicability to the special position of *black* women in white social structure. But these are the women who are subject to the effects of racism, sexism and class bias in combination (Lewis, 1977). This is, of course, to ignore the many parallels between discrimination against women and black people of both sexes.

Is this state of affairs deliberate? Members of an oppressed group theoretically constitute an interest-group whose shared interests derive from their common fate of powerlessness. However, it is extremely doubtful whether white professional women perceive themselves as having the same interests and problems as black women, sharing the same fate or being on the same deck as black women. To expect white professional women to champion the cause of black women whom they would employ as char women without the least qualm, as in the case of Carol and Martha (above), would be naive. It is uncomfortable for many white feminists to consider the racism suffered daily by black women in addition to the sexism they also suffer. Such discomfort arises because black women occupy different structural positions in society from white women. Black women, by virtue of belonging to a subordinate 'racial' group, are in structural opposition to white women, members of the dominant 'racial' group. Inevitably, white women, especially professionals, benefit from both racial and sex discrimination against black women. Furthermore, many feminists see themselves solely as victims of male oppression. They ignore their direct and indirect roles in the exploitation of other groups, particularly black women and men.

Black women also have less access than white women to deference (Lewis, 1977). White women, for example in their roles as 'the driving force behind every successful man', obtain a sort of second-hand prestige, even though they might prefer esteem for their own achievements. Black women, on account of black male exclusion from the economic and political domains, share with their men a more marginal position in white socio-economic structures; the menial and ill-paid jobs. White women have had access to power and resources, albeit indirectly, through kinship and marriage, for example, through their fathers, husbands and sons who do command power and prestige in society. Such analyses reveal why white professional women, including white women psychologists, pay only lip-service to racism. Achieving parity between black women and white women would necessitate a change in relations between the 'races', a change in the structural realities between black women and white women. This is a matter for action, not theory, as it entails the relinquishement of some of the gains achieved by dint of hard struggle by white women. The pertinent question is: are they prepared to do so any more willingly than did white men for them, however little it may be?

The failure of white women to address the needs of black women is pointed out by Reid (1988). This reflects a similar failure on the part of black groups dominated by men:

> Just as some black men have ignored the needs of black women as women and have rejected the notion that sexism is an important problem for them, white women have frequently ignored the unique needs of black women as blacks. This omission has been interpreted as rejection and racism. It is evident in many of the growing number of scholarly books in fields such as psychology, sociology, and history that *women* means white women, and that other women are treated as afterthoughts, if included at all. Just as white men have overlooked the attitudes, contributions, and perspectives of white women, black women have been similarly treated. . . . Greenspan (1983) did not give any consideration to racial factors in her book on women's therapy; neither did Scarf (1980) in hers on depression, nor did Notman and Nadelson (1978) in theirs on health care . . . consideration of ethnic differences remains unimportant to many white researchers, whether they are male or female. (p. 215)

Reid recalls that Gaertner (1976) defined the aversive racist as someone who 'tries to avoid contact with blacks'. Consequently, failure to be concerned about ethnic issues constitutes a form of racism. Most certainly, seeking to speak for minority groups risks being construed as paternalistic or patronising racism:

> Although the race and sex equity movements both claim that black women should join their ranks, each group has exhibited some extent

of discrimination against them. The results indicate that black women have
been most disadvantaged, economically and socially, when compared to the
other race-sex groups. (p. 218)

While we need not be too concerned about the validity of Reid's general
claims here, the way in which feminist writings have overridden the
perspectives of black women does warrant concern. Examples could
be taken: virtually the only mention of race in the well-known feminist
psychological text by Wilkinson (1986) is the suggestion by Condor
(1986) that some of the earliest research on sex role-related beliefs
emerged out of Adorno *et al.*'s (1950) work on the Authoritarian
Personality. This is hardly to take on board black experience.

But this is little different from the findings of Brown *et al.* (1985)
who analysed for content American textbooks on the psychology of
women. They obtained a sample of twenty-eight books fitting this
description which were then searched for references to black women,
black, minority, Negro, Third World, racism and lower class. The
contents of the books were then coded according to the following
scheme:

1. *Integration*: 'information about Afro-American women is presented,
   compared, and contrasted with information about other racial–economic classes of women and interpreted from an international/inter-
   cultural perspective'.
2. *Tokenism*: 'instances in which sentences or paragraphs about Afro-
   American women are included in at least two or more places in the
   book. References are usually brief.'
3. *Segregation*: 'when information about Third World, black, or minority women is presented in a chapter or chapters devoted exclusively
   to that material'.
4. *Exclusion*: 'no references to Afro-American women'. (p. 32)

The research found that 25 per cent of books were exclusionary in
character, 39 per cent tokenistic and 36 per cent in the segregation
category. There were *none* which were integrationist.

Commonly these books on the psychology of women covered a rather
limited range of topics addressing the experience of black women. The
biases of the white women writers were reflected in the topics chosen:
for example, the matriarchal black family, the 'double bind' of being
black and female, and the relationship between black women and the
feminist movement. Furthermore, the books rarely described original
research on black women but preferred to concentrate on white Euro-
American women as the focus of attention. Nor did the books attempt
to adopt a psycho-historical approach involving pre-colonial African
lifestyles and the transmission of African values and culture following

slavery. In terms of black experience, the textbooks on the psychology of women did little other than to reproduce the non-feminist tradition in psychology texts – but against black people rather than women:

> *The findings of one particular group are generalizable to individuals of other groups; therefore, the findings on Euro-American women are indicative of women in general.* . . . Just as women were forgotten, excluded, or ignored by writers of introductory psychology books, writers of psychology of women books have similarly excluded, segregated or given only token reference to the experiences of Afro-American and other Third World women. (p. 35)

It would appear that being a victim does not guarantee sensitivity to the needs of other discriminated-against groups. Among the reasons for this is the frequent inability of psychologists to take a metaperspective, divorcing their own viewpoint from that of others. This may be encouraged by psychology's tendency to deal in putative universals – in this case women's experience of sexism being equated with black people's experience of racism. Self-satisfaction with one's own world-view as correct and proper might be responsible for this egocentrism. To suggest that psychological theory is as determined by beliefs, values and ideologies as by dispassionate science is hardly new.

Discourse analysis of racism

Nowhere is this egocentrism more clearly revealed than in the discourse analysis approach to identifying language mechanisms involved in effecting the social reproduction of racism. Although discourse analysis-orientated academics vary widely in their methods and theories, some have spasmodically turned their attention to the matter of racism in speech and text. Of course, there are extremely important questions to be asked about how racist dialogue is constructed and this should not be detracted from. However, discourse analysts' views on racism largely rehearse ancient themes in the psychology of racism. At the same time, many fundamental problems are ignored. By focusing on the language of racism, discourse analysts inevitably assume its detectability through language, its reproduction intergenerationally through language and, most significantly, that discourse analysts have a theory of racism. All of these assumptions are questionable and fundamentally misleading premises which reproduce the trap of marginalising racism to the statements of readily recognisable racists.

Van Dijk (1987) presents a major catalogue of discourse analysis of putative racist texts. But significant theory is not an inevitable outcome of cataloguing. Despite some meanderings around the term (arguing that it should include 'ethnicism' which is 'racism' applied to ethnic groups), in this much-cited work Van Dijk simply avoids defining what he means by racism! He writes merely that 'Our usage of the term *racism* follows the traditional terminology'! This would be a remarkable lapse for a work which purports to identify and code the means by which racism is communicated. However, there is reason to think that it is essential to Van Dijk's approach that the matter of definition is not adequately addressed. By failing to define it, racism becomes anything which he chooses to identify as racist.

Several years later, Van Dijk (1991) chose to tackle the meaning of racism more directly:

> Contemporary racism is a complex societal system in which peoples of European origin dominate peoples of other origins, especially in Europe, North America, South Africa, Australia, and New Zealand. This relationship of dominance may take many forms of economic, social, cultural and/or political hegemony, legitimated in terms of, usually negatively valued, different characteristics ascribed to the dominated people(s). (Van Dijk, 1991, p. 24)

Despite this, the notion of racism as a complex societal system is virtually ignored. We are not told just how such a complex system is represented in language or whether language is racism's *sine qua non*. Lacking a theory of racism directly related to textual interpretation, inevitably the analyst becomes the arbiter of what is racist! Without strong criteria, how can the discourse analyst be confident? The following provides grounds to wonder: 'Somewhat later in the interview, the woman musician counters the interviewer's suggestion that sometimes people are also *intolerant* when they have no direct experience with ethnic minority groups at all' (Van Dijk, 1987, p. 94, emphasis added).

Van Dijk thus reproduces language structures which reflect racism since it is possible to be tolerant only of what is otherwise intolerable. It is not surprising, then, that discourse analysis, according to Van Dijk, takes the view that non-racism is possible:

> the prevailing nature of racism as a system does not mean that all white people are necessarily, let alone inherently, 'racist'. White group dominance, and hence racism, are part of a specific historical process which involves western imperialism, capitalism, and colonialism, among other fundamental factors. . . . Segments of the white group may well oppose and challenge racism, and thus become allies of minority groups, for instance in anti-racist teaching or political action. Again, such real or apparent exceptions to structural dominance do not debilitate the system,

but may sometimes even strengthen it. Exceptions make the system of dominance more flexible or less rigid. (Van Dijk, 1991, pp. 30–1)

But the question of why some people are unaffected by racist social systems is not even raised. Van Dijk merely insists that they are not despite there being research evidence to the contrary (Devine, 1989). Such a suggestion is self-serving rhetoric for academic liberals – after all, not one jot of evidence is offered. There is little point in Van Dijk or any other academic prematurely abandoning self-exploration in such an ideologically charged area. We are all familiar with a good many racist stereotypes so in what sense can we be held to be free of racism? What would it mean? Despite Van Dyke's (1991, p. 5) claim to adopt a 'critical, anti-racist perspective', this is hardly compatible with his view that some people are non-racist. Anti-racism normally accepts the importance of the notion of 'the anti-racist racist'. The implication being that the racism of our culture is bound to structure our thoughts and actions. Consequently, anti-racism should involve critical self-examination, not merely that of other people and other organisations. Van Dijk's thesis risks encouraging complacency in those of us who avoid overt racist language. He also appears not to see one of his interviewer's apparent collusion with racism:

Interviewer: Well, how do you like living here?
Woman: Well, unfortunately the neighborhood has changed very much.
Interviewer: In those 26 years?
Woman: Yes, unfortunately, it used to be a VERY nice neighborhood, but it has become terrible.
Interviewer: In what sense terrible?
Woman: Uhh, many strangers.
Interviewer: *'Is it, yes yes, I saw that on the street.'* (Van Dijk, 1987, pp. 100–1, emphasis added)

This illustrates why we should be alert to the risk of racism in our activities. We tend to see racism as being 'out-there', among the general public. So, in this sense, racism is someone else's problem, not our's.

It is, of course, a moot point whether anyone could infallibly detect racism given its capacity to transmogrify and change its superficial appearance. By what criteria is text to be judged as being racist? Van Dijk does not really tell us; he points to certain recurrent racist themes such as 'they have a different mentality', 'they do not respect women', 'they are aggressive', 'they are dirty, cause dirtiness and decay', 'they are a closed group; they keep to themselves', 'they must adapt to our norms, integrate into our society', 'they take our houses' and 'they profit from our social services'. It is likely that no special skills are needed to recognise most of these as quintessentially racist since even those expressing the views usually see these characteristics as sufficient cause for a hostility towards, or a dislike for, racial minorities. Readers of Van Dijk's work are unlikely to have difficulty in recognising most of his textual examples as racist at root from their personal perspectives. Consequently, the reader is not fed with ideas which might raise doubts about their own ideas and beliefs. They, after all, share Van Dijk's viewpoint. The lack of inherent challenge to the academic readership may leave us smugly confident about the correctness of our views.

This is confirmed strongly by an aficionado of this approach, the South African Louw-Potgieter (1989), who names various well-known discourse analysts (including Van Dijk) as providing the means of uncovering the more subtle forms of racism – what he describes as covert racism. Quite properly he dismisses the age-old questionnaire approach:

> An attitude questionnaire might yield only information regarding the denial of racism and be incapable of dealing with the linguistic subtleties in which racism is couched. Clearly, what is needed is a different and more refined measure to tap the true attitudes of 'closet racists'. (p. 309)

These are fine words with which it is difficult to disagree. However, the problem with the approach becomes manifest when we find that his prime example of this subtle, covert racism is the white man who moved away when a black woman sat next to him in a lecture theatre. If this is subtle, covert racism one wonders what need there is for finely honed methods of revealing it!

Wetherell and Potter (1992), also from the broad discourse analysis perspective, appear to rock the boat a little when they wisely suggest that the issue of prejudice in psychology:

> depends on being able to categorise individuals as prejudiced or *tolerant* types. However, in practice, people are adept at upsetting the dichotomy and muddying the categorisations and, when all of us become skilled at exploiting the rhetorical possibilities of the prejudice problematic, who is to say just which of us are the *tolerant* sheep and which the prejudiced goats? (p. 215, emphasis added)

But they then go on to criticise attempts to do something about racism through anti-racism training. Katz's (1978) approach to white racism in which groups are encouraged to examine their beliefs, attitudes, behaviours and institutions receives particular attention: 'critique and local action around specific issues, a strategy which some Maori and Pakeha groups have successfully practised for many years, particularly around opposition to South African rugby tours, seems preferable to Katz's rather solemn self-examination' (Wetherell and Potter, 1992, p. 220). Again this seems to reflect a contentment with one's own world-view which should not be shaken by an examination of the role of racism in one's own life. It becomes problematic for a discourse analyst to justify examining the discourse of other people if examination of their own is less worthwhile than protesting against rugby tours. Contentment with one's own views is not part of an anti-racist strategy.

The need for a positive stance

There is no simple correct position on racism. It is not possible to present a few 'rules' which, if applied, will eliminate racism. Characteristically, racism is capable of manifesting itself in an endless stream of forms. There are broad aspects of racist thinking and action which are relatively easily seen and understood. However, guarantees are not available. The liberal tradition is best seen merely as a reaction to the worst excesses of past racism. Rarely does it dig at the roots of racism. There is an aura of cosiness or complacency despite many fine words. It begs too many tough questions. Favoured is a sort of 'group spirit' of shared outrage at hands-off distance. But what gets changed? The illusion that racism is somewhere out there, expressed by those whom we ought not to be mixing with anyway, means that the rest need not see the locus of responsibility as much in their thinking and actions as elsewhere. But it has been shown in this chapter that such complacency is at best smug, at worst, dangerous. Men who change the baby may not be non-sexist paragons.

Chapter 4

Everyday racist psychology

> In their work-related activities, psychologists do not engage in unfair discrimination based on age, gender, race, ethnicity, national origin, religion, sexual orientation, disability, socioeconomic status, or any basis proscribed by law.(American Psychological Association, 1992, p. 1601)

Much of the racism of psychology occurs in psychologists' day-to-day work. Unlike some of the grandiose racist theory discussed so far, everyday racism is to be found in the research, therapy and beliefs of practising psychologists. It occurs in a range of settings spanning the entire discipline, including the psychology taught through textbooks to students. Everyday racism is to be found throughout the world – in South Africa, the USA and in Britain. Rather than being trivial aspects of psychology's racism, everyday racist psychology has a profound impact on black individuals.

Racism and clinical work

In South Africa, for example, Swartz (1991) studied what he calls the politics of the psychiatric ward-round. Membership of the team included psychologists and psychiatrists. Few of these clinicians spoke a black language so interviews with patients were conducted through interpreters. Rather than engage the patient, the focus of the clinicians' attention was on these intermediaries. Patients were rarely addressed directly and doctor–patient eye-contact was uncommon.

> At times there was even a feeling that genuine psychiatric difficulties were being forgotten as patients' problems were translated into issues having to do with Black customs and rituals. . . . Such advice was given generally speaking when it was felt that the patient would benefit by performing

rituals either to appease ancestors who were seen as not protecting the patient from the effects of being bewitched, or to facilitate the patient's journey on the path of *thwasa* to becoming a traditional healer. . . . On one occasion, a ward-round participant joked, 'Dr A. will love this – we'll write in the patient's folder Diagnosis – bewitched; treatment plan – dancing ritual!' (p. 232)

This is to define the patient solely in terms of the traditional black person's culture rather than as an individual from that culture. It is a stereotypical world in which the family and the community are seen as major sources of support for the black patient. Inevitably this is a diversion which, among other things, ignores the material poverty of the black patients. ' "Cultural essence" used in this way may well be seen as a weapon used against people' (p. 223). This is especially damaging, for example, when the recommended treatment involves a 500-mile trip which the poor patients cannot finance even with whatever help their families could muster.

There is nothing specifically South African about stereotypes harming therapeutic decision-making. In the USA, Lewis *et al.* (1979) described how interpretations of the delinquency of black children carried out by psychologists and psychiatrists stressed character impairments even where there was clear evidence of psychotic or organic disorders; similar symptoms in white children were seen as pathological. Hallucinations in black children were regarded as culturally appropriate; dangerous paranoid thoughts and behaviours as adaptive responses to threatening social circumstances; and extreme grandiosity was read as a manifestation of street bravado:

> The family of another black delinquent boy was described in clinical and probation reports as stable and close-knit simply because of the presence of the father in the household. After talking at length with the mother and the boy, we learned that the father brutally battered his wife and child and shot off guns in the house. The boy was eventually declared delinquent for running away and for assaulting his father. The child, not the father, was sent to a correctional facility. (p. 55)

They undertook an epidemiological study of children known to a juvenile court. Only 15 per cent of white children had psychiatric symptoms reported in their records compared with 26 per cent of the black children. Seventy per cent of the white youngsters with psychiatric symptoms were referred to psychiatric services and received treatment, yet only 18 per cent of the black children with similar symptoms were.

The case-notes of 92 patients compulsorily detained under the UK Mental Health Act over a fifteen-month period starting in 1982 were examined (Bolton, 1984). Of the white detainees, 25 were placed in a high-security unit and 17 on an open ward. For African-Caribbeans the ratio was 6:1, for those from the Indian subcontinent 3:2, and for Africans 6:1. Despite the small numbers involved, it seems clear that African and Caribbean detainees were substantially more likely to be treated in a locked ward. Patients described as aggressive in their case-notes tended to be transferred to the secure unit. Nevertheless, although all black patients described as aggressive were placed in a high-security unit, 'aggressive' white detainees often remained on the open ward. Fewer white patients were described as 'uncooperative' than black patients were. However, it was more usual for 'uncooperative' black patients to be placed in the high-security unit, whereas similarly 'uncooperative' white patients stayed on the open ward.

One study looked at racism in psychiatric diagnosis using a vignette method (Lewis *et al.*, 1990). This involved presenting virtually identical case-studies varying only in the race and sex of the 'patient' to experienced senior psychiatrists. The main features of the case-study were as follows:

A 23–year old woman has recently become unemployed. Her family called the police because she had damaged furniture, been acting in a threatening manner, and been verbally aggressive. She has no past psychiatric history but the family noted that she had spent more time in her room alone, reading religious books, which seemed to follow the death of a close friend. They also suspect that she had been smoking cannabis. . . . The only family history of mental illness is in an aunt who spent several years in mental hospital. She drinks two units of alcohol per week and denies drug abuse. . . . She is a fit white woman who appears agitated and paces around. She does not complain of depressed mood but says she heard a voice telling her that the world was ending. She also believes that the neighbours are plotting to kill her and that they are poisoning the milk. There are no other mental-state abnormalities. (p. 411)

Other versions described a black woman, a white man and a black man in corresponding terms. If race was not an influential part of the thinking of the psychiatrists, their clinical impressions would be identical irrespective of the patient's race. Although race made no difference to beliefs about the appropriateness of anti-depressants, statutory hospitalisation, and bereavement counselling among other things, this was not universal. For example, the black patient was seen to be a greater risk of violence against the staff, less in need of neuroleptic treatments, more likely to be suffering a short-term illness and deserving being charged with criminal damage. More marginally, black patients were less likely to be recommended for referral to a community self-help group, remand in custody and admission as day patients.

Whatever else may be said, these are not trivial differences. Being routed through the criminal justice system is in line with the experience of many black mental patients. Furthermore, that they are seen as violent despite having no history of this is stereotypical rather than diagnostic. However, the black patient was less likely to be seen as schizophrenic despite past claims that overdiagnosis of schizophrenia occurs for black populations. Perhaps the psychiatrists were over-compensating for this when they formed their judgements of the implications of hearing voices in black patients. Perhaps another stereotype was being activated when black patients were seen as having a 'pathological grief reaction'. Not referring black patients to community self-help groups might be an aspect of ghettoisation of black people.

Lewis *et al.* (1990) interpret their findings without suggesting that psychiatrists are racist – apparently because not all of the racial differences in treatment imply a pejorative attitude towards black people:

> The evidence for a racial stereotype provided here, irrespective of any implied inferiority, supports the view that race-thinking is prevalent among British psychiatrists. Race-thinking distorts all social interactions, including the psychiatric assessment, and thus undermines the 'objectivity' of psychiatric diagnosis and management. There is no indication that interpersonal aspects of care such as ability to establish a rapport, counselling and predicted compliance are prejudiced on grounds of race. Rather there is a tendency to expect brief, perhaps cannabis-influenced, violent psychotic reactions of limited duration in less neuroleptic medication. (pp. 414–15)

We are asked to believe that if intercultural communication is seen as problem-free by the psychiatrists, this in some way establishes that racism does not hamper psychiatrist–patient relationships. This is made all the more curious by being seen as acceptable despite some drastic misdiagnoses of patients. We are expected to use the phrase 'race-thinking' rather than racism to describe actions which classify people who show no sign of drug abuse as showing 'brief, perhaps cannabis-influenced [though there were no differences in beliefs about the influence of cannabis found in the data], violent psychotic reactions'. All this, simply because Lewis *et al.* are unwilling to call such things pejorative. They do not appear to worry that there is nothing more racist than to provide inadequate service to clients on the basis of racial stereotypes which receive no substantial support from the case history. The reluctance on the part of Lewis *et al.* (1990) to use the term racism to describe the judgements of these psychiatrists is explained when we read: 'The term "racism" may be applied to some British psychiatrists, but such accusations seldom change beliefs or behaviour for the better' (p. 415). Fernando (1991) criticises the adequacy of the vignette used in this study because it might prime the reader to think of the patient as being black which in itself leads to stereotyped thinking. This would reduce the apparent effects of the race of the patient. Furthermore, the American research on which this was based was more sophisticated and revealed racism more clearly.

All the examples cited above demonstrate that black people are more likely to receive inappropriate treatment merely as a consequence of the way in which skin colour is 'read' by psychologists, psychiatrists and others. Without doubt the studies do nothing to undermine the following views of Kobena Mercer of the Black Health Workers and Patients Group:

> we recognise the need for psychiatric services and in this sense our communities have not been in the business of anti-psychiatry. But at the same time we vigorously contest the current functions which these services fulfil. Rather than offering care, the psychiatric services have been seen as a basically custodial system. As a form of social control psychiatry uses both overt, coercive powers and more complex, subtle measures of persuasion which are involved in the organisation of *content*. (Mercer, 1984, p. 22)

The major lesson in all this is that while political and cultural considerations must inform clinical practice, they cannot replace sound professional judgements; people should not lose their individual richness and complexity. The danger of treating cultural caricatures rather then people must be avoided (Cooper, 1973).

It would be convenient to argue that psychiatry's problems are not those of psychology. Nevertheless both disciplines feed each other with ideas and knowledge bases. After all, it is psychology which makes psychiatry a special branch of medicine. Furthermore, psychologists as well as psychiatrists are implicated by the authors of some of the above studies specifically mentioning psychologists as being part of the problem. The question that we ought to address is how psychologists become part of the problem.

A case-study: split minds and split treatment

> Because of its historical biopsychosocial awareness, psychiatry has unique contributions for society in its search for remedies to the sickness of racial and ethnic intolerance. (McCleod-Bryant, 1993, p. 1128)

In recent years, a large body of research has revealed that schizophrenia is more commonly diagnosed among black people than white people in the United Kingdom and the USA. In the United Kingdom, for example, Cochrane (1977) reported disproportionately more immigrants being diagnosed as schizophrenic, especially African-Caribbeans and Pakistanis. Similarly, in Manchester, Carpenter and Brockington (1980) reported that diagnoses of schizophrenia were commoner for immigrants – once more especially so for black groups such as African-Caribbeans, Africans and people of Indian origin. Similar trends were found by Bagley (1971) and Dean *et al.* (1981). In the latter study there were five times the proportion of immigrants from Africa (mainly East African Indians) and three times the proportion of immigrants from India diagnosed as schizophrenic compared with British native groups. Other studies have reported similar findings (e.g. Cope, 1989; Littlewood and Cross, 1980). McGovern and Cope (1987) reported that African-Caribbeans enter the mental health system, mostly through the courts, at a much younger age than white people. Furthermore they are much more likely to be diagnosed as schizophrenic. The study also found that substantial numbers of African-Caribbeans were diagnosed as suffering from 'cannabis-induced psychosis' – a diagnosis not given to white people despite known high levels of use in this group. The chances of a young adult African-Caribbean being legally detained in a psychiatric institution by order of a court were 25 times greater than for the same age group of white people. Cope (1989) found similar trends but in addition demonstrated that for *second-generation* African-Caribbean males, the psychiatric admission rate was 29 times the rate for white people.

Another study (Harrison *et al.*, 1984) compared African-Caribbeans, with white inner-city dwellers. Black people were more often alleged to have attracted attention by causing a 'public disturbance' and the involvement of the police was more characteristic of their admission histories. Despite this, the black patients were less violent and less threatening before admission but no more violent on the ward.

Section 136 of the Mental Health Act of 1983 in England and Wales allows police officers to deal with persons who appear to be affected by a mental disorder by taking them to a hospital or another place of safety. An African-Carribean male is three times more likely to be treated in this way than a white man (Rogers and Faulkner, 1987). Disquietingly, psychiatrists and police agreed on the appropriateness of the section in every case studied in which black men were hospitalised in this manner. Some might see this as an indication of the collusion of psychiatric staff with the police's viewpoint. Indeed, Littlewood and Lipsedge (1989) have claimed that in Britain 'the police are overtly racist and selectively pick out non-mentally ill black people in the streets and take them to a psychiatric hospital under Section 136 of the

Mental Health Act as an alternative to arrest' (p. 273). It is doubtful whether they could achieve this without psychiatrists' collusion.

Examination of the case records of out-patients or domiciliary patients of a psychiatric facility revealed important racist trends (Littlewood and Cross, 1980). The patients included black immigrants, white immigrants and white British-born. Black patients were more likely to be diagnosed as psychotic, to be attended to by junior medical staff, and to be given powerful tranquillisers (even after allowing for different types of diagnosis). Sex and class were insufficient to explain the differences. Migrants were more likely to have received electric shock therapy without being diagnosed as depressive. Black patients were more likely to have long series of electric shock treatment. Littlewood and Cross interpreted their data as reflecting stereotyped attitudes. Quite clearly, black patients were especially subject to gross physical treatments in circumstances in which the native British are treated more kindly. Similarly, Shaikh (1985) reported that electric shock treatment was more excessively used on diagnosed Indian schizophrenics than indigenous patients so diagnosed.

Things are not much different in the USA. For example, Gary (1981) reported that black males in the USA had the highest in-patient admission rates to state and community mental hospital. They were also younger when admitted to mental health facilities. After admission, black men were three times more likely to be labelled schizophrenic than white men and more likely to be diagnosed alcoholic or drug addict. According to Gary, the US mental health system is especially risky to black men much as are the economy and the criminal justice system.

Explanations of black psychiatric over-representation

Among explanations for the differential treatment of black people by the psychiatric system are a range of approaches which vary in where the responsibility is placed. The *medical explanation* assumes that black patients indeed have a fundamentally different pattern of mental illness from that of white people. Thus their over-representation merely reflects natural psychiatric facts. The *procedural explanation* assumes that the admissions process itself is responsible for the excess of black people in compulsory admissions. Racism within the procedures and the psychiatric health services has been a factor in the response of professionals to black people (Littlewood and Cross, 1980). *Racism and racial stereotyping*, as we have seen, result in black people being seen differently from white people. Some researchers have described plainly how black people receive inferior and discriminatory service from the psychiatric and other health services in general (e.g. Cooper, 1986; Littlewood and Cross, 1980; Mercer, 1984; NAHA, 1988). Loring and Powell (1988) showed that psychiatric diagnoses were decided in part by the race of the client. Harrison *et al.* (1988), in a careful study, found black people to be more than twelve times more likely to be diagnosed as schizophrenic than white patients. They concluded that race alone accounted for a substantial proportion of the difference.

It is the routine nature of the discriminatory treatment of black people which glares through these data. The idea of isolated and occasional racist acts by racist individuals seems to describe the evidence poorly. There are many practical ways in which racism's effects on service delivery can be mitigated, as we will see in the final chapter. Some organisations have formal policies which are helpful in identifying the issues (e.g. MIND, 1993).

The politics of the psychology text

Texts are not simply 'delivery systems' of 'facts'. They are at once the results of political, economic, and cultural activities, battles, and compromises. They are conceived, designed, and authored by real people with real interests. They are published within the political and economic constraints of market, resources, and power. And what texts mean and how they are used are fought over by communities with distinctly different commitments and by teachers and students as well. (Apple and Christian-Smith, 1991, pp. 1–2)

While there have been several attempts to decipher the politics of school textbooks systematically (e.g. MacCann and Woodward, 1977; Zimet, 1976), relatively little attention has been paid to psychology texts. Ideology in psychology has been discussed many times (cf. Bramel and Friend, 1981; Howitt, 1991; Samelson, 1974) but the political agenda of psychological textbooks has been largely ignored. A recent major study of ageism yielded depressing trends in the contents of a large sample of undergraduate psychology textbooks published between 1949 and 1989 (Whitbourne and Hulicka, 1990). Relatively little change occurred over time in the numbers of pages devoted to childhood compared to adulthood and old age – though development was defined largely in terms of childhood. Numerous ageist comments were found such as: 'The old should not be "laid on the shelf" while they still have something to contribute to the welfare of society'! That psychology textbooks are routinely ageist is but one important finding. Perhaps even more important are the self-reproductive processes involved in maintaining ideas over generations of textbooks:

> Certain areas of focus within a field of psychology become perpetuated from edition to edition of a specific text and from generation to generation of a set of texts. . . . Large numbers of psychology students thus become exposed only to a narrow and prematurely fixed view of psychology that does not mirror the reality of the complexity of the discipline. As textbooks become 'McDonaldized', they provide the same standard fare to consumers across the country and perhaps the world. We hope that this disturbing trend can be reversed. (Whitbourne and Hulicka, 1990, p. 1136)

If 'McDonaldized' psychology is anything it is bland, palatable middle-ground fodder. Nevertheless, just as McDonald's fast food is an incarnation of American values, so is the McDonaldised text. Howitt (1991) looked at the treatment of drug abuse in psychological texts and found a sort of vague commonsense anti-drugs point of view which distorted any possible message from research. Similar processes are involved in the presentation of race in textbooks.

An arbitrary sample of the way race issues are treated in psychology textbooks is fairly illustrative of a rather dangerous blandness. The following is from Sabini (1991):

> In the 1940s New York department stores refused to hire black sales clerks because, they claimed, customers wouldn't shop in stores with visible black help. Some managers said that they themselves had nothing against blacks; they just couldn't endanger profits. Some, no doubt, were just giving an easy excuse for their own prejudice, but for others the claim was no doubt true. These managers weren't prejudiced, but they discriminated nonetheless. This sort of discrimination has been called institutional racism since it is a result of institutional pressures rather than a direct result of prejudiced attitudes. (p. 124)

This fundamentally misrepresents the nature of institutional racism and offers an anodyne image of personal racism. Notice first of all that no evidence is provided for any of the assertions made – in total contrast to the usual requirement in psychology to provide empirical proof. This allows Sabini to impose a point of view which is neither justified nor informative about the situation described. Is it possible that managers of stores who do not employ black people are merely holding their customers responsible for their own racism? This is clearly the case. Even if it was true that some customers would not shop at the store that had black sales assistants, this is merely to give direct support to the racist customer. Sabini has no evidence that the store managers were not racist – on the contrary, that they so readily did racist work implies that they were. He prefers to adopt the unworkable view of racism as personal prejudice and hostility. Nor does he have any evidence that there were institutional pressures on the managers not to employ black sales assistants. Normally, institutional racism is seen as being the ways in which the policies, practices and procedures of organisations lead to possibly unintended discrimination and disadvantage.

However, much of the racism of psychological textbooks is a broad assault on the nature of black cultures. Psychologists' writings often reflect nineteenth-century social anthropologists' images of black peoples (Howitt, 1991). That these images or ideas were rejected by anthropologists long ago does not seem to affect their pertinence to psychology. The concept of 'primitive' people, created by nineteenth-century anthropologists, simply 'turned Western society on its head' (Kuper, 1988). Western society was seen as characterised by mono-gamous marriage, private possessions and a political order which was bounded by geography. The antithesis of this, which defined 'primitive society' held it to be sexually promiscuous, communistic and nomadic. Psychoanalytic notions of the primal horde (Freud, 1950) reiterated this precisely. Freud believed that 'primitive', 'undeveloped' or 'savage' cultures were ones which had limited or no contact with European cultures.

Of course, rejection of such views does not mean that the broad cultures of different races are all the same. Indeed, the dominant values of European, Asian and African societies may be quite distinct. Namely it has been suggested that the three primary races exhibit an overdevelopment of a particular aspect of being: a *materially advanced* but spiritually bankrupt culture in the West; a *spiritually developed* and relatively socially stagnant culture in the East; and a developed *social consciousness*, but relatively undeveloped material culture, in Africa (Cook and Kono, 1977). Black nations, peoples and cultures are still described by some psychologists in such deprecatory terms as 'primitive', 'tribal', 'undeveloped', 'underdeveloped' and so forth. For these psychologists, parity in technology is the criterion of whether a culture is advanced or primitive. Such other important aspects of a culture (and hence humanity) as religion, morality and communal spirit are granted little significance. In short, there is a refusal even to admit to cultural diversity; everything which does not conform to the standards of white culture is banished to the realm of barbarism. This view of black peoples and their cultures has a long history. For example, Curvier (1927) described the black 'race' thus:

> The Negro race is confined to the South of Mount Atlas. Its characters are black complexion, wooly hair, compressed cranium and flattish nose. In the face, in the thickness of the lips, it manifestly approaches the monkey tribe. The hordes of which this variety is composed have always remained in a state of complete barbarism. (Quoted in Curtin, 1965, p. 231)

Remarkably, conceptions of black people as 'primitive' survive in textbooks today, although other claims about their inferiority are ignored now. Amongst the latter, Caroll, at the start of the twentieth century, compiled 'evidence that the Negro is not of the human family' and was convinced that 'all evidence indicates that the beast of the field which tempted Eve was a *Negress* who served her as a maid servant' (Burns, 1948, p. 22). In the 1920s, a French 'anthropologist', Levy-Bruhl, claimed to be primarily 'concerned with the thought processes amongst savages' (Parin and Morgenthaler, 1969, p. 188). He concluded that African thought belonged to a phylogenetically earlier stage since it was a 'pre-logical mentality' which relied on memory alone. He claimed that also lacking the capacity for individuation, Africans could not live independently of the European (Bulhan, 1985, p. 83). Others regarded Africans as less than fully human, without a full superego, and so they deserved to be owned or controlled like domestic animals or children. For example, Ritchie (1943) suggested that Africans are driven by two opposing forces: a benevolent force giving them everything for nothing, and a malevolent force depriving them of life itself. The resultant ambivalence and conflict were said to make the African dependent on a mother or mother-surrogate (read European).

Such views about Africans (and other black peoples) as described above still find their way into psychological textbooks, although very often expressed subconsciously. We have chosen the tenth edition of *Introduction to Psychology* (Atkinson *et al.*, 1990) to illustrate this persistence. *Introduction to Psychology* has been dominant in the psychology textbook market for many years. First published in 1953, it was originally authored by Ernest Hilgard of Stanford University. This phenomenally successful work has been translated into Russian, Spanish, French, Chinese and German among other languages. Indeed, the preface to the book boasts that 'Many young students studying the text to-day will have parents who used an earlier edition' (p. v). However, in this book, Africans and other human groups outside North America and Europe, along with apes and monkeys, are portrayed as savage, primitive and tribal. These terms are defined by *Chambers Twentieth Century Dictionary* as:

> *Savage*: wild, uncivilized, ferocious . . . a wild or primitive state; a brutal, fierce, or cruel person.
> *Primitive*: of an early stage of social development.
> *Tribe*: a race, a breed, a class or set of people; groups of animals usually ranking between genus and an order.

In addition, the term *tribe* is reserved for monkeys and black people to convey much the same meanings as primitive, savage or undeveloped. Through arguments, repetitions and juxtapositions, the text is fastidious in representing non-North American black people as (a) strange and other than Westerners, (b) an undifferentiated mass, and (c) primitive.

As will be seen, one of the means of doing this is to use repetitively the word *tribe* when referring to African cultures but *society* in connection with Western ones. However, one major exception is made. Bearing in mind Kuper's suggestion that sexual promiscuity is an attribute of 'primitive people', it is noteworthy how Atkinson *et al.* write differently when discussing African cultures with strong controls on the sexual activities of their youngsters. These are described as societies and *not* as tribes: 'very restrictive *societies* try to control preadolescent sexual behavior and to keep children from learning about sex' (p. 383, emphasis added). But, nevertheless, there is a problem when they then go on to suggest that 'among the Ashanti of Africa, intercourse with a girl who has not undergone the puberty rites is punishable by death for both participants' (p. 383). In these few words, like its eighteenth- and nineteenth-century forebears, the text presents a view of Africans as barbaric and savage. Despite their muted terminology, Atkinson *et al.* essentially describe the *Asante* (erroneously called Ashanti by the colonialists) as being murderers. We find this allegation very disturbing. One of us is an Asante, born and bred in Asante, in Ghana, where he lived continuously into his twenties. Since leaving Ghana he has kept closely in touch with his family in Ghana, and with other Asante people in Britain and other parts of the world. Yet never has he even heard of one such killing, nor has he met anyone who has. Extensive research has also failed to yield any evidence in support of this allegation. However, Atkinson *et al.* make no attempt to substantiate their claim. We doubt very much if they could name any Asante girl who has been killed in this way. Perhaps they think that this preposterous suggestion was self-evident to their predominantly white readership – Africans are primitive, savage, barbaric and murderous, aren't they?

According to Atkinson *et al.* Africans are also paranoid schizo-phrenics:

> For example, members of some African *tribes* do not consider it unusual to hear voices when no one is actually talking or to see visions when nothing is actually there, but such behaviours are considered abnormal in most societies. (p. 591, emphasis added)

As usual, no specific 'tribes' are mentioned. Throughout, the book gives the impression that the whole continent of Africa is inhabited by 'tribes'. Thus the implication is that the huge African continent is largely populated by paranoid schizophrenics. Little wonder, then, that research has shown the overdiagnosis of schizophrenia in people of African descent by Western mental health workers (e.g. Bagley, 1971; Carpenter and Brockington, 1980; Cochrane, 1977; Cope, 1989; Dean *et al.*, 1981; Gary, 1981; Harrison *et al.*, 1988; Littlewood and Lipsedge, 1989; McGovern and Cope, 1987).

The textbook illustrates the role of culture in human activity and experience by reference to pain threshold: 'The striking influence of culture is illustrated by the fact that some non-western societies engage in rituals that would be unbearably painful to Westerners' (p. 151). In this, one can see how the book uses a putative standard of white people by which to judge black people. It is the black person who is portrayed as odd or strange, not the white person as abnormally sensitive to pain. Again, by failing to state which societies are like this, the authors make a further licentious generalisation about black people and their cultures. Atkinson *et al.* drive home further the 'barbaric' nature of black people when discussing emotional differentiation:

> If we watch a film of African *tribesmen* making an incision in a young boy's body, we may feel outrage if we believe the men are torturing the boy but feel relatively detached if we believe the men are performing a rites-of-passage ritual. (p. 408, emphasis added)

In view of the readership, would not a Western example be more appropriate? For example political torture, child ritual sexual abuse, the gassing of black Americans in execution chambers and the lynching of black men in the southern USA are all examples in which outrage may vary according to context.

The attack on African people appears no less extreme when we note that the only other references to *tribes* concern savage pack animals: 'In another chimpanzee border war observed during the 1970s, a *tribe* of about 15 chimpanzees destroyed a smaller neighboring group by killing the members off one male at a time' (p. 427, emphasis added). This may seem innocuous at first sight, but consider the following. Firstly, nowhere in the book are white people associated with 'tribes'. Black people, on the other hand, along with primates (chimpanzees) are constantly referred to as *tribes*, *tribal groups* or *tribesmen*. It appears as if black people and monkeys belong to the same *genus* sharing similar social structures. Furthermore, nowhere in this textbook are white people associated with deliberate, non-political cruelty against other humans. On the other hand, black people and chimpanzees are linked to murder and other atrocities. An alleged 'genealogical link' between black people and monkeys is thus reinforced along with a stereotyped image of primitive, savage, barbaric and violent black people. In brief, black people are depicted as racially inferior in terms not only of culture but also of temperament. However, compared to the blatancy of the eugenicists and other biological racists, this textbook conveys subtle messages about other races which require close scrutiny to detect.

Black peoples are represented in other ways as 'not-quite-human'. Even in such universal human characteristics as the expression and differentiation of emotions, black people are depicted as inferior. So when reviewing some research evidence on the identification of emotions from facial photographs, surprise greets evidence that black people show human skills: '*Even* members of remote, preliterate *tribes* that had had virtually *no contact with western cultures* (the Fore and Dani tribes in New Guinea) were able to identify the facial expressions correctly' (p. 413, emphases added). The implications of this are quite apparent. Following the Freudian tradition, the book suggests that to be civilised, and therefore to be human, is to have had contact with Western cultures. The surprise at these 'primitive' peoples' capacity to distinguish between different human expressions of emotions illustrates this. The Fore and Dani people are not presumed to have the ability to recognise emotions, even though people credit their pet dogs and cats with the ability to identify their owners' emotions.

In describing the long-term effects of early experiences on human development, the authors write: 'Infants in an *isolated* Indian village in Guatemala are kept inside the family's windowless *hut*' (emphasis added, p. 79). From whom is the village isolated? Not from other communities in Guatemala. No doubt, 'isolated' is employed here as a euphemism for 'primitive' or 'undeveloped'. Furthermore, what makes one person's home a house and another's a hut? Would a thatched home in a European suburb or country village be described as a hut? These Guatemalan children are also compared with American children (p. 80) without justifying the failure to compare them with other Guatemalan children. We see this as the usual white psychologists' practice of setting a white 'norm' as the standard by which others are judged.

There are signs in this text, and others, that textbooks are 'politically correct' in their portrayal of multi-cultural *American* society, while at the same time remaining parochially racist when dealing with cultures outside America. Thus recent psychology texts, including Atkinson *et al.* (1990), present an image of black people as part of American society in terms of the pictures accompanying the text. A good example of this is Brehm and Kassin (1990), who mix black and white people, show pictures of black families and so forth. While this might be mere window-dressing in that some of the text reproduces traditional psychologistic views of racism, at least a publisher's editor or the authors are aware of part of the issue. One might contrast this with a publication for school children *How About Psychology?* which contains careers advice. Published by the British Psychological Society (1989), it contains pictures of a number of professional psychologists. While it does illustrate *one* black face, it is notable that this person occupies the least prestigious professional role in the publication – an infant-school teacher!

Textbooks such as these are too important to be disregarded. The massive and long-term sales of some of them confirm how extensively they have affected directly the training, thinking and practice of generations of psychologists world-wide. The knock-on effects for the professional training of teachers, social workers, lawyers, nurses and all others whose training involves psychology cannot be overstated.

The politics of the psychology journal

> Just as mainstream psychology was once accused of being 'womanless' . . . so too in the 1990s it is in danger of becoming 'raceless'. (Graham, 1992, p. 629)

Perhaps significant in itself, there have been few systematic studies examining the racism of psychology journals. Many journals publish little or nothing to do with race (even where it is appropriate). The neglect of race as a topic is one of the problems, as we will see. However, some specialties within psychology such as social psychology have focused directly on race and so are more likely to be at fault through commission rather than omission. Analyses of the content of social psychology journals form most of the available research. The roots of the social psychology of race treat it as a matter of individual attitudes (Jones, 1983). Increasingly scant attention was given to the cultural foundations of these attitudes during the twentieth century. Furthermore, psychology's obsession with the 'scientific method' meant that non-randomisable variables like race were deemed peripheral for much of this time. Having analysed the contents of mainstream social psychological journals published between 1969 and 1980, Jones found that 'only 11.2% of all articles in seven major psychology journals concerned race, ethnicity, or culture' (p. 130). During this period there was a strong, but curvilinear trend in the numbers of race-related articles. The figures increased between 1968 and 1973 but then quickly dropped back to the pre-1968 levels: 'social psychology has contributed relatively little in recent years to cultural (normative) analyses of nonwhite subcultures in the United States or to theories concerning intercultural relations' (p. 132).

One reason why this is significant is shown by Jones' reanalysis of data gathered by Sagar and Schofield (1980). These investigators showed both black boys and white boys aggressive cartoons in which the race of the aggressor was systematically manipulated. In the original interpretation provided by Sagar and Schofield, it was claimed that black and white subjects alike saw the acts performed by a black aggressor as the most violent. Jones re-examined the data in terms of comparisons made within and between cultures. Black youngsters had actually rated black aggressors at the same level of violence as white youngsters rated white aggressors. Significantly, black youngsters saw white characters' aggression as less aggressive; white youngsters saw black characters' aggression as more aggressive. For Jones, his reanalysis shows the data 'to be part of a cultural complex' (p. 138).

In a major analysis of the contents of six journals published by the American Psychological Association, Graham (1992) found much the same trends as Jones had a decade earlier. She selected journals from the major areas of psychology including some with basic research orientations and others dealing with applied psychology. The research covered nearly 15,000 articles published in the twenty years starting 1970. Over the entire period less than 4 per cent of the articles were about African-Americans. But the trend was even more disturbing in that there was a steady decline in the number of relevant articles; there were only 2 per cent of such articles during the last five years. Further evidence of the marginal status given to African-Americans in the research literature emerged. Articles on African-Americans were published disproportionately more frequently in the form of a 'brief' report – that is, given minimal space. Explanations of these trends include: (a) a possible diminishing pool of African-American psychologists – though their numbers appear to be constant in recent years – and (b) white psychologists' fears of the notoriety that research on ethnic minorities can bring. The upshot of these and other explanations, though, is that the predominantly white psychological profession of the USA is incapable of tackling research on African-Americans effectively.

A radically different approach to content-analysis was adopted by Howitt and Owusu-Bempah (1990). They drew on experience of anti-racism training to examine the racist strategies of journal articles. They chose the *British Journal of Social and Clinical Psychology* for this purpose. The journal was published between 1962 and 1980, after which time it was split into two separate publications. This period was a significant period in race relations in Great Britain with considerable changes in immigration policy as well as race relations being brought directly into public focus by intensive media coverage (Hartmann and Husband, 1972; 1974) and equal opportunities legislation. The journal dealt with both clinical and social psychology although it contained few or no discussions of race in the clinical articles. This is a remarkable omission in a psychology journal in a multi-cultural society which, presumably reflects the lack of submissions by authors. However, Howitt and Owusu-Bempah concentrated on the social psychology articles. Much like the American journals reviewed by Jones, there was a peak in the publication of race-related articles during the late 1960s and early 1970s. One can only speculate about the reasons, but it is likely that the topicality of race was an important factor.

Five essentially racist strategies were identified in the journal articles:

1. Stereotyping.
2. Marginalising racism.
3. Avoiding the obvious.
4. Neo-imperialism.
5. Blaming the victim.

Quite clearly there may be other strategies, but the evidence of the above tended to be the strongest and clearest.

1. *Stereotyping*: Not surprisingly, there was little evidence of the crudest forms of this. Nevertheless one article (Brown, 1973) may reflect a relatively simple form of racial stereotyping. This research used ratings by observers of the behaviours of black and white children towards each other. A special focus was on aggression – and warning bells ought to ring whenever race and aggression are raised together. It is a common stereotype that black people are aggressive (Duncan, 1976; Sagar and Schofield, 1980). Thus it cannot be argued reasonably that Brown's decision to research aggression in a racial situation was purely arbitrary. There are endless other matters he could have explored such as racial abuse or black people's experiences of discrimination, had he chosen. Turner and Sevinc (1974) also criticise this study. They argue that the race differences in aggression found in Brown's study were likely to be the results of a methodological flaw in which few black girls were included relative to the number of white girls. This seems to be the sort of methodological pitfall which psychologists normally would be adept at avoiding.

2. *Marginalising racism*. White people generally find it psychologically comforting to relegate racism to the fringes of society such as the activities of fascist groups. Relegated from centre-stage, the problem is essentially externalised and marginalised. Similar tendencies were

repeatedly found in studies which attempted to explore 'liberalism-conservatism' (Wilson and Patterson, 1968) and similar attitude dimensions. Despite there being very little evidence in favour of this in their research, some researchers persistently link racism with broadly conservative viewpoints. In a similar fashion, Eysenck (1971) tries to make racism a working-class phenomenon:

> Working-class people . . . emerge on most issues as conservative and tough minded. . . . Thus working class people, in summary, are nationalistic, even jingoistic, xenophoic, anti-semitic, racialist, inhumane, narrowly moralistic in sexual matters, and unconcerned with ethical or religious issues. (Eysenck, 1971, p. 205)

However, there were absolutely no social class differences in Eysenck's data (Eiser and Roiser, 1972). One has also to be very careful over imputed social class differences in racism. Often the differences lie in the way in which racist attitudes are expressed (Cashmore, 1987; Dummett, 1984; Littlewood and Lipsedge, 1989).

3. *Avoiding the obvious*: Some of the journal articles failed to come to terms with racism, and avoided calling clearly racist matters racism. For example, Vaughan (1963), using Maori or white interviewers, studied the attitudes of Maori and white children towards their own race. At about the age of twelve years, the Maori children *interviewed by a white person* showed a marked difference in attitude from when interviewed by a Maori person. Vaughan (1963) suggested: 'In any given instance, however, the provision of own-race experimenters should be considered an automatic control in ethnic attitude research' (p. 69). Howitt and Owusu-Bempah (1990) point out that rather than seeing the matter as a methodological nuisance, Vaughan's findings ought to have led him to recommend the importance of further exploration of the racial dynamics of New Zealand society.

4. *Neo-imperialism*: Several studies in the journal reported research which transported Western standardized personality tests to other cultures. There were no studies which attempted to study Ghanaian, Chinese, or any other people's personality structure in its own terms rather than through the use of Western artifacts such as the 16 PF or EPI questionnaires.

5. *Blaming the victim*: Signs of 'ingratitude' on the part of black people are often taken to demonstrate that the person has a 'chip on the shoulder'. Characteristically, in racist thinking, black people are held to be victims of their own genetic inferiority or pathogenic cultures. So to be ungrateful for 'sops' such as meagre employment becomes proof

of the responsibility that the black person holds for his or her plight. Dawson (1969) is a case in point:

> although individuals in Australian Aboriginal and Eskimo hunting societies tend to develop spatial skills and independence to a high degree, they do not appear to develop motivation for modern type work to the same extent as subjects in certain traditional 'strict' agricultural societies which are politically stratified, and in which subjects tend to develop a high degree of conformity and low spatial skill. It is thought that Aborigines tend not to do well in modern work situations because of this independent permissive hunting society orientation, which appears to be reinforced by extremely permissive child-rearing processes. (p. 139)

There seems little doubt where Dawson holds the blame to lie.

Once again, given the common assumption that racism is on the run in society and that we have made considerable progress in eliminating it, it might be suggested that our comments are raking over the coals of long-forgotten journal articles which represent an older era. It is interesting then that the publication of the review produced a flurry of correspondence challenging what had been written. So, for example, Wober (1990) defended one of the authors whose work was included in the review with the comment 'his feelings were amicable as was his behaviour' (p. 594) towards black people, as if sexism cannot be chivalrous.

Depth psychologies and superficialities

Most of the notorious instances of racism in psychology have been associated, as we have seen, with psychologists who adopted a 'hard-nosed' but short-sighted approach to their discipline. This helped to lead them to make unsustainable claims about the role of genetics in the social order. However, this does not mean that those 'soft' psychologists, whose stock in trade is the exploration of the depths of the human psyche, avoid racist traps. While it may be that the wooliness often assumed to be characteristic of such approaches might render depth psychologists less dangerous, this is far from the case. In contrast to the critiques of Freud for sexism (Figes, 1970; Frosh, 1993; Mitchell, 1974), the racism of depth psychologists is relatively unknown. Take the following comment, surely as patronisingly racist as could be imagined:

> The absence of black Jungians has been a remarkable fact in my experience of Jungian groups since I first became associated with our organizations in

1973. . . . Even as we admire cultural diversity and often *idealize 'blackness' as an attribute of earthiness, spontaneity, soul, or depth associated with the quality or color of black, we are without those colleagues who call themselves black in our society.* (Young-Eisendrath, 1987, p. 41, emphasis added)

The author is well aware of some of the racist comments made by Jung in his multitudinous writings but chooses to regard these as inconsequential historical frippery:

Jung's account of our 'Negroid' behavior seems mostly to be a charming, patronizing account of '. . . ways of feeling, reasoning, judging and behaving, of going on, discontinuous' with his own. Jung's world and ours were 'worlds apart' when he wrote the above passage, but what do his words mean now? (pp. 48–9)

Young-Eisendrath ignores the force of the case against Jung. According to Masson (1989), there is a consensus that Carl Jung, second only to Sigmund Freud in the entire psychoanalytic movement, colluded with the Nazis. He became president of the International Medical Society for Psychotherapy and chief editor of its journal. In 1933, the journal publicly announced the requirement that 'all members of the Society . . . have read through with great scientific care the path-breaking book by Adolf Hitler, *Mein Kampf*, and will recognize it as essential' (Masson, 1989, p. 135). Jung was moved to make statements concerning the differences between 'Jewish' and 'Germanic' psychologies 'which have long been known to every intelligent person are no longer to be glossed over, and this can only be beneficial to science' (p. 136). Or at a more general level: 'The Jewish race as a whole – at least this is my experience – possesses an unconscious which can be compared with the "Aryan" only with reserve' (p. 134). It is not intended to rehearse the full details of the case against Jung here. However, Masson makes an important argument about the impact of Jung's racist involvement with the Nazis on his psychological theorising:

What I find totally absent in Jung's accounts is any sense of all the tragedies that go on in people's lives. The real world is simply absent from his books. I cannot believe that Jung's patients never spoke about the real world . . . Jung could not afford to urge his patients to examine their pasts, for he needed to avoid thinking about his own past, tainted as it was by collaboration with the Nazis . . . Jung's psychotherapy was a screen behind which he could hide his own unpalatable past. (p. 164)

Whether or not the ahistorical aspect of Jung's theory influences the thinking of his followers has to be a matter of conjecture. Certainly Young-Eisendrath (1987) is willing to condone the abandonment of history by other Jungians:

> Probably most American Jungians would dismiss . . . racist comments made
> by Jung on the grounds of the prejudices of his culture. I have no objections
> to such a self-protective move; we are simply saying 'don't blame us for the
> past'. (p. 49)

Or we can point to Mattoon (1981), who writes in terms which
essentially hide Jung's past:

> Jung puzzled long and unsuccessfully over the question of how a presumably
> civilized and Christian nation could allow and, indeed, support the collective
> evil of Nazism. (p. 27)

> For Jung, a white person's disparaging attitude toward the darker races was
> a projection of the shadow [the psychic contents which a person prefers not
> to show (p. 25)] . . . Recognition of such a projection is a first step toward
> withdrawing it. (p. 267)

Perhaps even more damning than Masson's critique is that of Dalal
(1988). He identified Jung for attention because of his current popularity among psychotherapists and that his racism appears invisible
to current Jungian practitioners. Dalal discusses how Jung explicitly
equates:

> (1) The modern black with the prehistoric human
> (2) The modern black conscious with the white unconscious
> (3) The modern black adult with the white child.
> It is this that constitutes the racist core of Jungian Psychology on which all
> else is based. (p. 263)

In a thorough analysis of Jung's racist writings, Dalal provides numerous examples of the Jungian image of black people. None of these reads
as the charming patronisation of 'Negro' people as Young-Eisendrath
describes it above:

> I am now going to say something which may offend my Indian friends, but
> actually no offence is intended. I have . . . observed the peculiar fact that
> an Indian . . . does not think, at least not what we call 'think'. He rather
> perceives the thought. He resembles the primitive in this respect.' (Jung,
> 1921, volume 10, p. 527)

> The child is born with a definite brain, and the brain of an English child
> will not work like that of the Australian black fellow but in the way of the
> modern English person. (Jung, 1921, volume 18, p. 41)

> Racial infection is a most serious mental and moral problem where the
> primitive outnumbers the white man. (Jung, 1921, volume 10, p. 509)

> When I was a child I performed the ritual just as I have seen it done by
> the natives of Africa; they act first and do not know what they are doing.
> (Jung, 1963, p. 39)

the famous American naivete . . . invites comparison with the childlikeness of the Negro. (Jung, 1921, volume 10, p. 45)

Dalal suggests that Jung's race theories are a serious matter since Jungian therapists have no choice other than to treat black and white clients differently or abandon the Jungian perspective. 'Is it possible to rescue the concepts . . . from their racist antecedents? When psychotherapists and analysts use these concepts, are they aware of their racist roots? If so do they rationalise them away? Or do they accept them as facts?' (p. 278). Of course, Jung was neither the first nor the last to image African people as children. Nor was such a characterisation exclusive to psychology. Addressing adult black men as 'boy' by white people has been a significant feature of interracial exchanges on several continents.

But whatever the status of Jungian ideas in modern psychotherapy, it has to be acknowledged that for many psychologists this form of psychology is worlds away from their interests. As such they may well feel that here is more raking over of old bones – anthrax-ridden ones though they may be. They would be quite mistaken to think that. Similar sorts of notions appeared in the following newspaper article. The psychologist in question is an honorary lecturer at a British university. The article was published just a few days before the Gulf War against Iraq:

> Mr. Chesney . . . believes that the mind is made up of three separate states: The parent – which judges; the adult – which thinks; and the child – which is in touch with the person's feelings. In all of us one of these states is usually dominant. . . . Mr. Chesney today predicted that war was inevitable in the Gulf. Saddam and Bush are at opposite ends of the analyser's scale and are unlikely ever to find any common ground. . . . Bush 'the parent' has treated Saddam like a naughty kid by giving him a deadline to meet. . . . The Iraqi President . . . is the child in the plot. . . . His psyche has little to do with judgment – the parental influence – or thinking and rationalisation – the adult. His actions are more influenced by primitive instinct and satisfying himself – the child. (Astley, 1991, pp. 38–9)

We should make due allowance for this being a newspaper report which may have introduced a slant on the material which the psychologist did not intend. Nevertheless, the full article actually contains a brief but not too imprecise account of the Transactional Analysis perspective (Berne, 1964) on which the psychologist's thesis is built. There is something remarkable about perceiving Saddam Hussein of Iraq as a child with all the implications that carries – particularly the legitimacy of a parent disciplining or scolding him severely. The characteristics described as being typical of the child can scarcely be argued to apply to a skilful politician and manipulator of world status. It might be totally coincidental that Saddam Hussein, a black person, is construed as a child but the ideological significance of such a choice cannot escape us as a likely alternative.

While Transactional Analysis crudely applied can be used to perpetuate a view of black people as childlike, it would be somewhat unfair to suggest that this racist notion is inherent in Transactional Analysis itself. Stern (1987) reminds us that Berne himself provided concepts which might have helped the psychologists like the one in the newspaper story to avoid ideological traps:

> of special interest to this paper is Berne's little-used concept of *The Little Fascist* (Berne, 1972) which is the grabbing, oppressive part of us. . . . Berne himself related this concept directly to expressions of racism. The concept of the Little Fascist has gone largely underground in T.A. (p. 36)

Stern suggests that awareness of the Little Fascist in us is an important part of avoiding its expression.:

> He encourages us precisely to know this oppressive, sometimes frightening, but very human part of ourselves in order for us not to operate in the world from that source. . . . Perhaps we avoid examining more modern and subtle forms of racism in order to avoid knowing this aspect of ourselves. (p. 37)

Racism in practice

A psychology that fails to recognise its racism within, or one which takes no action to counter its racism, will inevitably succumb to discriminating against black people directly or indirectly. How racist psychological 'facts' from biased research become part of psychological practice depends greatly on context. Racism in practice is racial discrimination. It is the deliberate or unintended acting out of racial prejudice by one racial group towards another (Richardson and Lambert, 1985). We will go further and describe racism in practice also as 'not taking active steps to change a system that discriminates against black people' (Owusu-Bempah, 1985, p. 22). Practitioners whose practice fails to challenge the racial *status quo* are racist not simply by benefiting from the system but through colluding with it. By rocking no boats they also serve racism.

Chapter 5

Racism in theory

The racist is the normal individual in a racist society. (Dolan *et al.*, 1991, p. 71)

Psychology's value-ridden nature is hardly a secret (Bramel and Friend, 1981; Howard, 1985; Riegel, 1978; Sampson, 1981; Sarason, 1981; Williams, 1988). Close scrutiny of what appears to be objective, detached enquiry often reveals its clear ideological foundations. Given the pervasiveness of racism in Western thought, psychological theory is bound to be part of the problem rather than its solution. Critical examination suggests that the discipline delivers essentially comforting messages which deny the need for action; theories effectively encourage psychologists not to see themselves as part of the problem. Such a palliative message is as damaging in its way as that of the 'bad-gene' theories. This allegiance to the *status quo* clashes markedly with the impression of concern promoted by 'liberal' psychologists and by psychological organisations as a whole. There are exceptions, of course, but those who try to expose the ugly side of psychology are generally regarded as unscientific, emotive or simply political.

Psychological theory as a palliative

Psychology is instrumental in maintaining the societal status quo by (a) endorsing and reflecting dominant social values, (b) disseminating those values in the persuasive form of so-called value-free scientific statements, and (c) providing an asocial human image of the human being, which in turn portrays the individual as essentially independent from sociohistorical circumstances. (Prilleltensky, 1989, p. 800)

At the end of the Second World War the situation of black people in the Western World could be described simply: the United States of America practised racial separation upheld by the law – some, with justice, would call it apartheid; in Britain, despite the British passport being the right of all colonised peoples under the Crown, very few black people were settled there; in Australia indigenous peoples were dispossessed and deprived of basic human rights little short of genocide; everywhere in Western Europe, black people were 'in their place' segregated from white society.

What sort of psychological theory of racism was available to cope with such facts, which would at the same not rock the boat? A psychology which questioned the morality of the social system would not do. Neither was it (nor has it ever been) the function of mainstream psychology to offer even the mildest of challenges to the established social order. In Europe, the genocide of Jews, Gypsies and other ethnic minority groups created a social climate hostile to crude, bad-gene theory. However, simply rejecting bad-gene theory merely nibbled at the problem, it did little overall to challenge psychology's racism. Theory stressed that racism was characteristic of psychologically troubled and marginal individuals; equating racism with psychological abnormality forced racism as an issue away from society's mainstream to its margins. By directing attention on racism to corners of society, psychology protected racist social structures (and continues to do so). Today, smug complacency is still encouraged in those who do not recognise themselves in the icon of the racist sculptured by psychology itself.

It is not surprising then to find a multiplicity of psychological texts which hark back to Myrdal's (1944) *An American Dilemma*. Myrdal, a sociologist and economist, in his analysis of the North American social structure raised the contrast between American values like equality or justice and the racist reality. The solution to this dilemma, according to Myrdal, was not to be found in a fundamental change in a society which generates racism and thrives on it, but in changing racist individuals. A similar viewpoint was promoted in the run-of-the-mill psychological theories of racism popular at the time. Racism was regarded as a prejudiced attitude. Psychology had developed crude but influential means of measuring attitudes – attitude scales. Indeed the subdiscipline, social psychology, was largely a by-product of this achievement. Early authors of these attitude scales led the way on theories of racism. The Bogardus (1928) social distance scale, for example, was predicated on the notion that accepted social intimacy is determined substantially by racial and national characteristics – 'Would you live next door to or marry an Italian, Eskimo and African?' were the type of relationships employed to reflect differing amounts of social distance. Bogardus was a sociologist and it showed. His measurements dealt with the social system as it was, with segregation a major feature. The scale could, at a pinch, be used to make comparisons between people in terms of their feelings about significant racial or national groups. However, Bogardus preferred to dwell on 'league tables' of relative social ostracism of Russians-versus-the-Chinese-versus-the-French and so forth. In other words, it was used to produce a map of racial segregation in American society.

Thurstone (1928; Thurstone and Chave, 1929), however, was a psychologist and it showed too. He had been asked to investigate the influence of Griffith's film *The Birth of a Nation* on the racial attitudes of American youngsters; his brief did not include directly the racist social structure in which these youngsters lived. As such, Thurstone's approach was geared to individuals and changes in their racial prejudice. This was a crucial influence on later studies in that it presented racism as an individual matter, a quality possessed by individuals rather than society. This perspective excludes many aspects of racism which are not simply stereotypes or related in other ways directly to prejudicial beliefs. It makes freedom from racial prejudice distinctly possible since the problem lies in the thoughts of bigots, not in the social structure:

> Questionnaires which are intended to test racist attitudes are based on a stereotype of the classic racist, and on the notion that people who are racially prejudiced are of a special type. Those who pass the tests with a clean bill of enlightenment by asserting that they think blacks should have equal access to jobs, are adhering to popular liberal middle-class notions of race relations and perhaps merely provide a measure of their distance from racial problems . . . they resist the reorganisation or the redistribution of resources that could bring about a measure of racial equality. They defend the *status quo* though they claim not to be hostile to black people. (Cowlishaw, 1986, p. 6)

By providing such attitude measures, these early researchers supplied the means by which psychologists would continue to only deal with racism tangentially – by attempting to change attitudes identified by a prejudice questionnaire. The way to rid society of racism is to do those things which shift people's answers on an attitude questionnaire. By adopting a high moral tone towards the much disparaged deviant racist, psychology ignored 'normal' racism. Indeed, it would not be going too far to suggest that such attitude scales merely pilloried the self-aware racist. The thoughts of those unaware of the nature of their particular brand of racism were at the same time condoned.

Even more bizarre was the attempt to suggest that racism was largely hot air; when required to act in keeping with their racism, bigots essentially behaved reasonably, dispensing equitable treatment irrespective of skin colour. Unbelievably, generations of psychology students have been kidded into believing this when told that attitudes did not predict behaviour (e.g. Wicker, 1969). The famous study by a sociologist, LaPiere (1934), was eagerly seized upon by psychologists. This is a curiosity in itself since very little sociology traditionally passed disciplinary boundaries into psychology. Perhaps a 'law' of psychological immigration applies here – only let in foreigners when there is dirty work to be done. In other words we should be alert to the ideological acceptability and underpinnings of LaPiere's research. Essentially he wrote to hotels and the like asking whether they would accept a reservation for a Chinese couple. Overwhelmingly they said that they would not. However, LaPiere had no difficulties when visiting the same establishments, accompanied by a Chinese couple, in obtaining accommodation and services for them.

Traditionally psychologists have suggested that this is evidence that the attitude and action components of prejudice may operate differently. Situational factors may override the prejudiced notions of individuals. This is good news surely? No, for it is merely a variant on the 'some of my best friends are black' thesis in which rock-solid racism is excused by individual exceptions. Psychology restricted concern about racism by insisting that it was 'all in the mind'. But there is nothing more racist than the initial exclusionary decision of the hotel receptionists and managers who wrote to LaPiere to the effect that Chinese guests were not welcome. Had they been government officers processing immigration applications such an 'attitude' expressed in writing would be seen as a profoundly racist act. That the hotel staff were not upfront in their racism when confronted makes them no less racist. Furthermore, psychology's apologists for racism ignore the evidence of racial segregation in the hotel and restaurant trade throughout many of the states of the USA at the time. This was legitimate in law even much later in the 1950s. That hotels would not accept black guests was not an 'attitude problem' but a social reality. What should LaPiere's research be taken to imply – that, despite a few wrong words, minorities could expect fair treatment? Suppose in real life a Chinese couple themselves had written asking to reserve accommodation. Would they have gone to a hotel which had refused them in a letter? With a lifetime's experience of American racism, they would likely not. The racist work would have been done.

Gordon Allport was for many years just about the most important voice in psychology on prejudice. He stressed the prejudiced versus 'tolerant' dimension as the crux of the matter. If only the bigot could be persuaded to be more like the 'tolerant' person then all would be well was the assumption. After all, the main problem was the irrationality of the racially prejudiced. This is another 'goodies' and 'baddies' scenario which substantially obscures fundamental issues. Racially prejudiced people rush into mistaken attitudes, by Allport's account, in contrast with the reasonableness and rationality of the 'tolerant' individual. However, as already seen, by modern standards the 'tolerant' person may well be an archetypal racist. Certainly this is the case if we accept Allport's definition; a 'tolerant' person makes no distinction of race, colour, or creed' (Allport, 1954, p. 425). Nowadays this would be described as the 'colour-blind strategy'. It essentially disguises a failure to acknowledge the special needs of different 'races' or creeds. It is the mentality which in a multi-cultural society (as, of course, the USA was in the 1950s) would expect Christmas day to be a public holiday but expect or require members of another creed, for example Chinese employees, to work on Chinese New Year.

Katz (1991) describes Allport's (1954) book as a landmark. But Allport's argument is merely a testament to the idea that *the* problem is prejudice. Not only that, the very irrationality of prejudice alienates it from the thinking classes. Allport, in his way, carried on the search for the marginal bigot, ignoring the centrality of racism in all our thinking. It has rarely been doubted that this was a significant inroad into our understanding of Western society. However, we would maintain, it was a deflection or diversion from the clear centrality of racist thinking throughout society. After all, almost every psychologist, including Allport himself, recognised the source of racism to be in society, that it is a socially acquired phenomenon. One would therefore expect such a 'clever' academic/professional group as psychologists to know that the most effective solution to the problem lies at its very source. Allport's neglect of the racism of the rational was a vote of confidence in his class and profession, a repudiation of racist crudities. The general pathology of his culture was ignored despite its apartheitism, the cause was in the pathology of individuals. At heart, American society had a nucleus of healthy, non-racist minds – a convenient scenario for some.

Perhaps the most significant example of the ideological neutralising of psychological research is the transmogrification of the Authoritarian Personality theory by American psychology. The psychoanalyst, Wilhelm Reich, sought to explain the rise of fascism he was witnessing around him in Berlin (Reich, 1933). While trivial explanations such as the power of Hitler's oratory might satisfy some, Reich sought a deeper explanation. This he found in the character structure of working-class and lower-middle-class Germans: the strongly patriarchal family had reproduced within it the structure and ideology of the state; the family and the nation are thereby inextricably interlocked in a pathological social system; the repression of sexuality within the family generated yearnings for vague and mystical ideas; nation, duty, honour, religion and motherhood are aspects of psychological internalisation of the fascist state's politics; the citizen both reflects and ardently supports this fascist state.

The repression of Jewish thought in 1930s Germany led to the exodus of several important and psychoanalytically orientated members of the Frankfurt School to North America. These academics had developed their own notions, somewhat different from Reich's, about the role of the family in the development of fascism. In particular, Adorno focused on anti-semitism. Starting as the *fascist character* and through the *anti-democratic character*, the phrase *authoritarian personality* progressed to be one of the most familiar concepts in psychology. By holding that racism is integral to the social fabric and the family, a challenge was issued which claimed that society rather than the individual was the key to racism. Instead of the health of society being seen as affected by pathological racists in its midst, the notion that the state itself was pathological was a major shift in emphasis. The publication of the major work *The Authoritarian Personality* (Adorno *et al.*, 1950) was the most significant proclamation of this unacceptable message.

America was overtly racist and segregationist. Explanations of racism based on social structure, as Adorno *et al.* demonstrated, were not easy to reconcile with the notion of the marginal bigot. Thus a number of intellectual moves followed. One of these was already in train prior to the publication of *The Authoritarian Personality*. In 1943 Sanford and Levinson had received a small grant to study anti-semitism (Sanford, 1986), predicated on a radically different (and familiar) tradition. Sanford and Levinson asked themselves whether:

> people who were prejudiced against Jews were also prejudiced against other 'outgroups'; hence our Ethnocentrism . . . scale. After finding that this was indeed the case, and believing as we now did that among the sources of prejudice were deep emotional needs of the personality, we asked ourselves if these needs might be expressed in other ways as well – hence the F (for Fascism) scale. (Sanford, 1986, p. 211)

Opposition to right-wing ideologies had brought the USA into the Second World War. Not surprisingly, the claim that anti-semitism and other forms of racism were born of family structure did not have an easy passage in post-war America. In the Cold War era, the new enemy was communism not fascism. Joseph McCarthy's pogrom involving anti-communist witch-hunts claimed academics among its victims. In these dire straits, American psychology did not leap upon the radical aspects of *The Authoritarian Personality* as a rallying ground. Instead it reduced the issue to the academic but politically safe game of methodological critiques. Despite the theoretical foundation of authoritarian personality research, it was the matter of the adequacy of the questionnaires which attracted the spotlight. 'Yeasayers', 'naysayers', and acquiescence-response set were amongst the methodological stumbling blocks raised. Psychologists' attempts to rewrite the questionnaires continued for many years after Reich's original intent had been forgotten. By changing the task to an issue of measurement, once more, the profession equated the problem with extremism. Measuring differences in authoritarianism, anti-semitism and the like promotes the idea of a league table of high scorers on authoritarianism. The question of what a low score meant was generally dealt with in a cursory fashion. For us, however, the important question is that of what is to be made of low scorers on such measures. Do they reveal non-racists, low racists, circumspect racists or the goodies? Should they be absolved from blame while the high scorers are pilloried for their extremism?

A straightforward answer to the above questions is summarised by Littlewood and Lipsedge's (1989) dismissal of the myth that racism is a disease afflicting certain white psychopathological individuals. They argue that the theory of individual psychopathology fails to explain how society as a whole could be racist if only a (small) section of it suffers from this delusion. They argue further that racism is not a disease or a delusion; rather, racist beliefs are highly adaptive in a racist society; that in a racist society the racist is the normal individual. To single out the most prejudiced, those who most accurately mirror the societal view, and to label them mentally ill is, therefore, to find a scapegoat. They go even further to assert, rightly, that 'We excuse ourselves by using the very mechanism for which we condemn the racist. Everybody who benefits from a racist society is, in some measure, a racist' (p. 52).

For objections to the notion of authoritarianism, the prize could be awarded to Eysenck (1953; 1971). He argued that the authoritarian personality research was flawed since it ignored the fact that many political left-wingers demonstrated thinking processes which were akin to those of the extreme right, apart from certain aspects of ideology. So committed was he to this viewpoint that he describes his thoughts when being physically assaulted in the early 1970s over his views on the racial differences in intelligence as:

> When the attackers rushed at me, I thought: 'Here at last is conclusive evidence for the existence of the Left-wing fascists I had predicted in my 'Psychology of Politics', and whose existence had been vociferously denied by the sociologist at this very school of the University! (Eysenck, 1991, p. 37)

Eysenck's view was that what he termed 'tough mindedness' spanned the political world from right-wing fascist thinking to left-wing communist thinking. The style of thinking was not determined by the politics of family structure but by the vicissitudes of a constitutional psychology which held that the thinking style was largely a matter of certain personality characteristics, themselves largely consequent on biological inheritance. The F-scale advocates had got it wrong since they concentrated on right-wing issues rather than on a more universal cognitive style. Once again we have to ask ourselves what this manoeuvre achieves. It is, perhaps, the self-same one in so far as it marginalises the problem. Rather than racism arising from social structure, it is merely one amongst many attitudes which arise from extremes of personality, especially extraversion and neuroticism. As such the social structure cannot be the culprit – we are asked to believe.

A radically different device for reducing the impact of racism as a central matter for psychology emerged in the work of Rokeach (1960). Again taking issue with the idea of authoritarianism as the basis of certain styles of thought, Rokeach followed a similar line to Eysenck's in suggesting a different mechanism from the simple ideological one which accounted for the racism of the authoritarian personality. The open–closed mind dichotomy characterised thinking and spanned the left-right political continuum. There were closed-minded left-wingers just as there were closed-minded right-wingers. The *style* of believing was as important as its content. Taking the case further, Rokeach went on to argue that belief incompatibility was responsible for much of what passes for racial hostility. In other words, it is not black skin that racists object to but black beliefs! Twenty years later Rokeach was still confident in his viewpoint:

> When I first mentioned the work on race versus belief to a very prominent psychologist . . . He believed that the results would show that people would like a person of their own race who disagreed with them more than a person of the opposite race who agreed with them about something important, because everybody knows how important race is. When I told him that the vast majority of the subjects do exactly the opposite, he said, 'Oh, the reason why you got these results is because the subjects are at a liberal mid-western university, and you brainwashed them. They know what answers you wanted. If you were to repeat this study in a southern university, you wouldn't get this sort of thing.' (Rokeach, 1980, p. 117)

However, Rokeach had obtained such data to support his view, and goes on to poke fun at the unnamed prominent psychologist who would not accept Rokeach's thesis no matter what evidence was produced. We have sympathy with the disbeliever. There is a lack of credibility in Rokeach's thesis, whatever evidence he may call in support. The notion that belief congruence swamps skin colour in judgements of other people is not verified by the day-to-day experience of racism by black people. Should the black person, spat upon in the street, denied employment or beaten up walking home at night, simply philosophise: 'Oh shucks, its my beliefs that they didn't like; lucky thing I kept them to myself, it could have been worse otherwise!'? There is adequate evidence of prejudice and racial hatred being expressed against black people, simply because of the colour of their skin, to justify dismissing Rokeach as yet another academic apologist for racism. Frankly, it is unlikely that Rokeach could have designed research in which the full impact of skin colour could be measured. In the context of research on rational beliefs, it is easy to see how participants inhibit the expression of their racism. We will see the need for subtlety in research on racism later in this chapter. In the meantime, Rokeach was merely falling into the trap of equating racism with obvious hostility. No one would suggest that Rokeach deliberately sat down and fabricated excuses for racism any more than a fish makes the water in which it swims. However, there is a subtext in Rokeach's argument which is unacceptable. What Rokeach is essentially suggesting is that the way to reduce racial hostility is to bring diverse beliefs into alignment. In 1960 Rokeach should have known that black people were not welcome in many white churches and places of worship in the USA. Thus, since racism frequently demands the denial of blackness and black culture as the price for the ending of violence and other forms of oppression against black people, Rokeach's 'solution' is in fact the problem.

Of course, some have always chosen to be positive about relations between people of different races. Sherif (1953; 1967), contributed much to American psychology although it is notable that he was not a native-born American. Especially important was the robbers' cave experiments in which he demonstrated that groups, initially hostile to each other can, in appropriate circumstances, form positive relationships. They need to work together to reach mutually desired goals in order to achieve this. Sherif's research was some of the most widely reported research ever in social psychology. 'Pull together and the problem takes care of itself' is the basic liberal message. The cinammon and apple pie sentiment of this, at a minimum, provides a positive goal in the search of intergroup equality. It is a rather rosy view which has had only limited success in terms of studies of the improvement of race relations as a result of intergroup mixing. Nevertheless such a viewpoint has rather strong messages for society and social action, implying, as it does, that a solution to racism is in our hands. However, in Chapter 3, we saw how even this minimal hope was undermined by an attempt to substitute a view that intergroup hostility is not only common, but built into human psychology as a fundamental social process.

We are now in a rather different period for psychology and racism. The 1960s were a watershed in many respects. The European colonial nations, such as Britain and France, were forced to leave their colonies under pressures from those colonised nations for independence. Principles upon which the empires had been based were challenged by the colonised. For example, it was no longer the case that the British government believed in the view that everyone within the British Empire was equal. The rights of access to 'the mother country' of holders of a British passport were rapidly removed, for example. In the USA urban protests were making inroads into the question of the segregation of black Americans in urban social, educational, legal and employment ghettos impossible to ignore. These urban protests in America led to a range of government initiatives. Some of these, such as the pre-school compensatory education programmes, were indirect. Black protests occurred elsewhere, though what is referred to as 'rioting' was sometimes motivated by white racial hatred against migrant groups. But, of course, there were other changes to be dealt with. For example, for the first time in Britain, there was a long-term visible (though relatively small) black minority. This group was held largely 'in check' in menial employment. (Though it would be wrong to ignore the fact that racial hostility to groups such as the Jews and Irish had long been a feature of British life.) Equal opportunities legislation was soon to make crude expressions of racism more difficult in some countries by specifying certain forms of racism legally unacceptable. During this period, in parts of the world, there was clear evidence of a tight racist grip. In South Africa, for example, the political reality of apartheid remained strong with forced relocation of the black population and violent repression of protest. In Australia, 'whites only' immigration policies were still the order of the day, though it was gradually lifting.

The overall impression might be that, close to home, in Britain things were getting better for black people – overt hostility was on the wane. If legislation against racial discrimination and for equal opportunities was working then old-fashioned racial bigotry must be atypical of modern racial attitudes, it was generally believed. In the USA, it was possible to point to radical changes in public opinion concerning equality of opportunities and busing of school children (e.g. Simon, 1974). During the 1970s, psychologists and other social scientists had begun to claim that racism's nature had changed. A distinctly different form of racism was replacing the crude racial bigotry of the past. This new racism draws on basic American values as the vehicle to express sentiments antagonistic to black people. Beliefs are couched in terms of matters like 'fair play' and 'unfair advantage' rather than 'These niggers are forgetting their place'.

Sears (1988) retrospectively described Kinder and Sear's version of the 'new' racism:

> we proposed that a new form of racism had emerged in white America, which we termed *symbolic racism*. . . . This was not racism composed of derogations of and antagonisms toward blacks *per se*, or of support for formal inequality. Rather, it blended some antiblack feeling with the finest and proudest of traditional American values, particularly individualism. . . . We argued that old-fashioned racism was disappearing: relatively few whites still believed in the innate inferiority of blacks as a race or supported formal discrimination. (pp. 54–5)

Kinder (1986) presents his position on this new sort of racism:

> It . . . represents a form of resistance to change in the racial status based both on racial prejudice and on traditional values that are not in themselves racist. As the political agenda has changed over the last 40 years from an emphasis on equal rights and opportunities to an emphasis on compensation for past discrimination, issues have arisen that have evoked this mix of prejudice and values powerfully. (p. 152)

According to Sears, at least, the content of symbolic racism broadly falls into the following categories: (1) the over-fast social progress of black people, partly achieved through their use of political protests; (2) objections to 'special favours' for black people such as racial quotas in employment, welfare privileges for black people, and the like; and (3) denial of continuing racism on the grounds of the present achievements of black people in employment and elsewhere. Views which represent each of these different components of symbolic racism include:

1. 'It is easy to understand the anger of black people in America.' (Disagree)
2. 'Over the past few years, blacks have got more economically than they deserve.' (Agree)
3. 'Blacks have it better than they ever had it before.' (Agree)

The virtual dominance of this modern symbolic racism is so great that Kinder and Sears (1981) 'found so little old-fashioned racism among Los Angeles suburbanites that they did not even test its effects.' (Sears, 1988, p. 62). Not surprisingly, Kinder and Sears' formulation of a new racism received considerable critical attention. Weigel and Howes (1985) studied (a) the view that symbolic racism is a previously unknown form of racial prejudice, and (b) the possibility that symbolic racism measures just one aspect of a generalised tendency to disparage any out-group perceived as threatening established authority and established standards of conduct. They used a general population sample and found that traditional racism and symbolic racism correlated highly. Symbolic racism was also associated with self-reported conservatism. In other words, symbolic racism is not really different from traditional racism. This view was also to be found in the critique by Sniderman and Tetlock (1986a, b). On the question of the two types of racism, crude racial bigotry versus symbolic racism, they argue:

> First, the two forms of racism are strongly correlated. Second, every observed cause of the one has also been found to be a cause of the other; and every observed consequence of one has been found to be a consequence of the other. (p. 180)

Given this, it is then appropriate to ask questions about the role of the 'traditional American values' in the expression of the symbolic racism. Is it not more than possible that those expressing symbolic racism are merely dressing up their crude bigotry in fine clothes? Furthermore, the values involved in symbolic racism do not appear to be intrinsically different from those Myrdal had held to be core American values – i.e. equality and liberty.

But, as we might have anticipated, underlying the Sniderman and Tetlock criticisms are a swathe of ideologically founded concerns. Many of these are familiar in the objections to equal-opportunities initiatives based on a wide range of ideological foundations, especially by the so-called 'New Right':

> We strongly object, however, to treating opposition to such policies as *racist by definition.* . . . Kinder has no apparent qualms, for example, about operationally defining symbolic racism in terms of opposition to busing, quotas, or special government programs for minorities. (p. 182)

Sniderman and Tetlock argue that the research on symbolic racism amounts to little more than an agendum to change the meaning of racism. This they describe as a 'weakening' by replacing a valid old definition with a suspect 'new' idea. Sniderman and Tetlock clearly state what they mean by racism: 'Racism used to refer to genuine prejudice – a deep-seated, irrational insistence on the inferiority of blacks, and contempt and hostility toward them. It still does' (p. 186).

But this debate seems to be little other than a replay of liberal versus New Right stances on the matter of race. The wish to confine the concept of racism to irrational racial hostility is to reaffirm the marginality of racism as well as to ignore substantial developments in our understanding of the social context of racism. However, to follow Sears and Kinder's recommendations is to dismiss the experiences of black people on the streets, in employment, in the welfare system and elsewhere together with a mass of social research repeatedly demonstrating racial discrimination. That Kinder and Sears had diffi- culty in finding expressions of racial bigotry in surveys matches poorly our knowledge of the rates of crude racial attacks and other street- level indications that 'old-fashioned racism' is not history. Comforting as the liberal position is in so far as it suggests racism is 'on the run', it is only sustainable with a narrow focus on liberal causes and politics. Ultimately it ignores important developments elsewhere in psychology.

The discomforting side of theory

While much of psychological theory on racism has been either anodyne or, more obviously, palliative, there are a number of exceptions to this. Much more fundamentally challenging perspectives have been developed by several important theoreticians. These contain messages which the psychological community could usefully apply to itself. That this has not been done by the discipline is perhaps predictable, although these theories have not been entirely ignored in terms of their application to wider society. One common thread which emerges from these approaches, despite their radically different intellectual origins, is that the concept of non-racism is impossible to sustain given the evidence that racism pervades the thinking of even those appalled by traditional racism.

The threat from psychoanalysis

The psychoanalyst Kovel (1970/88) has painted a portrait of white racism which, while not couched in the language of academic psy- chology, warrants its attention. Psychoanalysis has long since ceased to be a major force in psychological 'science'. Nevertheless, for some psychiatric and psychodynamic approaches to therapy, psychoanalytic ideas remain central. The embarrassment for psychology is that Kovel's insights amount to a psychoanalytic view of the racism of psychology:

> Psychoanalysis can only grasp the full reality of racism if it is itself freed from *psychologism*, which for present purposes we may define as the location of significance within the construction of an isolated mind. (p. xcv)

For Kovel, racism is a product of aggressive expansionist activity by the dominant state which has sucked together different peoples of different ethnicities. 'It is the subjective reflect of imperialism' (p. iv).

Historically American (and other Western societies) have demonstrated major dislocations. The move from entrepreneurial capitalism to the industrial state reflects the expansionist nature of change. Kovel offers a remarkable metaphor:

> as a snake sheds its skin and assumes a new one when it passes a certain size . . . so too does racism provide boundaries within a culture. . . . As we grew more powerful, complex, and variegated, so did we become more racist. . . . Racism belongs . . . to the regulative aspects of our culture. (p. 26)

Taking an organic view of society, Kovel sees the moral and ethical attack on racism as part of the adaptation of society to its changing boundaries. With no gain in potency from change, there will be no change. Adaptation is to gain strength: 'the ethical condemnation has a function too, insofar as it is derived from the main sources of cultural power, and serves to regulate the evil, not to replace it' (pp. 27–8).

Within Kovel's theory exist four types of people in relation to racism. The first two are the 'ideal types' of racists and the third a shadowy 'non-racist' type:

1. *Dominative racists.* Such a person openly turns his bigotry into action. Representing the 'open flame' of racism, such a person manifestly seeks to maintain dominance over black people, through force if necessary. Kovel points out that this is the only type which corresponds to usual notions of racial prejudice.
2. *Aversive racists.* Such a person accepts the superiority of the white races. Usually there is a degree of awareness of this belief. Nevertheless such a person does not put the beliefs into manifest action. There is a conflict between the racist sentiment and the individual's conscience which rejects such views. The aversive racist defends against the conflict by avoidance. According to Kovel, 'Within this type we find at one extreme those individuals who, upon threat – such as when a black gets "too close" – lapse into dominative racism; and at the other, those who, impelled by a strong social conscience, consider themselves liberals and . . . do their best within the given structure of society to ameliorate the conditions of the Negro' (p. 55).
3. *No racist tendencies.* However, this person is ill-defined.

The dominative racist reflects slavery days best, the aversive racist best reflects post-slavery segregationalist America. But Kovel sees racism much as Freud saw psychopathology; the disease remains constant but the symptoms of the disease vary. Conceived as such, it is wrong to consider that the modern period is one which corresponds to Kovel's non-racist type. Instead Kovel sees the current situation as being best described as 'metaracist'. This is his *fourth type*. He claims that nowadays racial distinctions are regarded as out of date. Consequently, there is this new form of racism: 'they are not racially prejudiced – but metaracists, because they acquiesce in the larger culture which continues the work of racism' (pp. 211–12).

The metaracist is not someone who is above racism. The metaracist is the beneficiary of racism, someone who helps share out the spoils and endeavours to keep their hands clean at the same time. Whether metaracists are aware of it or not, they are leaving others to do the dirty work. That this is one of Kovel's *prototypes* is important since it may be hotly contested whether such an individual could remain unaffected by the racist society from which he or she benefits. Doubtless, however, in the identity parade line-up of racists, this type would be the last to be picked out.

Kovel's analysis warns of a number of things. Most importantly, it points to the changing appearance of racism despite its unchanging core. As such, a warning might be warranted. Great care needs to be taken against defining racism in terms of its superficial aspects.

The threat from psychology

While scorn may be an appropriate response to much psychological theorising about racism, it would be unjust to lump all psychological theories together. When allowed to do its best, psychology is capable of generating penetrating insights. Amongst the best critical approaches to understanding racism is Gaertner and Dovidio's (1986) notion of aversive racism. To a degree, they capture the essence of the racism of much of psychology while addressing a wider issue. It is suggested that the emotional basis of racial discrimination is not located in racial hatred *per se* but in rather different sorts of feelings: 'The negative affect that aversive racists have for blacks . . . involves discomfort, uneasiness, disgust, and sometimes fear, which tend to motivate avoidance rather than intentionally destructive behaviors' (p. 63).

Psychologically these negative feelings often go unacknowledged. How can they be admitted when they are characteristic of liberal individuals with a profoundly egalitarian value system? People with these feelings dislike racism, support liberal causes, are distressed by discrimination and promote equality of opportunities for minorities. These egalitarian views are both genuine and sincere. Far from being trivial aspects of the social persona, they are beliefs about oneself, others and society. Quite clearly there is an ambivalence in this.

Aversion to black people and egalitarianism are not normally compatible. Circumstances and situations in which the incompatibility is obvious to the individual, therefore, result in a victory for egalitarianism. However sometimes the warning signals fail or are not recognised:

> When a situation or event threatens to make the negative portion of their attitude salient, aversive racists are motivated to repudiate or dissociate these feelings from their self-image, and they vigorously try to avoid acting wrongly on the basis of these feelings. In these situations, aversive racists may overreact and amplify their positive behavior in ways that would reaffirm their egalitarian convictions and their apparently nonracist attitudes. In other situations, however, the underlying negative portions of their attitudes are expressed, but in subtle, rationalizable ways. (p. 62)

Gaertner and Dovidio's work is exceptional in that they are able to generate a number of testable hypotheses from this set of notions. Significantly, they consider that it would be impossible to develop useful questionnaires to measure aversive racism. Indeed, it would be a contradiction in terms since any questionnaire can only deal with what is known or made salient to the individual. Aversive racists are unaware, most of the time, of their own racism. In a very real sense, underlying the psyche of the liberal may well be irrationality not too dissimilar to that Sniderman and Tetlock (1986a, b) ascribe to the traditional conception of racism. In aversive racism theory, distaste for racial bigotry is not sufficient to ensure freedom from the self-same bigotry.

The hypotheses based on this theory are as testable empirically as any others in psychology. One hypothesis argues that the aversive racist may behave in a racist fashion in circumstances where socially appropriate ways of behaving are not clearly defined or where the racist act can be rationalised as being caused by some non-racial factor. Dovidio and Gaertner (1983), for example, found in an experiment that when someone volunteered to assist white college students the offer was more likely to be taken up if the volunteer was black than if the person was white. However, when it was necessary to ask for help from another person, the white students chose to ask another white person rather than a black person. This occurred despite the fact that those taking part perceived no differences in terms of competence or willingness to help between the black and white persons. Gaertner and Dovidio suggest that to reject help that has been freely offered violates social convention and so is frowned upon. Besides, it is black people's traditional role to be at white people's service anyway. In these circumstances the aversive racist accepts the offer so as not to behave inappropriately. On the other hand, failing to ask for help would violate no social conventions, but soliciting help from a black partner transgresses the tradition of white superiority.

In another hypothesis, Gaertner and Dovidio proposed a process by which another person's race affects how salient non-race-related aspects of a situation are. In other words, justifications are provided to account for a racist act which could have been applied (but would not have been) if that other person was white (or vice versa). This was demonstrated in the work of Faranda and Gaertner (1979). They used a mock court-room situation. In this, a weak prosecution case was sometimes accompanied by an extremely damaging piece of hearsay evidence. The judge instructed the jury to disregard this evidence. Traditional bigots behaved broadly in line with their overt racism. Much more important in this context was the response of the low-authoritarians or 'liberals'. When they heard the inadmissible evidence they rejected it in line with the judge's comments and were favourably disposed towards the defendant. At least, this is what happened when the defendant was white. When the accused was black they failed to disregard the inadmissible evidence so were more inclined to see the black defendant as guilty. 'These [liberal] subjects later reported that they were angry with the prosecution for trying unfairly to introduce this hearsay testimony. They did not express this anger, however, when the defendant was black. Thus, low authoritarian subjects demonstrated a pro-ingroup bias' (p. 79). Studies by Howitt and Owusu-Bempah (1990c) and Owusu-Bempah (1994) support Gaertner and Dovidio's hypotheses.

The notion that racism remains hidden, revealing itself in some 'liberals' only in circumstances which are conducive to its unrecognised expression, also underlies *regressive racism* (Rogers and Prentice-Dunn, 1981). Circumstances in which an individual's social persona is stripped away are particularly conducive to acting out of the profound, racist reality of the white character. Anything which encourages this process of deindividuation will tend to facilitate acting upon deep-seated racism. Again it is dependent upon the idea that there is a new norm amongst white people of 'unprejudiced egalitarianism' which guides dealings with people of other races. This contrasts markedly with the new norm among black people of militancy and overt hostility towards white people which replaces the historical deference exhibited in their presence. In order to demonstrate this experimentally, the standard Berkowitz type paradigm (Berkowitz and Geen, 1966; Berkowitz and Rawlings, 1963) was used. In this an individual's aggression against another person is measured by the amount of obnoxious electric shock that the individual gives in the context of an experiment. *Deindividuation* was manipulated by failing to address the participants in the research by name, telling them that the experimenter would not know the level of shock given, the researcher assuming full responsibility for a pseudo-subject's well-being and not allowing the participants in the research to meet the pseudo-subject. The *individuation* process was roughly the reverse of this. As is typical in this sort of research, some participants in the research 'accidentally' overheard disparaging comments about them by the pseudo-subject:

> when white subjects were not insulted, they expressed less aggression toward black than white victims; however, if the white subjects were insulted they expressed more aggression against black than white victims. (pp. 67–8)

An earlier study by Wilson and Rogers (1975) indicated that black people react differently and show no reverse racism. The suggestion is that under conditions of emotional arousal both black and white people regress to the behaviour patterns of an earlier age. White American people show racial aggression but African-American people a passivity towards white people:

> Regressive racism . . . may be found in the members of any race. To a large extent, black and white Americans take a Janus-faced view of interracial encounters, one face looking forward but the other face focussing grimly on the past. (Rogers and Prentice-Dunn, 1981, p. 71)

With such demonstrations of the elusive quality of much of racism, psychologists ought to be constantly aware that traditional methods of assessing racism through direct questioning are unable to predict the subtlety of the expression of racism in action. Our beliefs are no guide to our actions on such an ideologically complex matter as racism.

Defining racism

Definitions in the social sciences serve a purpose. However, rarely, if ever, can they specify the distinctive essence of something; usually they largely exclude certain things from consideration. As such, they provide a vehicle for the metatheory of the discipline. Bearing this in mind, it is perhaps to be expected that there is no universally accepted or commonly employed definition of racism in psychology. Granted that psychology has generally equated racism with individual beliefs and ideology, perhaps it is not surprising to find one useful but limited definition of racism which holds it to be 'the belief in the inherent superiority of one race over all others and thereby the right to dominance' (Lorde, 1984, p. 115). That this relates to easily measured things which are used to label individuals matches perfectly the traditional psychological approach. However, racial prejudice and beliefs reflect incompletely what we have already discussed as racism. They may well be aspects of racism but in themselves they are neither sufficient nor necessary to define it. There is something unrealistic about trying to piece a few words together into a sentence which tells us what is and what is not racism. Nevertheless, it is worthwhile exploring the range of available definitions of the term.

Racism = prejudice + power

This simple formula has proved popular outside academia ever since it was proposed by Katz (1978) in her book *White Racism*. It encapsulates the viewpoint underlying Katz's highly influential approach to the use of group work in experiential anti-racism training. The exercises that she supplies form the basis of a programme to tackle the racial knowledge, beliefs and behaviours of white people at both the individual and the institutional levels. As an intermediary step between a purely psychological definition of racism and a sociological one it has commendable features, particularly in so far as it dwells on the importance of a discriminatory outcome and not simply racial hostility and bias. However, its strengths also determine some of its weaknesses. The formula can be taken to imply that there is no racism unless there is prejudice. Furthermore, if an individual has no power to act upon his or her prejudices at a given time or in given situations does that mean that they are not racist? It is notable that members of disadvantaged minorities sometimes use the Katz formula to argue that they cannot be racist (e.g. McLaren, 1989). After all, while women and the white working class are held to be socially disadvantaged and consequently powerless, surely they cannot be racist? However, power is not indivisible or an all-or-nothing quality. The ability to harm others is not confined exclusively to the dominant groups in society. Quite clearly, a white woman employer is just as able to discriminate against black applicants as is a white man. Equally, an Indian Hindu landlord may well discriminate against a Chinese family, or *vice-versa*.

Each individual has a variety of roles and relationships which differ in terms of their potential to harm others. Merely favouring a shop owned by a Bangladeshi rather than one owned by an African-Carribean contains the seeds of a situation which might be profoundly racist. Arguing that the disadvantaged cannot be racist is merely an example of distancing oneself from racism, an avoidance ploy. A black man, arguably, cannot be sexist according to Katz's logic.

Probably no better summary of the problems of power in relation to racism is to be found than in the following:

> You can be a racialist but still not discriminate, because you've got no power to discriminate: you're not a boss; you haven't got a house to sell; so you shout abuse at children and hold racist views. But you are not a discriminator. . . . You can be a discriminator even though you don't personally hold racist views; you do it out of sheer ignorance. Or it has always been done this way, so you continue to do it this way, as a lot of institutions do, because you are responding to the racism of the people you are with, the people you employ or the people you house. You know how they will react if you bring in blacks to this kind of job or this kind of area, therefore you're going to adapt your policy so that it doesn't happen. This link is a reaction to racism, rather than you actually holding racist views. Unfortunately many people in positions that affect the lives of others respond to racist views of others in what they do. (Cashmore, 1987; p. 224, quoting an interview with a Commission for Racial Equality official.)

Yet another definition of racism which has gained some recent popularity (e.g. Condor, 1988) is that of Husband (1982). This definition, apparently heavily influenced by the notions about intergroup relations of the time (e.g. Tajfel, 1978a), focuses on how racial group members are seen as possessing relatively fixed and discernible characteristics 'Racism is the application of "race" categories in social contexts with an accompanying attribution of invariable characteristics to category members' (Husband, 1982, p. 19). While this definition will most certainly identify certain sorts of racism, it moves little beyond the notion of stereotyping in which certain characteristics are held to be typical of racial categories. Unfortunately for proponents of this sort of definition, research has shown that there is no easy way of assessing how racial stereotypes function cognitively. It is difficult to believe that there are many in society who are unaware of racial stereotypes. Racial stereotypes are part of the argot of the culture, let alone foisted on us all as 'entertainment' by the mass media. How could one escape the influence of this? Certainly when researchers have asked people to list stereotypes of racial groups they are well up to the task (e.g. Devine, 1989). Our own experience in racism awareness training was that when participants were required in role-play to generate stereotypes of 'black people' for about three minutes, they managed this with ease (and pleasure) without exhausting their supply of stereotypes.

After all, who has not heard of 'working like a black', 'as lazy as a black' or 'The blacks are coming here to sponge off of the welfare system'? What research has shown is that some people, including those who like to think of themselves as free from racial prejudice, may respond on the basis of stereotypes when they have not been alerted to the possibility. Devine (1989) found in a sample of white American students that the following racial stereotypes were well known: criminality, low intelligence, laziness, sexual prowess, athleticism and being rhythmic. When asked to interpret a passage which was somewhat ambiguous in content, all subjects tended to respond on the basis of stereotypes irrespective of their measured levels of prejudice. Things were different, however, when the participants in the research were presented with the opportunity to list their thoughts about black Americans. These comments ranged widely: 'Blacks are free loaders' to 'My father says blacks are lazy, I think he is wrong'. In these circumstances the potential for expressing racist thoughts was clear to the participants. This time the type of response made varied according to prejudice as measured by a standard psychological test – those racially prejudiced made more hostile comments than those who were not.

Gilbert and Hixon (1991) argued that there is no automatic relationship between having a stereotype and its being activated. They devised ingenious studies in which the amount of mental work being done in a situation likely to provoke a stereotype was varied. A busy person, doing a lot of thinking, may not respond stereotypically towards a member of an ethnic minority. However, in circumstances where the stereotype has been activated, the mentally busy person is more likely to apply that stereotype.

These psychological studies make it difficult to separate racism from the situation. In other words, given the universality of many racial stereotypes, one cannot regard the use of those stereotypes as being predictable from racial hostility. The question, however, is whether circumstances are such that they will be applied. There is nothing unusual about this. After all, knowing the stereotype that women make bad drivers and also believing it to be false because of statistical evidence, does not stop us from applying the stereotype when a female driver cuts us up on a motorway.

Husband's definition is at root a psychological one, this becomes clear when one considers Brown's (1985) suggestion:

> Racism is based in material conditions in that most or all white people benefit from their superordinate position relative to blacks . . . [it] can be regarded as 'culturally sanctioned, rational responses to struggles over scarce resources'. (p. 67)

It follows from such an analysis that a racist social system requires constant and routine reinforcement by social institutions as well as individuals. Brown (1986) describes aspects of the work of the careers service in England. The front covers of the young clients' files, for example, might have one of two written codes based on information gathered at the initial interview. One symbol gave the client's preferred choice of occupation, the other the careers officer's judgements about suitable and realistic jobs. A discrepancy was a clue to 'overambition' though the advisers' choices were based on a working knowledge of racism within their community. While the upshot is that such actions can hardly be said to be the result of personal racial prejudice, the effect is to exclude black school-leavers from parts of the job market.

Experience of this led Brown to proposes a typology of racism. The dimensions of intent and outcome allow four basic sorts: intent may be prejudiced or unprejudiced, similarly the outcome discriminatory or non-discriminatory. Of the four types, *prejudiced intent* with discrimination as the outcome corresponds to traditional ideas of racism – *individual racism* or all-weather illiberalism; unprejudiced intent which leads to discrimination corresponds to the notion of *racist non-racism* or fair-weather liberalism (Berry, 1958). The other two possibilities which do not lead to discrimination are described by Brown as *non-racism*. For Brown, quite clearly, the outcome determines what is racist or not.

> Racist Non-Racism' . . . refers to the ways in which (white) people can understand their daily actions to be 'non-racist'. That is, they seek to disassociate themselves from their conception of racism as being the result of the accumulation of . . . 'Individual Racism' . . . The distancing from the stereotypical racist provides a way of getting off the hook when faced with the uneasy daily resolutions between generally 'liberal' outlooks/ideas and racist outcomes. (pp. 390–1)

Brown gives as an example of this, taken from a letter to an Australian newspaper, the topic of Asian immigration there: 'a country and its people have every right to defend their heritage, way of life, culture, traditions and morals from the likes of Asian migration without the fear of being branded racist' (p. 397).

As might be expected, there are many ways of classifying racism. For example, Halstead (1988) claims to have detected six different types in recent writings on the topic. Some of these will be redolent of aspects of the definition of racism which have already been discussed in this chapter and elsewhere:

Type 1: *Pre-reflective gut racism*: This contains elements such as fear of strangers, a need to feel superior to others, and ignorance of racial minorities. This syndrome easily attracts to it the acceptance of 'race myths' such as 'black children in a class ruin the education of the white majority'.

Type 2: *Post-reflective gut racism*: Rationalisation and justification of racial prejudice define this type. Included in this would be sets of beliefs which, if true, might justify discrimination. An example of this is the notion that Europeans possess the drive and initiative for self-enhancement and that of their group. Halstead also includes the racism based on inadequate scientific theory in this category.

Type 3: *Cultural racism*: This is characterised by attribution of inferior cultures to ethnic minority groups. Matters such as leisure, social customs, manners, religion and moral beliefs would be included. Racist attitudes are justified in terms of cultural inferiority rather than inferior or subhuman biological potential.

Type 4: *Institutional racism*: This reflects how many traditional systems, practices, procedures and structures of social organi-sations fail to meet the needs of multi-cultural society or effectively deny access to, or disadvantage, black groups in society. The extent to which institutional racism is unintentional may be a matter for argument, but if traditional ways of acting are maintained after having been challenged as racist then unintentiality ceases to be defensible.

Type 5: *Paternalistic racism*: Here, the white majority takes it as their right to decide for black people how black issues are to be tackled. There may be an element of tokenism in this, but in essence it denies black people authority over their own lives.

Type 6: *Colour-blind racism*: As we have already seen, this rests on the belief that acceptance of differences among racial groups is racially divisive. Consequently the different needs of different groups are dismissed in favour of treating everyone the same irrespective of needs. In a sense it is unintentional racism in that the intent may be 'good' but the outcome as harmful as any other form.

The existence of these different types leads to the conclusion that the origins of racism do not lie in any simple psychological mechanism. Indeed, some of the above types of racism are little to do with psychology. For example, institutional racism seems radically different from the crude racial bigotry and stereotyping which underlie much of the debate in psychology.

Pushing the definition in other directions, King (1991) raises the notion of *dysconsciousness* which essentially accepts the present social order without question. Social inequality and racial exploitation are uncritically accepted:

Dysconscious racism is a form of racism that tacitly accepts dominant White norms and privileges. It is not the *absence* of consciousness (that is, not unconsciousness) but an *impaired* consciousness or distorted way of thinking about race as compared to, for example, critical consciousness. (p. 135)

She evaluated student essays attempting to explain why American society had got into such a state that twice as many African-American children die in their first year of life. Notably, very few of the essays failed to defend the present system. Two broad categories of explanation emerged. The first is *conservative assimilationist ideology*. This holds cultural deficits of African-Americans responsible for their condition. In the words of one student, during the times of slavery, black people 'were not given the luxury or opportunity to be educated *and each generation passed this disability on*' (p. 137).

The second major category of explanation essentially involves devaluing diversity since it ignores the importance of accepting and displaying majority norms and values achieving. A simple thesis of the American Dream is implied – anyone can make it given the chance. An example of this is:

> Because of segregation . . . Blacks . . . have had less access historically to education and jobs, which has led to a poverty cycle for many. *The effects described are due to poverty*, lack of education and lack of opportunity. (p. 137)

No matter how 'dysconsciously' racism is expressed, it results in a failure to come to terms with the centrality and pervasiveness of racism in society. The emphasis is moved away from racism to matters of slavery and inequality of access due to history.

While none of this necessarily identifies the thinking of psychologists particularly well, cognate examples abound in the writings of academics specialising in race. Take the following:

> For example, let us consider the well-documented fact that people of Caribbean and Asian origin in Britain are more likely to be unemployed than people of indigenous origin when the economy is in crisis and there is a shortage of jobs. . . . There is firm evidence that this is, in part, the long-term consequence of exclusionary practices based on negative stereotypes. . . . However, in the 1980s, it has also been determined partly by the fact that workers of Asian and Caribbean origin are more likely to have been employed in the textile and clothing industries which are more vulnerable to restructuring and therefore abolition than others, as a result of which they have been overrepresented amongst those made redundant. (Miles, 1989, p. 56)

In this, once again, we are being invited to de-emphasise racism as the prime cause of inequality until we have rejected other 'explanations'. So if a black person is made redundant by an ailing factory we should not see this as a consequence of racism! How come black people were over-represented in a weak industry? Were not many people 'imported' to do factory and other menial work which white people did not want in the first place? If racism is to be the last-ditch explanation of social inequality then surely we are following the same ideological path as King's students; we are, in effect, denying its existence, or our role in its maintenance.

Accepting that the treatment of racism in psychological research and theory has been an essentially self-serving exercise rather than a means of promoting understanding and raising consciousness, the following comment is apposite. It comes from a practising psychologist meeting with ethnic minorities as a group for the first time:

> I had been working for several years in an area with a very mixed population and I was careful to keep in mind what I knew about testing in relation to ethnic minority children. . . . I had thought that, with the exception of incidents involving extremists such as the National Front, things were not too bad. . . . I also came up against the perceptions of black people about education, about my profession in particular and the very real pain and resentment which were placed at our door. (Booker *et al.*, 1989, p. 126)

Chapter 6

The Eurocentrism of psychology

> Asked point-blank if white researchers should be removed from black communities, a thoughtful observer might concede that in the interest of furthering the cause of racial justice and opportunity, a goodly number must go. He might also concede that a small but growing number of black researchers must also leave. (Brazziel, 1973, p. 41)

Psychology and imperialism in Africa

Psychology served imperialism on the African continent in two ways (Bulhan, 1981): firstly, by reinforcing the myths of African dependency (*psychological colonialism*); secondly, by direct involvement in the exploitation of black workers (*psychological neo-colonialism*). These two functions were somewhat separated by time, the watershed being the period of rapid decolonialisation during the 1950s and 1960s when many colonies won political independence, but not freedom from economic exploitation.

The earliest psychological work carried out by Westerners in Africa mainly sought to advance the material interests of Euro-Americans and their self-knowledge. So among justifications for doing research in Africa were Doob's (1960) claim that such work might facilitate the entrance of the 'less-civilised' into 'civilisation', and Reuning and Wortly's (1973) suggestion that the study of 'earlier' ways of life helps put civilisation's problems into perspective. Note the avoidance of references to 'exploitation' in these justifications; one should not be fooled, however:

> Just as his material resources and human labour have been exploited to build sophisticated technologies and institutions, thereby *developing* Euro-America while *underdeveloping* Africa, the African 'subject' for research

becomes a means through which answers are sought for every 'controversial' issue – as exemplified by the debate on nature vs. nurture. And just as those improved technologies and institutions help in their turn to bolster the forces continuing to oppress him, so more and more refined psychological theories and instruments serve only to rationalise and make more effective the African's exploitation. (Bulhan, 1981, p. 27)

The influential psychiatrist, Carothers (1951), suggested that black Africans were much like lobotomised Europeans, sharing some characteristics with psychopaths. In this he merely reflected the view of Africans as undeveloped children, needing a firm parent figure – white colonialists doubtlessly. Similarly, Haward and Roland's (1954) claim that Africans loved repetitive routine activities simply slotted black people into their 'proper place in the natural order of exploitation'. And this made a perverse sort of sense. For example, in just one small corner of the continent, Zaire (the French Congo), 9 million Africans had been forced to gather and process rubber for a handful of European entrepreneurs (Bulhan, 1985).

Parin and Morgenthaler (1956/7, reprinted 1969), using field observations, psychoanalytically 'studied' the character of 'primitive' Africans, as they called them. However, they never bothered to learn any local languages so were entirely dependent upon claims made by European colonialists and Africans who spoke some English or French. The following was among the stories which led them to claim that African employees were lazy, lacked a sense of duty and had no pride in their work:

> An employee in a timber-exporting business in the southern part of the Gold Coast was building with the help of about 300 workers (mostly Mossi and Ashanti) a 40 km. stretch of roadway with many wooden bridges over it. . . . Only a few hundred yards were still left to be done, together with the completion of a bridge, presumably a few days' work. After the last payment of wages about 90 per cent of the workmen gave in their notice; they did not feel it worth their while to stay just for two or three days' pay. When it was pointed out that the work done by them all in common would, if left incomplete, be quite unusable, this failed to make a single workman change his mind. (p. 195)

History is silent on whether Parin and Morgenthaler rushed to take over from these 'irresponsible' labourers and even whether they bothered to check their sources. They quite clearly sided with the timber exporting company though no information is provided about how it treated its employees and its contribution to the good of the country.

The 'industrial psychology' attributed to the African was very simple. Their behaviour at work was governed only by the pleasure principle. It was fortunate for their colonialist exploiters that 'Only such factors as command from an external authority; imitation of, and identification with, a prestige-bearer (a white man); reward and punishment were of some efficacy' (pp. 194–5). Parin and Morganthaler conceded that some of the Africans they observed included intelligent and well-educated teachers, nurses, midwives and civil servants. This, nevertheless, did not stop our European 'researchers' from describing these black people as 'primitive', 'savage', 'infantile' and 'neurotic mimics' lacking in self-control.

With decolonisation, psychologists continued to provide services and assessments to neo-colonial business interests rather than African interests. According to Bulhan (1981), this was without malice and due to '[a] limited historical perspective, narrow technical fascination, as well as financial dependency on grants from business cartels and governments' (p. 38).

Bulhan indicates the importance of the National Institute of Personnel Research of South Africa in this neo-colonialism. This organisation, regarded as relatively liberal by some (Louw, 1987), was attached to the South African Psychological Association. The Institute received most of its funds from the apartheid government. However, a third of its income came from British/American companies involved in the mining of gold, diamonds and iron. A crucial aspect of its work was developing performance tests of ability for sustained physical labour. One of the tests required job applicants to strong-arm a large weight up several steps and then drop it down one of three chutes. This, taken together with simple physiological measures, was a reasonably good predictor of ability to shovel rock. One stated intention of the Institute was to assess the extent to which the behaviour of the African worker could be changed. A range of other tests were developed to ensure that the workers employed were as efficient and compliant as possible.

This exploitation of black labour could be contrasted with the situation in French-speaking Africa. There, Bulhan (1981) suggests, psychologists more typically used their skills to understand how the educational potential of African workers could be fulfilled. Examples of exploitative relations could, nevertheless, be found in these parts of Africa. However, the overall contrast does stress how the apparently reasonable desire on the part of employers to ensure the efficiency of their workers can disguise an uncompromising process of exploitation in South Africa. The fact is that these Africans were not being helped to achieve their potential. If they were not the strongest and most co-operative of labourers, they were locked into unemployment. A racist state using psychology in this way quite clearly brings psychology's racism off library shelves into the real world with a vengeance. A wider perspective, therefore, leads Bulhan to the view that in Africa Western psychology:

> confirms the historical truth that the scholar's choice, formulation and interpretation of social issues are not, to any fundamental extent, out of tune with the basic motives and rationalisations of the ruling classes. (p. 29)

Such tendencies are clearly expressed in Robbertse's writings (1967, 1971) – when describing the policy of the Psychological Institute of South Africa. Dawes (1985) describes how Robbertse called for the use of psychology to enhance the popular acceptability of apartheid South Africa's government policy and to unveil the psychological characteristics of different races. This sort of work clearly supports 'separate development' – apartheid:

> Members of the Psychological Institute of the Republic of South Africa are encouraged to undertake research in this field on a greater scale because it concerns the scientific basis of separate development and strikes at the root of our continued existence. (Robertse, in Dawes, 1985 p. 58)

It is worth noting that some South African psychologists provide a 'glossy brochure' account of the flourishing psychology of South Africa compared to that of the rest of Africa (e.g. Raubenheimer, 1993). However, others note the human costs involved in this 'achievement' (Foster *et al.*, 1993; Howitt, 1993).

Encouragement for other separatist racial policies are found in the writings of a white Australian, Ray (1974). He has published extensively in fields related to race, basing his arguments loosely on questionable psychological theory. The following *tour de force* in the use of psychology in exclusionary racism appeared in his *In Defence of the White Australia Policy*:

> Let us face the fact that large numbers of even educated Australians do not like Jews or 'Wogs'. This is not concentration camp mentality. It is simply the perceptual discrimination of identifiably different characteristics in these people and the personal preference of not liking such characteristics. The concept of national characteristics stands in somewhat of a bad odour today but for all that it remains true that people who travel overseas have no difficulty in naming what those characteristics are. . . . I once knew even an ardent neo-Nazi who regarded the white race as the only one with a right to exist. One of his best friends and most constant associates was a Pakistani who was nearly as black as the proverbial ace of spades. Some exceptions don't necessarily disturb a rule. Following this line of reasoning through, if Australians like English migrants most and Asian migrants least, it is English migrants we should choose. This may be ethnocentric but it is not racist. (p. 70)

Ray continues to publish (e.g. Ray, 1988a, b) and remains an extensively cited academic, although fiercely criticised (Eckhardt, 1988; Sidanius, 1988), and so clearly influential in a sense. That he does not recognise the attitude of not liking 'Wogs' as concentration camp mentality is surprising, especially considering the appalling treatment received by Australia's aborigines at the time (Broome, 1982). Perhaps Ray lets his defence slip totally when he writes: 'I advocate enlightened self interest and an Australia not torn by racial tensions. At present I can walk alone at night through the streets of Sydney without fear. I would like to keep it that way' (p. 71).

Eurocentrism and the nature of psychological theory

Eurocentrism describes the orientation of much of the social sciences, especially psychology (Joseph *et al.*, 1990). It is a special case of the term ethnocentrism which means seeing other cultures from the perspective of one's own culture. Such perceptions are usually evaluative and encourage a belief in the superiority of one's own culture as the 'natural' way of things. As a way of conducting research and developing theory, the description 'ethnocentric' ought to be an anathema to psychology. Such a doctrinaire psychology essentially violates most of the basic principles of the discipline. Words like 'objectivity' come to mind here. However, despite this, and the rather obvious risk of doing so, the vast majority of psychology is carried out purely ethnocentrically. Of course, Eurocentrism might not matter if the object of today's psychology was the search for universals in human action and experience. While that once may have been its quest, fewer now believe this to be a desirable or feasible agendum. Pursuit of universals helps to deny the importance of a culturally specific psychology, perhaps a preferred course for the discipline to run.

None of this is to suggest that psychology has ignored the cross-cultural. This would be to neglect the extensive literature on cross-cultural psychology. But being cross-cultural in itself is no insurance against Eurocentrism as psychology's extended sojourn into Africa demonstrates. Indeed, an important question is whether Eurocentric psychology can ever hope to achieve the sensitivity required for a genuine understanding of cultural diversity. Nor is it axiomatic that psychologists from cultures outside Europe and North America will automatically produce a more culturally sensitive psychology. The Eurocentrality of much of today's psychology provides all psychologists with a discipline which inevitably obstructs a completely non-Eurocentric research.

Furthermore, how much do the metatheoretical perspectives of psychology themselves provide a structure for a particular view of the world? One is reminded of the debate between Chomsky and others concerning whether philosophical aspects of certain sorts of psychology make them prone to racism. The following, dating back to Hume in the eighteenth century, is an illustration:

> I am apt to suspect the negroes . . . to be naturally inferior to the whites. There never was a civilized nation of any other complexion than white, nor even any individual eminent either in action or speculation. No ingenious manufactures amongst them, no arts, no sciences. . . . In JAMAICA indeed they talk of one negroe as a man of parts and learning: but 'tis likely he is admired for very slender accomplishments, like a parrot, who speaks a few words plainly. (Hume, cited in Squadrito, 1979, pp. 105–6)

Classic racist stuff! Chomsky (1976), following Bracken (1973), suggested that the Empiricist philosophy which was integral to early psychology rose concomitantly with capitalism which was supported by a philosophy of individualism. This happened in a period of imperialism with its consequential racism, buttressed by empiricist philosophy.

> But a deeper look will show that the concept of the 'empty organism', plastic and unstructured, apart from being false, also serves naturally as the support for the most reactionary social doctrines. If people are, in fact, malleable and plastic beings with no essential psychological nature, then why should they not be controlled and coerced by those who claim authority, special knowledge, and a unique insight into what is best for those less enlightened? (Chomsky, 1976, p. 132)

Chomsky notes that colonialism was responsible for the development of racist notions. Some of the most important empiricist philosophers, including Locke, were even actively involved in the adminstration of colonialism. It is possible that other philosophies are similarly less amenable to racism:

> Cartesian dualism raises . . . 'a modest conceptual barrier' to racist doctrine. The reason for that is simple. Cartesian doctrine characterizes humans as thinking beings: they are metaphysically distinct from non-humans possessing a thinking substance (*res cogitans*) which is unitary and invariant – it does not have color, for example. There are no 'black minds' or 'white minds'. You're either a machine, or else you're a human being. (Chomsky, 1979, pp. 92–3)

That is, in plainer language, in Cartesian terms you either think and therefore you are or you are not because you do not think. Since the essence of humanness is in thought, aspects of a person which are unrelated to this are but accidental features. In this way the Cartesian approach is antipathetic to racism, which is dependent on physical features in the first place. However, some see this argument as inadequate. Squadrito (1979), for example, disputes that Cartesian philosophy is a brake on racism whereas Empiricism oils racism's engine. Likewise, we can concur with Hodge (1990) and argue that racism, like other forms of oppression, is sustained by Cartesian dualism. It contains assumptions which enable those accepting it to believe that they have greater moral or intellectual worth than those whom they oppress or exploit. For instance, the Cartesian dictum *Cogito ergo sum* has been employed in the service of racism (and classism) to mean 'Some think more than others therefore some are more worthy "beings" than others'. This is most evident in the manner in which power and resources are allocated in society.

Psychologists have tended to regard racism as being a feature of the 'hard-nosed' scientist. Superficially there is good reason for doing so. Psychological racism has been associated with innatism and psychological testing. Both of these fields have established complex empirical and theoretical underpinnings which, whether deserved or not, appear to be effective technologies and, possibly, scientific. Kimble (1984) wrote of two different cultures in psychology. One of these cultures is *humanistic* in nature. In this the main objective of psychology is seen as improving the human condition. The other culture values highly the *scientific* approach. But there is nothing inherent in either position which guarantees a stand against racism, they merely express their racism differently. Moreover, although it might be tempting to accept that humanistic psychologies would be sensitive to culture, we have seen no evidence that the major figures in 'non-scientific' psychology have been historically less inclined to racism.

An example of a seemingly strong claim for a branch of psychological science is in Jenkins' (1989) paper 'The liberating value of constructionism for minorities'. Despite the hyperbole of the title, the substance is far slighter. Adopting the standard contructionist view that knowledge is created partisanly to serve dominant interest groups, it is easy to see why Europeans associate derogatory themes with blackness. But understanding how knowledge is constructed does not prevent understanding how things could be different. Jenkins points to Malcolm X's autobiography as an example. As a child, Malcolm X confided to a supportive teacher that he wanted to be a lawyer. At this the teacher dressed him down a little for not being realistic and suggested that a skilled labouring occupation would be appropriate for him. For the first time he realised that being a lawyer was seen as an inappropriate role for a 'nigger'. He also knew that he was smarter than most white children. This began his career as a black militant.

But it was Malcolm X who did this, not social constructionism. Inevitably it becomes more than a little patronising that social constructionism, developed largely by European and American scholars, is held to be the key to what the youthful Malcolm X did for himself. This impression is confirmed when we read: 'One goal of human enlightenment would be to make people more aware in the sense of recognizing their individual capacity to contribute to changes of that reality through the power of their dialectical imagination' (Jenkins, 1989, p. 167).

Psychological Imperialism

> Power is the right to have one's or a group's definition of reality prevail over all other people's definition of reality. Military forces, police, weapons, prisons, abuse, instructions, laws, rituals and such like are simply the tools by which one definition of reality can be made to prevail over others. (Masson, 1989, p. 16)

The consequences of the continuing European hegemony in psychology, according to Joseph *et al.* (1990), have been the following:

1. Black countries are damaged because of the 'colonisation' of black psychologists by Eurocentric thought.
2. The lack of attention to alternatives to mainstream knowledge leaves the discipline impoverished.
3. The dominance of Eurocentric psychology helps legitimise world-wide inequality.

At the level of the content of psychology, rather than in terms of outcomes, the Eurocentric psychology characterises human nature in a manner which reflects poorly on black people. An example is moral development. In Eurocentric psychology morality is held to reside in the individual who possesses or constructs the rules required for moral activity (Rich and DeVitis, 1985). All of this is internal to the individual, and external regulation of actions is seen as unnecessary since it is presumed to be already incorporated into the psychology of the individual:

> Studies of morality in India have the unenviable task of trying to 'explain away' uncomfortable behaviour. Individuals in India appear to act guided by external gratification rather than internal norms alone. The psychoanalytic literature describes this as a failure in the development of internal controls,

somewhat akin to the weaker superegos attributed to women generally, and
a consequent development of a 'communal conscience' instead of individual
conscience. (Joseph *et al.*, 1990, pp. 14–15)

A non-Eurocentric conception of intelligence has also been raised.
Even at the height of the 'bad black genes' controversy over intelligence
around 1970, some were recommending that the cultural specificity
of concepts similar to the Western notion of intelligence needed
consideration. The Western–Anglo-Saxon–Protestant concept essentially involves the skilful playing with ideas with little thought to turning
them into action. In contrast, the Islamic notion of intelligence, for
example, is of a religious quality and involves trying to know god:

> Children brought up in a system exclusively emphasising this concept might
> not score so well on Raven's Matrices, but this would tell us nothing of their
> potential to have learned such tricks had they been brought up by parents
> with Eysenck's or Jensen's ideas. (Wober, 1971, p. 40)

While in some respects a radical suggestion, this does not abandon a
Eurocentric view since it reaffirms the importance of psychologists'
conceptions of intelligence in Western–Anglo-Saxon experience. It
assumes no racial differences in genetic potential to 'pick up tricks',
but it ignores the inseparability of intelligence from cultural experience.
Reified notions of intelligence such as this are part of the problem.
One radical black psychologist's position of the 1970s illustrates how
truly topsy-turvy is the Eurocentric approach to intelligence (Nobles,
1986). Based on arguments that African peoples are evolutionarily more
advanced than the white race and that African cultures are historically
more developed than white cultures, a redefinition of higher intelligence
was proposed: the more black skin pigment in the body the greater the
person's intelligence. It takes a little thinking to see the logic of this but
why should Europeans impose their values on an arbitrary notion such
as intelligence? Normally Western intelligence tests are biased to create
the impression that genes for whiteness determine intelligence.

Psychology forms part of a cultural imperialism just as do the mass
media and other institutions of the Western world. It is used as a
tool to make the European definition of reality prevail over those
of the rest of the world. It is exported throughout the world in a
number of different ways, including textbooks. Some of these are
world-wide sellers and translated into numerous languages, as we
saw in Chapter 4. Psychology is exported in a one-way stream. It
is also exported in the form of other artifacts such as psychological
tests and measures. Howitt and Owusu-Bempah (1990) noted that
it was fairly common to find Western personality measures applied
in other parts of the world, notably Africa. Typically these were

Cattell's 16 Personality Factor and Eysenck's Personality Inventory. It was usual for the authors of these studies to conclude that the measures behaved in much the same way as they did in the Western societies where they were developed. By no means were all of these researchers of European origin. That some of this Eurocentric research was conducted by black researchers is of no particular significance to the general problem. Europeanisation via professional socialisation accounts, in a large part, for some black psychologists' Eurocentric approach to psychological research. While there is some justification for such studies, irrespective of who conducts them, it is the research which was *not* done that highlights the problem. Fundamentally the studies are Eurocentric in that they take tests developed in Western cultures for use on Westerners, and then apply them with little or no adaptation to different cultures. No studies attempted to explore, for instance, Ghanaian or Chinese personality structures in their own terms rather than through these Western tests. Equally, no studies were found which attempted to understand Western personality using tests which originated in Africa or China, for example.

Kline's (1967) study illustrates these points well. He examined the structure of the Eysenck Personality Inventory and Cattell's 16 Personality Factor questionnaires in Ghana. Using a highly educated sample in this former British colony less than nine years after independence, he found that the factorial structures of the measures applied to Ghanaians tended to be similar to those of the Western standardisation samples. While this is somewhat odd as cross-cultural research, even stranger is his claim for a genetic basis for personality and what this implies for the maintenance of Eurocentric approaches to research: 'the results . . . in no way run counter to the hypothesis for the hereditary determination of these factors and may be regarded as tentative evidence for them' (Kline, 1967, p. 106).

Another of Kline's studies (Kline, 1969) attempted to use a questionnaire to compare the anal personality in British and Ghanaian respondents. There was only a difference of about 1 to 2 points (i.e. one or two more anality items agreed with) between the British and the educated Ghanaians on this measure. The variation in the scores of the British was larger than for the Ghanaians. Despite such severe limitations, Kline adjudges the Ghanaians as more anal but then claims that this was due to the pressures of the educational system which only the most determined and compulsive (i.e. anal) could overcome. In other words, beware of the educated black person – they only succeed because of their socially undesirable personality traits.

Remarkably, some psychologists who choose to take white racist psychology into black communities can feel that they themselves are the victims. Scarr (1988) pleaded her case to her colleagues in American psychology, suggesting:

> For those of us who have incorporated race into research designs, there is a great danger in the outcome. If one deliberately sets out to investigate racial or gender differences that have unfavorable possibilities for the underdog, one is in danger of ostracism and worse from one's socially well-intentioned colleagues. The messenger with the bad news seems to be blamed for having invented the message. (Scarr, 1988, p. 56)

> Only dishonest investigators can promise that the results of their investigations will hew to any party line, but I believed then and believe now that only by asking fair questions and seeking honest answers can one make a contribution to science and to one's society. (Scarr, 1988, p. 57)

Scarr's research compared the school progress on black adopted children in black and white families. Quite clearly it did not try to understand the adopted black child in the black family, since it was intended to make comparisons between black and white families. The research did not have to be in terms of black versus white comparisons. In a very real sense Scarr did invent the message for which she disclaims responsibility. Hers was more research which involved black people only as a contrast to white culture. That Scarr's focus compared the black and white community does not make the research fundamentally different from research comparing black and white children on scholastic achievement. That she felt aggrieved at adverse criticism points strongly to the compelling one-sidedness of Eurocentric thinking.

It is not uncommon to find the Eurocentricity of psychology operating within a culture rather than simply cross-culturally. An important case in point is Baldwin's (1979) analysis of the white-centred view found in the notion of black 'self-hatred'. Research and theory on self-concept has largely stressed the importance of social interaction on self-perception. This goes back to early works by Cooley (1902) and Mead (1934). Cooley's idea of the looking-glass-self basically asserts that how we see ourselves is largely a reflection of how we are seen by significant other people in our lives. Later writers applied this to black people's identity development (e.g. Bulhan, 1985; Dollard, 1937; Fanon, 1967; Myrdal, 1944; Pettigrew, 1964). They argue that black people form their self-identity from the way they are seen by white people. Others (Banks and Gramb, 1972; Clark, 1965; Proshansky and Newton, 1968; Tajfel, 1978a) extended this by suggesting that objective economic and social disparities between black and white people are used by black people to form a view of their social and individual worth. This means that to understand the black self-concept one looks to see how white society sees the black person. In other words, white society, with its ideas of black inferiority, merely serves to form the image reflected in the social mirror to black people. The precise mechanisms suggested have varied over time but, according to Baldwin, the central thesis is that there are damaging effects imposed on black people by the way dominant, racist white society regards them.

But there is a problem with this formulation. It posits black self-concept as due solely to the influence of white society, and nothing to do with black people themselves; namely, white society's unfavourable attitudes towards them are presumed to be internalised almost without an intervening black mind. This means that in developing a self-concept, the black person takes the role of the manipulated rather than the manipulator – black people constitute the classic *tabula rasa*. This, of course, is hardly the case. Black people can, and do, recognise the inherent racism of the white community and refuse to adapt to the mirror held up by white society. Rather, they regard their own (black) community as their significant social milieu, in much the same way as the white working class do (e.g. Heiss and Owen, 1972). Banks *et al.* (1977), for example, found that black students tended to be unaffected by adverse feedback from a white person, though the same feedback from a black person had a measurable effect on their self-evaluation. However, positive feedback from a person of either race had similar effects. Whatever else these findings imply, they suggest that the white-centred society is not a universal determinant of black self-concept because the black person is a much more involved actor in the process.

Following an extensive review of 'black self-hatred' Baldwin (1979) concluded that the vast literature suggests a fundamental 'Eurocentric' posture in psychology and social science. This matches the frequent lack of scientific ethics and responsibility in much research conducted on black people; Eurocentric beliefs and assumptions do not permit the exercise of objectivity in relation to black people (Guthrie, 1976). This appears to be the case especially in studies involving black children's self-identity. In this area, investigators have a particular tendency to selective reporting. Studies which contradict the notion of self-hatred amongst black children are ignored as are those where white children show signs of this characteristic.

Evidence abounds, of course, from studies of doll choice which claim to have revealed that black children see themselves as being similar to a white doll much more frequently than white children do with a black doll. Clark and Clark's (1939; 1947) evidence on this is commonly cited in psychology textbooks. Similar findings have been reported elsewhere. For example, in Britain, Pushkin (1973) found that a third of three-year-olds and four-fifths of six-year-olds 'at a tea party' were rejecting or deprecating of black dolls. Milner (1973) also found that half of five- to eight-year-old black children identified with white dolls and even more preferred white dolls. A decade later Davey (1983) and Milner (1983) confidently reported that a majority of West Indian and Asian children would prefer to be white. This is by no means a novel claim. In 1930 Jung asserted that: 'The Negro. . .would give anything to change his skin; so too, the white man hates to admit that he has been touched by the black' (Jung, 1930, p. 196).

Of course, that a white child will overwhelmingly choose a white doll over a black doll may tell us an awful lot more about white racism than about black self-hatred. The worrying thing is that so many of us are familiar with such research findings but ignorant of contradictory evidence. The research on the question of racial preference in dolls, drawings and the like is actually remarkably inconsistent. Baldwin describes how Hraba and Grant (1970) and Ward and Braun (1972) found that black children preponderantly chose a black puppet as being the nicer or having a nicer colour. Also, Baldwin refers to Beckham's (1929, 1934) studies of over 3,000 black people. Overwhelmingly, those sampled expressed the view that they were happy being black. A fifth rejected this however.

Further relevant research findings include the following: Fox and Jordan's (1973), which demonstrated a significant positive shift in black racial identification compared with Clark and Clark's data – the majority of the black children involved in this study expressed own-race preference; Datcher *et al.* (1973) also found that black children preferred black dolls to white dolls, and white children preferred white dolls to black dolls; furthermore, white children in multi-racial schools preferred white dolls significantly less than white children in a monoracial school. Somewhat similar findings were reported by Greenwald and Oppenheim (1968), who gave black and white nursery schoolchildren a choice of three, rather than two, different skin colours with which to identify. They found that the inclusion of an intermediate alternative reduced black children's 'misidentifications' significantly. Moreover, there did not appear to be any significant difference between black and white children's misidentifications. Greenwald and Oppenheim concluded that there is nothing unusual about black children's misidentifications.

The above studies add weight to Baldwin's (1979) comments about the perspective of white researchers on black self-concept:

> given the multicultural nature of American society, we must be extremely cautious in interpreting the experience of Black people. . . . Such a perspective recognizes that American society encompasses a variety of systems of cultural definition (or sociocultural orientation), some of which

are fundamentally different in nature. Within this sociocultural context one must be cautious not to use the framework of the experiences of one racial–cultural group to interpret and explain the experiences of another. It may very well depend upon which racial–cultural system of definitions is operative as to what kinds of observations are made and the types of explanations and interpretation ultimately derived. (p. 52)

The notion of black self-hatred superficially demonstrates a degree of sympathy for the plight of black people in a racist society, but is itself racist. To recognise that racism is rife and adversely affects black people might appear a good starting point for an anti-racist argument. However, the argument also alludes to the view of black people as helpless puppets incapable of thinking and acting independently. Black people are held to derive their view of themselves from white racist society, and not from their own community. This is a reversal of the adage: *alter ipse amicus*, a friend is another self. Significantly, no one has, as yet, postulated that the white working class suffer from 'self-hatred' despite the stark social, economic and political disparities between them and their upper- and middle-class counterparts. The persistence of the notion of black self-hatred is due mainly to its racist functions to society. It combines the victim–blame and the avoidance strategies thereby enabling white people to blame black people for their plight and the same time eschew responsibility for ridding society of racism.

Essentially following Baldwin (1979), Foster-Carter (1986), reviewing evidence of black self-hatred, suggested that research inadvertently reinforces ideas of white superiority. For instance, she suggests that Milner's (1973; 1983) influential studies and interpretations reinforce an insidious and potent Eurocentric myth that black children are 'inferiorised' and would prefer to be white. Extreme case studies and individual literary histories are often used to provide support for the idea that black children suffer from damaged self-esteem together with the introjection of white racist attitudes, she argues. So the occasional case of a black child attempting to bleach their skin or amputate a limb to achieve love (e.g. Alhibai, 1987) is often used to make a general case. Or, when Goldberg and Hodes (1992) in trying to explain adolescent suicidal behaviour through poisoning suggest 'racism is an attack on the individual which is reproduced by overdosing as an attack on the self' (p. 65).

When pointed out, racist thinking is often readily recognised by people strongly opposed to racism in any form. Unfortunately, this is not protection in itself against such thinking. So embedded are racist ideas in Western culture that they can encroach, unrecognised, into the thinking of many who are horrified when it is pointed out to them.

Psychological ideas about the black family readily filter into professional thinking about black people. So, for example, the false notions about the inadequacy of the black family may influence decisions made about such families. This is not surprising as psychological theories often have their roots in the 'common sense' of racist societies. Some may require proof of the failure of professional training to deal effectively with racism. Research on the (in)adequacy of the training of psychologists is uncommon, that on the racist thinking of trainees even rarer still. Nevertheless, there is relevant research. Owusu-Bempah (1994) found evidence of racist thinking about black families in a study of postgraduate trainees in social work. Many of these students would have been undergraduates on social science courses including psychology. Furthermore, in Britain, social work education is relatively advanced in terms of offering an anti-racist and anti-discrimination stance. Consequently, such a group of trainee professionals, many of whom will have already worked professionally as unqualified social workers, perhaps provide an acid test of the influence of racist social science literature and ideas on their thinking and/or practice.

Three descriptions (vignettes) of children were prepared. These differed solely in terms of their racial or ethnic origin. In one case, a white boy was described, in another a black boy and in the last a boy of mixed parentage. The vignettes describe a thirteen-year-old youngster who has a history of behavioural difficulties both at home and at school, including theft and damage to property. There is a double history of divorce by the mother and the boy is the oldest of three children, the others being half-siblings of his. He has never met his father and his mother tells the boy little about him. The trainee social workers were asked to identify possible social and psychological factors associated with the boy's behaviour and emotional problems; what could be done to help the boy change his attitudes and behaviour; and what sort of professional intervention might be the most helpful to the boy. Race was highly influential in terms of the respondents' comments. Identity crises, for example, were held to blame by 25 per cent for the white child, but 85 per cent and 59 per cent for the mixed-parentage child and the black child respectively. Family circumstances were held to blame in 69 per cent of the comments involving the mixed-parentage child, 59 per cent for the black child and only 30 per cent for the comments about the white child. In terms of action to be taken, rather fewer suggested that the white boy needed activities to deal with identity issues. The white boy was not seen as needing cultural information but the other two boys were seen as needing this and a disciplinary adult male model. The child of mixed parentage was seen as being in no need of therapy compared with the other two.

The only difference between the boys was skin-tone; black and white children will be treated in very divergent ways on the basis of the most dubious of psychological theorising.

Harking back in part to our discussion of white feminism, it is interesting to note the following comments of a social worker and a psychologist included in a powerful feminist critique of orthodox thinking on sexual abuse:

> It is also necessary to recognize the impact that racism can have on the meaning of the event. *A Black child who has internalized racism may equate being Black with being bad*, and the guilt that all abused children experience may confirm those feelings. She may also find it harder to 'tell', since it may feel like an even greater betrayal of her family than it is to a white child. (MacLeod and Saraga, 1988, pp. 44–5, emphasis added)

That the argument so easily elides into a variant of the self-hatred theme without one jot of evidence is further confirmation of the routine nature of such race thinking. The child has internalised racism but not sexism!

Sometimes it is extremely difficult to understand quite what the underlying thesis is. Weinreich (1979), for example, describes a case-study of a black youth who gets a lot out of his association with white people but firmly rejects a great deal about black people:

> Seen from one vantage point, John has 'improved'. His self-evaluation is becoming more positive and his own behaviour is becoming more controlled. However, from another vantage point, things are far from well. He dislikes his own skin colour and he dissociates from much of his own community. An understanding of how John's identity structure is made up would appear to be at least as important as attempting to define him in terms of mental health. The other conclusion follows directly from the understanding achieved of his identity structure. Should it be deemed necessary, therapeutic aid, formulated on this kind of understanding, should come from a black therapist. (Weinriech, 1979, pp. 174–5)

Weinreich claims this boy suffers from an identity crisis, though it is difficult to understand what the problem is. After all, the boy's identification with the white community is resulting in a more 'positive self-evaluation'. That he does not identify with the black community seems to be a bigger problem for Weinreich than for the boy. There is no suggestion that white people who do not identify with the black community should see a black psychiatrist. Nor is it claimed that white boys with mostly black friends need therapy from a white therapist. If a black child lives in a predominantly white community why should their efforts to broaden their social milieu be seen as symptomatic of mental ill-health?

Care should be taken to avoid the assumption that the experiences of black people in Western cultures follow the USA and British model in which there is a dominant majority of European origins. Just across a national border there may well be a substantial change in the social structure which invalidates the findings of US research. For example, in Canada things are very different from the rest of North America. Thus Berry (1983) offers this caveat:

> Another error occurs when we employ imported theory (and methods) to study and explain local phenomena. For example attempting to understand multiple intergroup relations in the Canadian ethnic mosaic by the main-stream–minority American concept would have been fruitless . . . ; in Canada we simply do not have a single mainstream to which minorities relate one by one in neat dyadic interactions. (p. 452)

Berry points out the experience of a hapless postgraduate student whose thesis was under review:

> it was predicted that the self-esteem of non-European immigrant students to Canada would be lower than that of native-born students; this expectation was based entirely on the U.S. literature with black and Chicano children. However, lower self-concept was not found, and the author squirmed to explain why his Canadian findings did not fit the American theory; nowhere did he attempt to relate his results to the idea of support for self-concept of ethnic group members which is available in multicultural societies. (pp. 452–3)

In spite of his useful advice or caution, why does he assume that the US situation was actually different from that of Canadian ethnic group members? On what grounds does he imply that Canada is a multi-cultural society but the USA is not?

None the less, Berry suggests that there are three important steps to take to avoid the universal application of Euro-American experiences:

1. The decentring of psychological theory and method from Euro-American influences.
2. Recentring the discipline on the cultures being explored.
3. Integrating various cultural psychologies to achieve 'a truly universal psychology'.

The first two seem axiomatic, the meaning of the third has to be unclear at least for the present time. The fixedness of a universal psychology makes it difficult to envisage as an attempt to do a better service to cultural diversity. The history of universalistic or Eurocentric psychology is not a happy one for black people. Through the abuse of power – education and training, together with rituals such as some aspects of clinical practice – psychology has historically expedited the imposition of white people's definition of reality on black people. In short, it traditionally acts more as an instrument of domination than a liberating discipline. By now the extent of the historical complicity in global oppression and exploitation should be becoming clear. Psychology has been part of the armoury of domination and conquest.

Thomas' (1973) view perhaps speaks loudest:

> It is . . . fixation of beliefs which shapes and sustains white scientific activity. By thus supporting fixed beliefs in society the modern psychologist rationalizes the contempt in which the dominant culture holds all nonwhites. And the inability of psychologists to base their activities on an alternate value system permits the maintenance of conventional assumptions about themselves and others. (p. 58)

Psychology as an organised discipline, as taught and practised, ascribes little value to the experiences of black people. They are important only in so much as they reinforce white people's sense of superiority. Out-and-out Eurocentrism permeates the assumptions, outlook and instruments of this psychology. But it is this psychology that has stormed through the world to be adopted even by black nations, uncritically and wholesale. In a world of cultural and racial heterogeneity, the proliferation of this Eurocentric psychology raises the fundamental concerns over cultural imperialism. In this cultural invasion, the cultural and intellectual resources of another group are penetrated and their potential ignored. One dominant view of the world is imposed and creativity is inhibited by curbing its expression. Cultural invasion, thus, serves the ends of conquest (Freire, 1972).

A century ago, Hegel (1894) argued that only through recognition by others do people become conscious of themselves. The masters/ mistresses are to be found among those who attain recognition without reciprocating: those who recognise but are not recognised become the slaves. In this dialectic not only do the masters and mistresses gain recognition but they also reduce the slaves to mere instruments of their will. 'In that other as ego I behold myself' (Hegel, 1894, p. 202). This remains what Eurocentric psychology attempts to impose on black people. Black people are forced to see themselves in white people without the latter's reciprocating. 'I cannot be aware of me in another individual . . . I am consequently bent upon the suppression of this immediacy of his' (Hegel, 1894, p. 202). This, in a nutshell, epitomises the Eurocentric psychology–black people dialectic.

Is Eurocentrism inescapable?

The failure of the traditional school is, of course, in its devotion to primarily informing us about what White people are doing to Black people. . . . As such, it provides us with very little insight into the intrinsic psychological reality of Black people. (Nobles, 1986, pp. 70–1)

It is important to ask the extent to which the characteristics of Eurocentric psychology are intrinsic to the business of psychology itself. In other words, is it really possible to develop, say, an Afrocentric psychology which is materially different from its Eurocentric cousin? This is a tough question, beyond a brief answer. It is simpler merely to explore the progress of non-Eurocentric psychology. One of the difficulties, of course, is that psychology is a complex web of activities, decidedly economic in nature. If Western psychology is largely about meeting the needs of industrial society, we should not expect it to be very different when transposed elsewhere if the same economic links apply. Alternative psychologies cannot compete without similar levels of resources and different economic links. To make direct comparisons between the achievements of an army of professional psychologists and the non-professional psychologies of other communities is probably nonsensical. After all, it is not a fair comparison to make between the 'gentlemen' scholars who largely contributed to the development of psychology prior to the twentieth century and the discipline's modern workforce. Nevertheless, it is a superficially reasonable question to require some evidence that a systematic psychology of other cultures would be radically different from dominant Euro-American psychology.

Some might retort that this is not essential. One does not expect to know what to replace a headache with, one seeks to get rid of it. Similarly, we are not seeking to replace racism with anything; it is simply to be got rid of. It follows then that in order to understand Eurocentric psychology it is not necessary to have details of the characteristics of viable alternative psychologies. More crucial is understanding the nature of the white culture which generates most psychology. In this way, rather than psychology being schisms moving in parallel, there might be more of a joint enterprise which enables psychology to rid itself of its Eurocentrism and to get closer to meeting the needs of all sectors of society. Ponterotto and Casas (1991) describe the white American value system as characterised by a number of features. Clearly, these need not apply to all white European peoples but it is worthwhile noting some of them as they at least make the problem a little clearer. Amongst examples of those mentioned are:

1. *Individualism*: The individual is held to be independent and autonomous ideally. Furthermore, groups including the family are seen as composed of individuals.
2. *Competition*: This is a highly valued characteristic.
3. *Achievement*: In white culture the accumulation of wealth and position are highly valued. In some traditional native American groups, in contrast, integrity depends on what has been given away.
4. *Time-emphasis*: A strict, linear time- and appointment-keeping system is employed which emphasises the future since time 'mismanaged' is time lost.
5. *Non-verbal and verbal behaviour*: Looking a person in the eye may be a signal of disrespect in a native American, but to the white American not to do so signals shiftiness or shyness.
6. *Nuclear family*: This is characteristic of white Americans but may not match the experiences of others where the extended family is much more important. Thus grandparents, priests and others may be invited to a family therapy session, something which would seem rather odd amongst white Americans.
7. *Written tradition*: Having things in writing is highly important in white society, but other societies may have a much more oral tradition.

Nevertheless, there have been growing attempts to create black psychology as an institution in the USA. Dating the origins of black psychology is as fruitless a task as dating the origins of mainstream psychology. Nobles (1986) offers 4,000 years ago if we mean the first recorded attempts by black scholars to apply their understanding to human behaviour. Alternatively, 1920, the year when the first black person, Francis Sumner, obtained a doctorate in psychology, could also be a legitimate starting point. Another possible contender is 1968 when the Association of Black Psychologists was founded in the USA. It is very much a matter of how terms are defined. What a black psychology is equally becomes a matter of definition. It could mean a psychology opposed to the racism of Eurocentric psychology; or the peculiar psychology of black cultures from ancient African origins to urban Euro-American experience; or a psychology serving black people as Eurocentric psychology has served white people. The first two have been the prime objectives.

According to Nobles, there are three broad approaches:

1. *Deconstructionism*: This highlights the inadequacies of Eurocentric psychology as a means of understanding black people.
2. *Reconstructionism*: Essentially this includes attempts to reshape mainstream psychology into more sensitive models.
3. *Constructionism*: This involves the creation of new techniques to unravel the psychology of black people.

In themselves, it is doubtful whether any of the above is necessary or sufficient to provide the sort of psychology which will enable a radically new approach to black psychology. The reason is quite simple. Each of them is useful for reinforcing the idea that there is no single, correct way of understanding society and individuals in it. In addition, they provide the intellectual stimulus to baulk at mainstream thinking. However, what they cannot do in themselves is to provide the alternative knowledge and ways of understanding. They risk replacing one ideology with another little different in overall implications. Using the analogy above, it would be like trying to replace a toothache with an earache. But we can share Nobles' enthusiasm for approaches which provide a focus for the need to replace traditional Eurocentric understanding with more sensitive and culturally appropriate ones. The danger, of course, is that confusing the replacement of one racist world-view by a superficially different one may be mistaken for a major shift away from racism and Eurocentrism. This has been a familiar error in the history of the racism of psychology.

Psychological racist jokes

In an important journal, *The Psychologist*, published by the British Psychological Society the following appeared:

> So he wasnae a psychologist then, this Freud?'
> 'No by today's definition, no.'
> 'And Anthony Clare – he's no' a psychologist either?'
> 'No. Anthony Clare is a psychiatrist.'
> 'So whit's the difference between a psychologist and a psychiatrist?'
> 'About fifteen thousand a year, I should think.' (Sik, 1989, p. 224)

The Scotsman parodied in this is portrayed as stupid, a person who warrants only a dismissive joke in answer to a serious question. He spoke:

> in a stereotypical Scottish accent, which the author seemed to judge necessary to underline the image of the 'ordinary punter' which he was trying to convey. . . . It appears to me that, for the author . . . and many others, rejection of racism is not a principle which is held and applied generally. Instead, they need to have every group which is the victim of racism and every form of racism pointed out to them. (Leiser, 1989, p. 445)

In the context of race relations such superficially harmless acts as racist jokes serve to reinforce our collective hostility towards members of other groups. They are spoken in contexts which enhance the common group membership of the teller and the audience. Without knowledge of shared hostility or disparaging beliefs about other racial groups, racist jokes are meaningless.

As Freud (1905) observed, jokes are often hostile, serving the purpose of aggressiveness. The main purpose of racist jokes is the satisfaction of a drive (i.e., hatred or contempt) which otherwise could not easily be gratified because of social constraints on the expression of aggression. In so far as we feel that we are members of one group, distinguishable from other groups on the basis of skin colour, sex, social class, profession and so forth, when we are in the presence of our kind we feel safe to verbally aggress against other groups. In other words, we use jokes licentiously to vent hostility and contempt upon groups of people whom we hate or despise. Thus, by means of jokes, indirect verbal hostility is substituted in the place of direct forms of aggression. By making and telling jokes which make black people appear small, subhuman, inferior, despicable, stupid or comical, we achieve indirectly the pleasure of overcoming them, of putting them 'in their place'. It enables us to treat them with contempt; and more importantly, as Billig (1982) has suggested, it systematically desensitises us to the physical (racial assaults) and emotional (racial harassment) abuse they are subject to, and to acquiesce to their economic and political exploitation and oppression by others. Racist jokes evade social barriers against aggression and are sources of sadistic pleasure which, otherwise, are inaccessible. People simply do not wish the extent of their potential for racial aggression to be apparent.

It is, then, perhaps not surprising that Milgram's (1963; 1964; 1974) famous studies which demonstrated that most people will, in the context of a scientific experiment, hurt another human being with painful or even dangerous electric shock, became reduced to an argument about method by many psychologists. Methodological critique is a common sign that the message is unpalatable. A forceful detractor is Mixon (1972), who argued that people in the real word would never do such a thing and they merely had fallen for the prestige of a scientific experiment which they failed to question. Orne and Holland (1968) also argued that the research has nothing to do with real life. These are ludicrous positions for anyone capable of opening a daily newspaper to adopt. The tragedy for psychology is that it needed demonstrations such as Milgram's of the depths to which humanity will sink. For Milgram, his findings could be likened to the concentration camp 'medical experiments' reported to have been carried out under the Nazi regime. Instead of implying that sick perverts were responsible for such inhuman acts, Milgram's studies clearly demonstrated that ordinary people will do inhuman things when the times and circumstances encourage it. The seriousness with which the generalisability or the societal implications of these findings should have been pursued were aptly summarised by Etzioni (1968): 'most people can become – with surprisingly little external pressure – "cogs" in a concentration camp apparatus' (p. 280). In other words, the apparent concern about methodology would appear to be but a red herring introduced to let psychologists and others neatly off the hook; to avoid posing the same questions as Milgram did, for example, in the context of race relations.

This raises a further question: what makes individuals surrender to authority against their will or beliefs? Billig (1982) suggests that this is achieved by society or those in authority making ordinary people commit first mild and then more sinister acts of 'bad faith', i.e. of denial of individuality and responsibility in the performance of their roles, thus paving the way for submission to authority. They may then become forced into a vicious cycle of embracing the authority of their superordinates or leaders rather than admitting to the contradictory nature of their own behaviour. Racist jokes are such sinister acts.

It is part of an anti-racism stance that individuals accept responsibility for their own thoughts and actions. Although racism is not endlessly re-created afresh by individuals but something passed on culturally, it is in the gift of each and every individual to examine their own personal racism. While we all need help with this, the buck stops with each and every individual but with no individual in particular. As Billig (1976) has argued, to attribute the generality of institutionalised cruelty to the perversion of a few individuals is no more persuasive or illuminating than attempts to reduce the causes of group conflict to the irrational motives of their leaders. The perversion is universal.

Racist language

Language, like jokes, is intrinsically a vehicle through which racist ideology is transmitted. Where psychologists have acknowledged the cultural transmission of ideology through language, their focus has largely been sexism. Much of the battle against sexist language has been won and many psychology journals will routinely refer back to the author materials which, for example, use 'he' as a generic pronoun for both males and females. This is only to be applauded. However, our concern is that the same is not applied so thoroughly to racist language. For example, the British Psychological Society (1988b) published extensive guidelines on the use of non-sexist language, but has no guide to racist language as such. The guidelines do make reference to minority groups but only in a very limited way. At the end of a set of principles for non-sexist language, the authors classify ethnically biased language as a matter of either designation or evaluation. Problems of designation largely arise because ethnic groups change over time on how they wish to be addressed. The solution is to seek the advice of the group in question bearing in mind that the designation might be controversial amongst the group itself. There are also problems of evaluation which we can recognise as Eurocentric in nature: 'The majority of instances of implied irrelevant evaluation seem to occur when the writer uses one group (usually the writer's *own* group) as the standard against which others are assessed' (p. 54).

It is then suggested that it is important to avoid language which is essentially an evaluation in disguise. For instance, the phrase 'culturally deprived' should be taboo when it is used as a designation of a single group rather than a comparison between groups. The justification for this is:

> Using the term to describe one group of subjects *without the supporting data required in scientific writing* implies that one culture is a universally accepted standard against which others are judged. As a test of implied evaluation, substitute another group (e.g. your own) for the group being discussed. If you are offended by the revised statement, there is probably bias in the original statement. (p. 54, numerous typographic errors corrected)

Despite the aura of common sense in such pronouncements, we should not be lulled into the belief that they avoid a negative value position. For example, just what needs to be missing from a culture for it to be culturally deprived? Instead of dealing with this, the guidelines reinforce the notion that there are aspects of culture essential to a quality of life or development. Not saying what these are leaves the danger of imposing an ethnocentric standard on another group. Just what could provide the supporting scientific data for establishing cultural deprivation? Since these criteria apparently need to be 'culture-free' to be scientific then the problems of definition become intractable. Finally, note the 'hand washing' in the advice 'seek the advice of the group in question'. Contrast this with the firm posture adopted in the case of sexist language.

Kloss (1979), basing his work on Kovel (1970/88), carried out a thorough, psychoanalytically based review of the language used of black people. For example, he noted that the word black has numerous negative connotations for the average person – including evil, sin, excrement, mystery, loneliness, hostility and violence. Referring to the dictionary, we found 55 *negative connotations* of the word black as compared to only 21 for the word white. Conversely, we found

9 and 19 *positive connotations* of black and white respectively. Kloss went on to examine the use of words to refer to black people. Three different groups were identified. The first group basically provided a fantasy of black people as animals: ape, buck, coon, jungle bunny, hoof. The second group largely were a sexual fantasy. Kloss points out that words like piccaninny and boy largely serve to emasculate black men and sees them as motivated by fears of the sexuality of black men. The third group of words contained primarily reference to colour: blackbean, crow, darky, Jim Crow, licorice stick, snowball and ebony are all examples. These, it is suggested, are a faecal fantasy. There is no simple solution:

> The persistence of these derogatory names, their multitude, their character – all indicate a deeply acculturated prejudice that is difficult if not impossible to eradicate. But it is not the job of the linguist to root out racism. To even suggest 'Don't use the words' seems futile, for, in a very deep sense, the words are using us. Unlike Alice conversing with Humpty Dumpty, one does not wonder 'whether you *can* make words mean so many different things'; they do. Like Humpty himself, one does wonder 'which is to be master – that's all'. (p. 96)

Cultural stereotypes

There is a rather complex process by which inadvertently stereotypes may be confirmed simply through the choice of topics for research. Researchers may feed social stereotypes by opting to research issues subject to stereotypes. One of the most obvious examples of this can be found in Trimble's (1988) discussion of research on the native American. Drunkenness is a stereotype which is as apparent in Hollywood films as elsewhere:

> those who prefer to cling to their notion of the Indians as 'drunken and suicidal' are not likely to be influenced by contradictory evidence. But a deemphasis on suicide and alcoholism themselves and a corresponding emphasis on the role of treatment and prevention sensitive to the Indian life-style can help erode the pejorative implications of those stereotypes. . . . On the one hand, the number of research citations on Indian suicide rates and alcoholism acts much as does a lightning rod. Indians and some non-Indians alike are deeply concerned about the problems, and because of the enormity of the topics, researchers and practitioners are drawn to them to seek explanations and solutions. . . . Yet, the attention given to the topics serves to confirm the self-serving stereotypical images of many racist-minded non-Indians, in whom no amount of factual evidence will alter deep-seated prejudicial convictions. (p. 192)

Such a situation is naturally difficult to resolve. A key aspect is that of the style rather than the subject matter of the research. So, for example, one needs to ask the extent to which the research actually studies something which intrinsically requires the involvement of Indian people. If the research does little more than provide information which feeds the stereotype then one needs to question why the research is necessary in the first place. However, if it attempts to answer questions which help deal with something which is especially pertinent to Indian people's needs then there is at least a *prima facie* case that the research is necessary.

Assumptions abound about the proper nature of research on socially disadvantaged groups. Much of the work of psychology is done behind the scenes by largely anonymous reviewers of papers and books submitted for publication. This is the 'peer review process' which is conventionally held to be a quality check. This is one of its major functions but it is also abundantly clear that the process serves as a control on the publication of ideas which are 'out of line' with the mainstream perspective (Howitt, 1991). Korchin (1980) describes how the process can be used to ensure that the dominant view that minorities should be evaluated in relation to white people can prevail in the peer review process:

> Recently Quincy Griffin and I . . . completed a study of the nature and determininants of personality competence in black youth. We compared two groups of black men; the first, nominated by their community-college teachers as being particularly competent; the second, a reasonably matched group of more average black students. The report of the resulting findings was submitted to a major psychological journal and rejected. In the opinion of one consulting editor, the study was 'grievously flawed' – there was no white control group. . . . What would happen, might we suppose, if someone submitted a study identical in all respects except that all subjects were white? Would it be criticized because it lacked a black control group? (Korchin, 1980, p. 263)

It is impossible to document the extent of such decisions in the profession, partly because of the secrecy of the process. Indeed, psychologists who have sought to explore how decisions are reached have come under considerable pressure and hostility (Mahoney, 1987). Normally, of course, the race-thinking of the anonymous reviewer is protected by the system. Furthermore, one should not imagine that this is essentially a matter for the individual reviewer. The editor of the journal quite clearly should have seen the remark for what it was. That it was allowed to pass as a reason for rejection illustrates that racism is not the prerogative of isolated individuals in psychology. But do not think for one moment that this was a rare exception.

This characteristic behaviour of white people generally, and white psychologists particularly, involves judgmentally comparing different people to themselves, using themselves as a standard, has been reported by other black psychologists. This Eurocentric bias presents a practical problem for black psychologists studying black people, but who are subject to Eurocentric hegemony: it is expected and often required that data on black people be compared to data collected on white people, which, it is further expected, will be used as the standard data or reference point data (Azibo, 1992).

Azibo narrates a personal experience to illustrate the point:

> Interviewing for a psychology post . . ., I presented empirical studies on African Self-Consciousness (Black personality). . . . The first question of the Q&A period from a European was '*Why* didn't you use a White *control* group?' (p. 19)

'Why' is emphasised because it illustrates the expectation and 'control' because it illustrates the assumption that the European is the standard reference point. However, in reply to this question, amongst other things, he explained to the all-white panel the difference between a comparative and cross-cultural approach, as well as pointing out to them that 'Whites or Europeans are no longer the standard by which the psychology of people is judged' (p. 19). (Azibo chooses not to say whether he got the job!) Another experience Azibo had with his graduate research on African personality is dumbfounding. He was asked by a white psychologist: 'This is interesting, but when are you going to do some human research?' (p. 19). What sort of mind-set would produce a question like this which essentially denies the integrity and humanity of Africans unless Europeans are involved? Azibo asks.

It is not only the collection of data on black people which must be authenticated by white people, but also the language in which black people's reality or experiences are expressed. On a number of occasions we have been told by white journal editors that the language we use in academic papers is unacceptable and has to be toned-down or removed as a condition of acceptance for publication. This even goes to the extent that one of us, for example, was not allowed to refer to the pugnacious racism of William McDougall as bellicose! On another occasion, one of our papers was accepted for publication by its reviewers but eventually rejected because the managing editor of the journal felt that the language was too strong for her predominantly white readers. These, then, are the basis of the practical problem of white hegemony: Azibo's research lacked validity in Eurocentric psychology because it was about black people instead of white people; in our case, the experiences of racism was dismissed because the language in which it was articulated was 'too' strong, and hence unpalatable to white ears. It appears that to the white psychologist, when it comes to racism, 'a spade should cease to be a spade'. At the same time, the black person is subject to racism in the street, at work, in books and on television. And they should not be angry! They are hurt by all this, but they should scream silently.

Without sensitivity to the intellectual, cultural elements and experiences of black people, white psychologists and social scientists have often proceeded as if what is correct for white people were, and should be, correct for everybody (Asante, 1987, p. 172); in other words, their definition of reality overrides that of everyone else.

This is not to suggest that research involving racial comparisons should not be undertaken. Rather the epistemological basis of such studies should not violate John Stuart Mill's 'method of difference canon'. Fundamentally, this canon 'requires that the two groups be equated, that is, equal in all respects . . . on relevant variables . . . known or believed to [have] influence' (Plutchik, 1974, quoted by Azibo, 1992, p. 20). Azibo suggests that if the comparison groups are not equated as specified in the canon, then the observed difference has only descriptive value – there can be no meaning or interpretation given to the difference, nor can causality be inferred.

According to this canon, therefore, in racial comparisons, the most important 'relevant' variable for equating purposes becomes culture. Nobles (cited by Azibo, 1992) has defined culture as patterns for making sense of experiences, a general design for living. Nobles sees this 'grand' design as consisting of folkways, language, behaviour, values, beliefs and so forth. Thus, according to this definition, culture is important because in a scientific enquiry, as in everyday observations, it determines the meaning, and therefore the validity, of observed facts.

Three general axioms (Azibo, 1992) are fundamental in guiding research in order that meaningful racial comparisons may be achieved:

1. The racial groups are equivalent on every relevant variable, most significantly culture.
2. If racial groups are not equated on any relevant variable it is improper to do other than simply describe any differences between races.
3. Culture itself will have an important bearing on the nature of the psychological constructs used in reporting the research.

Inevitably these axioms severely limit the applicability of comparative research, particularly because they register the importance of culture in determining the meaning of observations.

They are as applicable to research by black psychologists as much as that by white investigators. Thus Baldwin (1992) has warned psychologists, especially black clinical psychologists, that their Eurocentric-orientated training has virtually rendered them incapable of providing any type of truly culturally relevant services to black people; that they have often ended up treating black people as if they were 'white people in black skins', with only their experience of white racism being viewed as their distinguishing psychological characteristic. Baldwin's liberating message for black psychologists is:

> We must recognise that the basic nature of the European world-view (upon which psychology is based) is diametrically opposed to the psychological development, survival and liberation of Black people. . . . [T]he European world-view is 'anti-Black/anti-African', . . . it is 'anti-Us', and we must therefore reject it once and for all. (p. 54)

The wrong solution

The lazy solution to the Eurocentrism in psychology is to hand over the problem to black psychologists. Essentially this is the equivalent to holding rape victims responsible for the elimination of rape. This is unacceptable, not in the sense that black people are incompetent to provide alternatives, but in the sense that it provides white psychology with a most convenient excuse not to do anything about itself; the Eurocentrism of psychology becomes the problem to be dealt with only by black psychologists rather than psychology as a whole. It is also tokenistic in the sense that black people are employed to carry out the race relations and equal-opportunities work of organisations. This provides a precarious niche on the periphery for a few black people and leaves white people to get on with the 'serious work of the organisation'. It can also be seen as 'window dressing'. It also ignores, as we have seen, that some black psychologists are completely imbued with the Eurocentric discipline of psychology. In other words, they do the same work as the Eurocentric white psychologists, just as many women in the past have held to male-centred psychology and promoted its teachings.

Jones (1981) describes how, as recently as 1972, black people were used in the USA as guinea pigs in an experiment on the effects of syphilis. This study, known as the Tuskegee Experiment, was carried out by the United States Public Health Service, and under the auspices of various health agencies. Untreated syphilis is highly contagious, affecting internal organs as well as the nervous system. Death is the consequence. In spite of this, 400 black men with syphilis were identified and studied with their families for 40 years (from 1932 to 1972). This study is infamous in medical ethics for the way in which these black families were duped into taking part in a study whose avowed aim was to study the debilitating and even fatal effects of syphilis. Kept ignorant of their infection, they were deliberately left untreated. But there is another significant feature. A *black* community nurse, also kept ignorant about the true purpose of the research, was employed to administer placebos and collect data. Indeed, the experimenters admitted that but for the help and dedication of the black nurse the study would have failed. The ways in which black professionals such as psychologists, psychiatrists, nurses and social workers actively participate in the oppression and subjugation of black people, albeit unwittingly, have been recognised and highlighted by various writers (e.g. Fernando, 1988; Littlewood and Lipsedge, 1989; Owusu-Bempah, 1990; 1994). Bulhan (1985) uses the term *auto-colonialism* to describe this phenomenon – 'the highest stage of oppression in which the victim actively participates in his own victimisation' (p. 44).

Chapter 7

Business as usual

Racism and the institutions of psychology

> To be a psychological scientist who is using conventional methodology exclusively is a heady experience because it sanctifies laboratory control and manipulation in order to provide an illusion of certain, mastery, and power. This fantasy environment in which the scientist abides provides insulation against conscious awareness that what makes sense in the laboratory may become a travesty when applied in vivo. (Dana, 1987, p. 11)

Psychology's individualised conception of racism has widespread ramifications. Especially disturbing is that it tends to obscure the racism of psychology's institutions. Professions have collective responsibilities which cannot be sloughed off by blaming individuals for racism. Whatever regulatory functions professional institutions accept in relation to ethical and procedural matters in general, they establish standards expected of psychologists on numerous moral-cum-ideological matters. These include the betrayal of clients' confidences, having sex with vulnerable clients and deliberately misleading participants in research. But standards also need setting on racism and the provision of services for ethnic minority groups. Failure to provide culturally sensitive psychotherapy may be as disastrous for clients as ethical failings. Although they relate to competency, psychology as a whole has failed to address many issues related to race. In this very real sense, therefore, psychology has not simply colluded in the denial of the needs of culturally and racially diverse groups, it has trained psychologists unfit or incompetent for work in a multi-cultural society. Furthermore, psychology's flagship organisations should set the highest standards on all matters; not doing so inevitably sends its own signals to practitioners.

It is high time that the role of psychological organisations in encouraging racism is recognised. In our earlier discussion of racism in psychological journals, the focus was on individual authors or groups of authors who promoted, inadvertently in many cases, racist theories of a fairly pernicious sort. But is it a question of *who* or one of *what* is responsible? The identities of responsible individuals are easily found. They are the journal authors, reviewers and editors. However, these are not just identifiable individuals, they are clearly defined roles within psychology's institutional structures. Editorial boards of the journals, for example, can be seen as having a collective role which transcends that of their individual members. Psychology's professional bodies themselves publish some of the most prestigious psychology. For example, psychological societies in Britain, Australia, the USA and elsewhere publish best-selling psychology journals. Furthermore, house journals such as *The American Psychologist* and *The Psychologist* are distributed to all members world-wide, so presumably they are the most widely read of all psychological publications. How come, then, that professional societies can publish relatively crude racist propaganda? Just what is the special contribution of psychology's corporate bodies to racism?

This cannot be understood without distinguishing between racism as it is usually narrowly regarded by psychologists and conceptions which relate it to social structures. For example, Jones (1972) has identified three distinct forms of racism which are mutually reinforcing: individual, institutional and cultural racism. *Individual* racism is the personal attitudes, prejudices and behaviours which individuals use to prejudge other racial groups negatively (and their own positively). Without the power vested in them by institutions, many people are unable to express these feelings in direct action against minorities. *Institutional* racism involves the policies and practices of organisations which deny black people access to resources and power, often by construing them as pathological in some way or holding them to blame for their predicament. For example, it might be claimed that 'black people do not join the organisation' without questioning why this might be so or what features of the organisation might deter black applicants. Such institutional policies and practices, actions and inactions, maintain black people in disadvantaged positions. Finally, *cultural* racism consists of the values, beliefs and ideas, usually embedded in our social representation or 'common sense', which endorse the superiority of white culture over that of others (Barker, 1981) – this is akin to ethnocentrism or Eurocentrism. Intractably linked, these three forms ensure that racism is ubiquitous. They enable its penetration into the daily routines and lives of psychologists – in their teaching, writings and practices.

Knowles and Prewitt (1969) stressed the importance of studying the functions, manifest and latent, of organisations as a prerequisite for a proper understanding of institutional racism. Institutions have the power to reward and penalise. Rewards are provided in the form of career opportunities given only to some people and denied others. Organisations also reward by the selective distribution of social goods or services, by deciding who receives training and skills, medical care, formal education (and to what level or standard), self-respect, employment, fair treatment from the law, decent housing, and a secure future for oneself and one's children. A proper understanding of institutional racism reveals the many subtle ways in which black people are disadvantaged in these important sectors of society. This applies equally to the institutions of psychology.

Psychology is an institution which exists within a broader community and makes special claims about itself. In Britain, for example, freedom and justice for all are presumed to be enshrined in the 'British way'. But Britain is a nation with a shameful tradition of racism and racial exploitation, as well as many contemporary manifestations of racial prejudice and discrimination. Inevitably, without considerable efforts to prevent it, British institutions mirror this inequality and are often microcosms of racial injustice. Despite the UK's Race Relations Act of 1976 and previous ones, research shows that British institutions are blighted by discrimination against black people in virtually every important sphere: employment, education, housing, health, criminal justice and so forth (e.g. Brown, 1984; Brown and Gray, 1985; CRE, 1987a, b, c, d; 1988a, b, c; Home Office, 1986; Landau and Nathan, 1983; Littlewood and Lipsedge, 1989; National Association of Health Authorities, 1988; and Smith 1977). Most of these, like the health service, education, public and private industry, commerce and the criminal justice system, are major employers of professional psychologists and others trained in psychology. That racism is endemic in these major institutions further shows racism is not an abstract issue, but one which bears directly on psychology as a discipline and practice. Nothing in being a scientific and professional body in itself can reduce the risk of taint. On the contrary, academic expertise, science and learnedness may be accolades which shield psychology from the full impact of its own racism.

Without an understanding of the structural context within which attitudes occur, their meaning cannot be grasped (Wellman, 1977). In fact, as Wellman argues, once racism is embedded within the structures of society, the prejudice of individuals ceases to be the problem. Racism is not about attitudes alone, but about 'institutionally generated inequality'. A culture of racism, racism which forms the kernel of society, does not need prejudice for its survival. Institutional racism therefore denotes the extent to which racism is embedded in the 'dominant' organisations and power structure of society, resulting in distinctive patterns of social disadvantage. Thus, what happens in practice (how the 'facts' gathered from biased research are actually utilised) depends on the context in which psychology functions. A psychology which therefore fails to recognise the racism within it, or takes no action to counteract that aspect of its own culture, must itself succumb to racist practice – racial discrimination. Williams (1947) described *discrimination* as the differential treatment of individuals considered to belong to a particular social group. It should be stressed, however, that discrimination may occur without the accompanying feeling of prejudice (Simpson and Yinger, 1958). Hence, for example, a group of practising psychologists may refuse to appoint a black practitioner because to do so might injure the business. They may not be prejudiced themselves but feel that the business must be put before other considerations. Conversely, a racially prejudiced white employer may hire a black person 'because it is good for business'.

Not too much time needs to be spent over questions of intent and malice in relation to institutional racism, they may be involved but not necessarily so. More important is to show how institutional racism works. The London St George's Medical School case was a significant example and a clear demonstration of the unimportance of intent in institutional racism. In this instance, a computer program was developed in order to reduce the administrative task of selecting interviewees from among applicants to study medicine at the school. This effectively 'aped' the original labour-intensive, subjective selection procedures. In other words, it had been shown that this computer chose very much the same applicants as did human selectors, so effectively replaced human selection for several years without difficulties. Eventually someone realised that the computer's mimicking of subjective decision-making involved giving extra priority for selection for interview to males with British-sounding names! Things had happily been left to a computer program which was resolutely discriminatory against black and female applicants (CRE, 1988b). Not all instances of institutional racism are so dramatic. So what has this to do with psychology? Psychology, like medicine, is a social institution mirroring societal values, including racism. Besides, the professionalisation of psychology was largely a phenomenon of the late nineteenth and early twentieth centuries, a period of unmitigated racism, empire building and white dominance. Institutions in this racist epoch inevitably served white society's interests – they were created to do no other, and the blueprint remains.

It is not easy to find substantial accounts of the racism of psychological institutions. So it is with some foreboding that one comes across publications such as Thielman's (1985), which deals with racism in a psychological organisation, the American Medico-Psychological Association which became the American Psychiatric Association in 1921. Thielman's paper documents the association's involvement in American immigration restrictions on peoples of 'bad' stock between 1880 and 1930. However, a closer examination shows that the racist pronouncements and activities of individual members is its focus. While, in a sense, this confirms our concern about the individualisation of racism, it contributes nothing to our knowledge of institutional racism in psychology.

Psychology and state racism

> One of the reasons we do not understand racism is because to analyse it properly means to analyse ourselves and our own institutions properly: it is safer and far simpler to seek an obvious scapegoat – a Hitler, a Mussolini – than to say that modern states and their organisations are at fault, anachronistic or inefficient. This is too threatening, too close to home. (Lampley, 1980; p. xix)

Apartheid South Africa has presented an awkward problem for Westerners. It is rather too much like home and the product of Western history. Europeans have practised throughout modern history, much the same kind of separatism and denial of rights to black people. Indeed the British themselves had repressed the Boers. More pertinent here, the South African Psychological Association (SAPA) was formed in 1948 with an entirely white membership (Louw, 1987). In 1956, an Indian woman, J. Naidoo, applied to join the association. Opinion within the organisation was canvassed by its president, Biesheuvel. Mrs Naidoo was offered the opportunity to be registered within the Association as an academic psychologist, but she was refused membership proper. The colour of her skin was so important that, in 1959, special standing committees met to deal with the matter of race in each of the four regions of South Africa: Natal, Western Cape, Transvaal and Eastern Cape. Different recommendations were made by each committee.

The National Party became the government in 1948 and set in motion the process towards apartheid. The prime minister at the time, H. F. Verwoerd, was a former professor of psychology and is generally held to be responsible for inventing and implementing apartheid. Verwoerd was born in the Netherlands but emigrated with his parents to South Africa, where he gained his PhD in psychology in 1924. He was a staunch supporter of white supremacy which he saw as a religious duty, a Nazi sympathiser and ardent anti-semite (Bulhan, 1985). Verwoerd and the rest of the governing Afrikaner Nationalist Party learnt their methods from the Nazis and then implemented them in South Africa after 1948. The formalisation of the apartheid programme after 1948, and its effectiveness, was due to the applied psychological expertise and skills of Verwoerd (Lampley, 1980). Even after becoming prime minister he remained an honorary member of the South African Psychological Association. In 1960, Verwoerd insisted that professional associations mimicked apartheid by becoming racially segregated.

Two years later, in 1962, Afrikaans-speaking SAPA members consulted with Verwoerd, who made it clear that a mixed-race membership was against government policy. Forcing the point home, Verwoerd resigned his honorary membership of the Association the day after this meeting. This resulted in a 'breakaway' organisation, the Psychological Institute of the Republic of South Africa (PIRSA). The principles upon which PIRSA (an all-white organisation) was founded were spelled out by A. J. La Grange, head of psychology at Stellenbosch University:

> First, La Grange postulated that there was a 'natural need for self-protection'. . . . The best way to fulfil this need was to strive towards a healthy, industrious, and happy commonwealth of separate nations in South Africa. . . . South African society would [consequently] be characterized by mental health, prosperity, and happiness. Second, PIRSA was founded because of the commonsensical revolt against egalitarianism and racial integration. La Grange quoted from William McDougall's *Group Mind* . . . : human happiness is . . . in 'obedience to the elementary law of nature that brings together those who belong together on the basis of common inherited characteristics'. . . . A third factor La Grange mentioned was the 'natural' striving toward self-actualization, which he apparently borrowed from Abraham Maslow. This striving was based on self-knowledge, self-acceptance, and a need to develop one's potentialities to the fullest extent, all of which required social circumstances in which the process of identification could take place. . . . Racial integration would destroy the identification process, leading to a disturbed mental condition and an unbalanced, disharmonious personality. (Louw, 1987, pp. 348–9)

In other words, a racially exclusionary psychological association was justified using Western psychology's racist theories. Nowhere else is the relationship between racism and psychology's institutions so formally laid down. However, when Louw (1987) suggests that the 'split simply cannot be understood outside the unique societal constellation that set them in motion: racial conflict in South Africa' (p. 351) one wonders quite why he uses words which share the blame between black and white people. State racism and apartheid were responsible. To imagine otherwise is to blame slaves for slavery. Furthermore, Louw's thesis that the South African split was determined by unique factors should be firmly rejected. It reflects precisely the overlapping consensus in psychology which abhors racism, while engaging in it, and leads to occasional skirmishes within a broadly racist commune.

As a coda, the two associations devoted to psychology amalgamated in 1982 without any apparent difficulty. A new organisation, actively opposed to apartheid, was set up the following year by some psychologists.

It is interesting to note the philosophy of Biesheuvel – the president of the South African Psychological Association who took the initial exclusionary stance against the Indian psychologist which culminated in the split. He normalises national difficulties by defining them as a universal: 'Mankind is not in very good shape anywhere, as we all know' (Bieshuvel, 1987, p. 1). Then he resorts to psychological theory of intergroup relations in order to argue that interracial conflict of the sort found in South Africa is natural:

> Prejudice appears wherever groups with conflicting interests or values have to share the same territory or facilities. It is not confined to racial or ethnic confrontations. . . . I believe that the roots of this phenomenon must be sought deep down in the nature of man, in the discontents created by the very fact of civilisation. . . . [T]he development of bloodfeuds, so dramatically portrayed by Shakespeare in *Romeo and Juliet* . . . , is one of the fundamental aspects of behaviour which psychology should be investigating more fully than it has done. (pp. 4–5)

While this is a gross distortion of Sherif's psychology of intergroup relations (1953, 1967), in the sense that it omits Sherif's belief in the possibility that shared long-term objectives can result in reduced intergroup hostility, it is a very clear expression of racism as something in-built into the human condition. Such a philosophy clearly gains succour from psychology as La Grange had preached a quarter of a century earlier. But South Africa does not have a monopoly of racism in its institutions. Before apartheid, it should be added, Biesheuvel (1943) wrote a book critical of racist interpretations of research on biological racial differences in psychological test scores. Quite clearly the rejection of evidence of innate racial differences is not incompatible with exclusionary actions towards black people of the sort Biesheuvel effected.

Contracting whose compliance?

Sawyer and Senn (1973) recorded their view that *business as usual* is racist. By this they meant that organisations which persist in the old, traditional way, and do not directly or actively combat racism, act in support of racism by omission. There are so many forces in society supportive of racism that simply to 'go with the flow' is not enough. There is so much work to be done in the fight against racism that mere knowledge of the racist history of an organisation is insufficient in itself. Sawyer and Senn should know. They were part of a battle with the American Psychological Association to ensure that suppliers were not racially discriminatory. At this time, the American Psychological Association was paying the Lancaster Press in Pennsylvania more than half a million dollars annually to print a number of its psychology journals. Withdrawal of this income would be a substantial blow to any business. In a town with a population of over 60,000, of which about 5,000 were African-American people and 6,000 Puerto Ricans, the black employees of the Press were just one black wash-up man!

An action group, Psychologists for Social Action (PSA), raised the matter with executives of the American Psychological Association. Their response was to argue that black people's educational standards were a problem, that the unionisation of the plant made equal opportunities difficult, that the Lancaster Press was better than the norm in the industry, and that the Press had signed a letter of non-discrimination. Such vague assurances by the Press seemed to satisfy the managing committee of the American Psychological Association.

Members of the PSA action group visited the plant and made a number of suggestions based in part on consultation with the minority communities in Lancaster. Their only pressure on the Press was the likelihood that they would lobby the American Psychological Association on the matter. Nevertheless, the Lancaster Press quickly changed its employment practices substantially. For example, half of its new employees were black despite the previous 'obstacles'. In fact, the Lancaster Press became a 'model' employer in this respect.

Presented in this form, the process seems easy. However, the account omits frustrating attempts by the PSA to persuade the American Psychological Association of the need to do something about the problem – or even to convince them that there was indeed a problem. One episode is a rather dramatic illustration of the antipathy towards the activities of the action group. Sawyer and Senn submitted a report of the events for publication in *The American Psychologist* – the major publication of the American Psychological Association which is received by all members. The editor of the journal took the unusual step of circulating the text to the membership of the executive board of the Association:

> Although the members of the APA Board are individuals with favorable general attitudes toward racial equality, these persons were here acting in institutional roles where they displayed strong and sincere differences on how racial equality related to APA's practice. (Sawyer and Senn, 1973, p. 77)

The comments received included the following (both reported in Sawyer and Senn, 1973, p. 77):

> what have Sawyer and Senn done to use their skills to help Lancaster Press move toward recruiting blacks? An angry, unfair report, written before the facts were gleaned.

> The tone of the paper remains objectionably hortatory, propagandistic and jingoistic. It is unfit for publication in any professional journal.

Apart from many comments like these, there were some more positive ones. Whether the hostility was justified can be judged by consulting the text of Sawyer and Senn (1973), which contains virtually the original manuscript. The American Psychological Association refused to publish the paper although a rather different and much shorter note was published (Senn and Sawyer, 1971).

At the centre of all of this, there is the issue of the self-presentation or image of the professional organisations. By their very nature, such societies, apart from their information dissemination function, serve to negotiate between the profession and the state. Consequently, one might expect little enthusiasm for 'system bucking' pressure groups whose aim is to unveil an unacceptable face of the organisation.

Of course, events from so long ago can only be indicative of the current situation. They cannot tell us how things operate at the moment. By the nature of things, accounts like Sawyer and Senn's of institutional racism in a professional society are unlikely to get an easy public airing – especially as the professional organisations control many of the major journals and other channels of communication. One should not read too much into the relative infrequency of accounts of this sort.

A more recent example might serve to confirm that this process of vilification of those responsible for criticism of a professional organisation is no historical artifact. Owusu-Bempah and Howitt (1990) submitted for publication in *The Psychologist* (the house journal of the British Psychological Society) an article critical of the Society's record on equal opportunities and anti-racism as well as other matters related to the racism of the psychological community. For example, at the time the article was submitted the Society showed no significant progress towards an equal-opportunities policy. Given that this was 1990, two decades after the first legislation against racism, and six years after the publication of the Commission for Racial Equality's code of practice in employment (CRE, 1984), this 'omission' was significant and needed attention drawing to it. The article was sent to reviewers for comment and their eventual recommendation was to publish it. Publication looked set until a few months later when an editor requested a totally different paper. This would essentially laud the Society for its embryonic moves on equal opportunities which had been made during the long delay in publishing the article. (It must also be said that Owusu-Bempah and Howitt's paper formed part of the documents cited by the group charged with formulating the Society's equal-opportunities policy.) However, as the equal-opportunities policy was merely a policy to have an equal-opportunities policy, besides being *a posteriori*, Owusu-Bempah and Howitt felt that this was scant progress and hardly addressed the meat of their paper. Consequently they declined the invitation to write a bowdlerised version of their work and asked that their paper be published as it was accepted by referees. Whereupon the editor wrote to colleagues on the Editorial Board of the publication making new charges which in no way reflected comments made by the reviewers or previously by the editor. Now 'chip on the shoulder' rhetoric was used which portrayed the article as aggressive:

> My purpose in writing is to ask you to consider the question somewhat differently. It will be clear, I think, that I had always supposed that *the authors of the paper would want to be reasonable*, present their case in the best possible light, be seen to be taking relevant factors into consideration. It appears *I was wrong about this* . . . the authors strongly desire publication of this *aggressive paper*. . . . In the light of . . . *the fact that this dispute will be used to fuel the flames of anti-Society sentiment*, I think we should consider whether or not it might be preferable after all to publish this paper as it stands. . . . We could then *control the context in which these opinions are expressed*. (Mapstone, 1991, emphases added)

Not surprisingly, given the way the case was put, the Editorial Board chose not to publish Owusu-Bempah and Howitt's paper. Twenty years later, and 4,000 miles away, Sawyer and Senn's experience had been repeated.

The concept of institutional racism transcends any account of the activities of individual racist persons. Institutional racism does not raise questions about the anti-racist stance of individual members of any institution, many of whom no doubt have strong anti-racist views. For example, individuals, as such, are not responsible for the training of psychologists – institutions are. Equally, one should not accept 'window-dressing' or 'image management' as evidence of a significant anti-racist commitment in any organisation. Token gestures are commonplace amongst fundamentally racist organisations. Simply to have an equal-opportunities policy on paper without genuine concern to examine systematically practices, policies and procedures may do more harm than good although it is not an uncommon practice (Owusu-Bempah, 1989). Anti-racism cannot be achieved by tokenism of this sort and may be damaged by it. An integrated approach at all levels and in all activities of the organisation is necessary. An organisation with few, if any, black employees in a city which is approximately a quarter black in population can have all the equal opportunities policies (on paper) in the world, yet remain suspect. In our view, this more or less precisely describes the British Psychological Society.

Psychology, wherever it is taught and/or practised, has a very clear responsibility to service the whole community, however diverse that community maybe. It is therefore an important matter to ask how well the institutions of psychology in Western societies have acted to meet the needs created by cultural diversity. Bender (1990) provides a partial answer to this when he suggests that:

> If clinical psychology services are to be delivered effectively to the various ethnic minorities, the profession will need to be well informed about the beliefs and attitudes of the various cultures, not only in terms of what is appropriate personal and social behaviour, but also in terms of belief about handicap and disadvantage. This is especially important for mental illness services. Clinical psychology service users from ethnic minority groups will need to be assured that they will be welcomed and respected rather than suffer the racial discrimination which characterises many other areas of society. (p. 250)

In Britain, clinical psychologists are trained either under the auspices of the British Psychological Society or with the final examination carried out by the Society. The Society has an entire division devoted to clinical psychology. Surprisingly then, in order to study the provision of clinical psychologists of ethnic minority background, Bender could not obtain his figures from the Society, which apparently keeps no records. He had to resort to another, less adequate but more pragmatic, procedure. He contacted informants who had been on different clinical courses for information about the ethnic composition of their fellow students. The period covered 1957–84. Of 921 students identified, 96 per cent were white, 3 per cent Asians and 0.9 per cent African-Caribbeans. In the general population, 5.5 per cent of 20–44-year-olds considered themselves to be Asian or African-Caribbean at the time of the study. While this is in itself underrepresentation, we have also to bear in mind that the black psychologists in training had to service the full age-range of the community since there was no older generation of practising psychologists. In other words, the underrepresentation actually reflects a considerably worse situation in the community. Overrecruitment would have to occur if the supply were to reflect the need. There was also evidence that black students had greater difficulty in completing the course. The reasons are unclear. White students had a drop-out rate of 4.5 per cent, but Asians were about three times and African-Carribeans four times more likely to drop out. Examination failure itself was relatively rare. So in 1990, about two decades after the major equal-opportunities legislation in Britain first came into force, Bender was recommending to the professional institution of psychology in Britain active ethnic monitoring of the composition of undergraduate and graduate psychology courses!

Playing the science card

> The most damaging consequence of the scientific posture is that it gives scientific sanction to the use of pre- and nonscientific concepts as a means of explaining the behavior of black people. It provides white psychologists with a license to give scientific credence to their autistic creations. (Hayes, 1980, p. 40)

Organisations caught out over their racist practices resort to a range of exculpatory strategies and arguments. The dynamics of institutional racism depend very much on the failure to accept racism as an issue. Dominelli (1989) describes various strategies employed by organisations which effectively defuse racism as a potent issue requiring drastic revisions of policies and practices. They are offered here partly as a means of understanding elements of the general debate on racism. Not all of them are necessarily typical of the thinking in psychological associations. Among these strategies are:

1. *Denial*: rejecting the existence of cultural and institutional racism in favour of the view that racism is confined to personal prejudice in its crude manifestations.
2. *Colour-blind strategies*: the spurious notion that all people are the same and ought to be treated accordingly.
3. *Patronising approaches*: giving lip service to racial equality as an ideal to strive for, but ensuring that white people remain 'top dogs'. In other words, accepting the notion of racial equality in the face of blatant inequality between black and white people.
4. *Decontextualisation*: acknowledging the presence of racism in general terms, but denying it in specific instances involving daily routines and interactions.

5. *Avoidance*: accepting that racism exists, but denying the particular responsibility of the individual to do something about it.

Some of these we have already seen to be manifest in the psychological profession. One would guess that the colour-blind strategy is the most typical of psychology as an institution. Rist (1974) has defined the colour-blind perspective as the belief that racial and ethnic minority membership is irrelevant to the way individuals are treated. For example, it is hard to find evidence world-wide that psychology as a body of professionals has undertaken initiatives aimed at developing understanding of the multi-cultural needs of the profession's clients, the problems of training and attracting black students and advocating the development of psychologies of cultures other than European ones. Individual members, on the other hand, are more likely to find decontextualisation to be a more convenient strategy.

Regarding *avoidance*, for example, the British Psychological Society's stance on apartheid South Africa readily reveals the sophistry of its position. There is apparently nothing wrong with individual psychologists being employed by or maintaining links with overtly racist and oppressive regimes:

> It would be incompatible with its own Code of Conduct for the Society to adopt any kind of blanket ban on links with individual South African psychologists simply because they are employed by a government funded agency . . . they have to be judged on their individual beliefs and actions. (BPS, 1988a, p. 328).

We see this as a feebly concocted excuse for doing nothing. Without clear guidelines about acceptable beliefs and actions for psychologists to adopt in the context of apartheid, little corporate action can be taken against anybody or anything. The Society's stance merely legitimises psychologists' work in the service of racist governments. But perhaps that was intended.

Just what would the apartheid South African psychologist need to do and think to warrant the Society's censure? Would a psychologist's acceptance of Rushton's (1990) views on the criminality, genital size, 'overbreeding' and so forth of black people be sufficient grounds for their exclusion? Or, to put it another way, would it be right to work as psychological advisers to a fascist party if we affirm our belief in democracy, freedom and justice? How can organisations seeking to promote psychology for the good of humanity do anything other than reject those who collude with apartheid? The psychological and other forms of harm such a system does to people would be sufficient reason. And it is these very institutions which impose ethical standards on individual psychologists when dealing with research participants and clients. Why not for states? Why should injecting a black person with a saline solution have to be justified ethically when, in the name of science, it is alright to advocate that this same person's race is morally, intellectually and constitutionally inferior, and ought to be treated accordingly?

Psychology's institutions have one important card which cannot be played by many other organisations – *science*. Societies of psychologists are the guardians of the discipline, the armoury of legitimating practices which it has developed. Science brings with it a raft of characteristic activities which are accepted as being rigorous, objective, honest and truthful together with other features which give psychology status and esteem greater than that of a baked-bean factory. No matter how often psychology appears to be demonstrably value-laden, faith in psychology is hardly dented. Indeed, within its mainstream ideology, the value-laden nature of the enterprise is probably as much an asset as a detraction. This notwithstanding, there is a very real sense in which psychology has lauded notions of its political and value-neutrality as part of its claims for professional autonomy:

> the value-neutral idea predisposes the public to accept psychology's asser-
> tions uncritically and to regard them as apolitical truisms rather than
> sociohistorically conditioned statements . . . the notion of 'value-neutral
> psychology' has been used to advance ideological objectives. (Prilleltensky,
> 1989, p. 797)

The ruse of hiding behind the skirts of science becomes obvious when an organisation is under fire. That Sawyer and Senn (1973) were criticised by the establishment of the American Psychological Association for using angry words and hortatory arguments makes no sense unless judged by the criteria of what 'good' science is. But passion in many other contexts is regarded as a positive thing. Who needs a dispassionate priest? Nevertheless lack of emotion is a characteristic of 'good' science. Ward (1988) draws this out in relation to race relations research. While reading Gilroy (1987), he noticed how a police officer discussing a black protest against the handling of a racist incident used phrases like 'hundreds of rampaging niggers', 'they should be shot' and beast- and animal-related comments. Gilroy describes such words as 'an interesting insight' into the racist ideology of police culture. Ward writes:

> I was struck by this because of a disjunction between the language of racism
> and the language used to understand it. Someone calls you an animal and
> believes you to be subhuman, and you find it 'interesting'. It is as if the
> restraint used in this sentence was to prove that you are not really an animal
> – 'Look at my syntax, I'm not even angry.' As if this very 'interest' in the

phenomena is trying to keep at a distance the knowledge that the police actually *believe* blacks to be 'rampaging niggers', 'animals', 'bestial', etc. – and what it *feels like* to be treated like this. . . . What language is racism written in? It is written in an *emotive* language. What language do we need to understand it? At the very least, a language which pertains to emotional life. (Ward, 1988, pp. xi–xiii)

From this perspective, the characteristics attributed to science seem less than a blessing. While one element of all of this is how psychologists choose peculiar notions of science, we should not forget the strategies used to make anger over racism impotent. The suggestion that the angry person has 'a chip on their shoulder' in effect alleges the unreasonableness of black people's intolerance of racism. Attention and responsibility are thereby diverted from racist society to the individual, often a victim of racism. Describing Sawyer and Senn's work as 'angry' blames them for being 'bad boys' and not doing things the way that society and science expects. The desire to treat racism as a matter for the head and not for the heart seems widespread. It is a common experience in anti-racism training to find participants intellectualising about issues as a means of avoiding the emotionally charged nature of the material.

A graphic example of hiding behind the skirts of science occurred with the publication of Rushton's (1990) theories in the house journal of the British Psychological Society. Rushton's claims about the biological basis of putative black cultural deficits (Chapter 2) inevitably raise the ire of psychologists antagonistic to the 'bad-genes' theorists who have long-since so publicly embarrassed the profession. The full history of the events has not been made public but they started when Flynn (1989) published an article critical of Rushton's ideas in the house journal. Even this was a curiosity as nothing had previously been mentioned in the journal about this aspect of Rushton's work. So although Flynn was heavily critical of Rushton's theories, he was also providing a forum for them and the kudos of a serious-minded review. This is a fairly rare accolade for any psychologist's work. Flynn's paper provided an effective forum for Rushton's views. Furthermore, he was excused for having such views:

Rushton has been the target of much abuse and labelled a racist. . . . [T]he truth can never be racist, nor can telling the truth as you see it, assuming there is no evidence of wilful neglect of evidence, an accusation Rushton need not fear. (Flynn, 1989, p. 363)

Zuckerman (1991) and Fairchild (1991) and earlier papers point to several instances of where Rushton erroneously claims the support of the research of other academics or disregards aspects of their work which is at variance with his theories. Fairchild writes that 'the empirical data bases are frequently misrepresented' (p. 101). Whatever Flynn's remarks were intended to mean, their inadequacy ought to have been spotted by any critical expert reviewer: that they were not points to the lackadaisical approach the profession has towards racial issues. The publication of this article also provided an opportunity for Rushton to excuse himself and justify what he had written in a number of publications. Rushton's (1990) reply to Flynn produced an outcry from those who objected to the anti-black implications they saw in Rushton's theories (e.g. Antaki *et al.*, 1990; Cochrane, 1990; Fatkmilehin *et al.*, 1990; Flynn, 1990; Halstead, 1990; Lea *et al.*, 1990; Lindsay and Paton-Saltzberg, 1990).

However, at precisely the time of the publication of the offending article, the president of the Society wrote to a number of key psychologists involved in the publication of the Society's house journal requesting them not to speak with the mass media about Rushton's work! In case they chose not to follow this 'directive', they were to read the following to reporters:

> As a *scientific* learned society and publisher of *scientific* books and journals, we are bound by our Royal Charter, Status, Rules and Code of Conduct to publish and disseminate *scientific* papers within the broad spectrum of the *science* of psychology. . . . The article by J. Philippe Rushton . . . like all *scientific* articles . . . was refereed by independent authorities. . . . The Honorary Editors then decided to publish on the basis that *scientific* evidence should not be withheld from the *scientific* community. (Morris, 1990a, emphases added)

Well, this just about clinches things. Seven references to science in a brief letter surely confirms that the proper standards of the SCIENCE of psychology had been met. The poor editors had little choice but to publish the paper. Experts had read it and recommended its publication. This is all well and good but it was inaccurate. The article had *not* been refereed according to Breakwell and Davy (1990), the honorary editors involved. Immediately a new letter (Morris, 1990b) was issued by the president which asked the recipients of the above letter to destroy it! This new letter dropped the claims that the usual refereeing had been applied. Now the excuse was: 'It is usual practice in scientific publications to allow a researcher who is criticised, the right of reply' (Morris, 1990b). This, the recipient was told, is attributable to 'a society spokesperson' and there is a marked drop in mentions of science. However, despite this, it is our experience that the right to reply is not treated by The Society as a right for all individuals. In the haste to show that everything was proper and above board, the facts were the immediate victim. The normal practices as required by 'Royal

Charter, Statutes, Rules and Codes of Conduct' had been waived. No heads rolled!

As a coda to this, just in case it is thought that there is a big logical jump between the scientific concerns of psychological institutions and the beliefs held about their own activities by individual researchers, the following might be mentioned. One of us received through the post in 1993, unsolicited, a package of three papers on racial (and gender) differences in brain size (Ankney, 1992; Andreasen *et al.*, 1993; Rushton, 1992) together with a scribbled note written on Rushton's compliment slip. It read

> Science,
> not racism!
> not sexism!
> Wishful thinking will not help.

Of course, it would be foolish to assume that identical situations apply in every psychological association throughout the world. For example, the situation in the USA has been made radically different because, there, white–black relations have historically been a domestic matter compared to their primarily colonial basis in the United Kingdom, for example. In Britain racism had domestically involved nationalism and anti-semitism. Black migrants were not common until after the Second World War. Inevitably, Britain and the USA are drastically different in terms of the numbers of black psychologists. Black people are more likely to be determined in their anti-racism than their white liberal colleagues. Partly, the history of anti-racism in the USA has involved the activities of black scholars and psychologists opposed to the biological racism of American psychology (Franklin, 1980):

> These black researchers were aware of the research in the field of mental testing, received the necessary training and carried out their own experiments and investigations, disseminated their findings and conclusions in the leading educational, psychological, and popular journals of the period; and eventually had their conclusions accepted generally in some sectors of the social scientific community. (p. 213)

In addition, in the USA a more radical institution for psychology was to be found in the Society for the Study of Social Issues. The history of this society outside and within the American Psychological Association is documented in a number of publications (Finison, 1986; Harris, 1986; Klineberg, 1986; Morawski, 1986; Stagner, 1986). Suffice to say that members were amongst the more vociferous opponents of racist interpretations of racial data.

The American Psychological Association as long ago as 1963 had a committee on equal opportunities in psychology; in 1969 it had a commission on accelerating black participation in psychology; in 1974 a minority fellowship programme which sought to encourage cultural diversity in psychology departments; and in 1985 a continuing committee on ethnic minority resources development amongst other initiatives (Ponterotto and Casas, 1991). Not surprisingly, therefore, more progress appears to have been made to set the American Psychological Association on an anti-racism path than elsewhere. However, the extent to which this has filtered into psychological education, training, research and practice is unknown. Although it is not intended to stock-take on the anti-racist and equal opportunities activities of psychological institutions, it is appropriate to look at initiatives which might signal progress. Partly this is a worthwhile exercise in its own right, but further it allows comparisons between organisations.

Concern over the attempts in the USA to impose English as the sole official language is a good example. Padilla *et al.* (1991) point out the associated concerns of the so-called English-only movement. They say that the movement has close connections with groups fighting for immigration restriction. Padilla *et al.*'s (1991) paper was prepared to support a *Resolution Against English Only* submitted to the American Psychological Association. They point out some rather familiar arguments: 'There is a strong consensus among school psychologists . . . that language-minority children's schooling aptitude may be seriously underestimated if testing is conducted only in the English language' (p. 125). Of course, there is an element of poacher turned gamekeeper in this. American psychologists, after oppressing and excluding minorities with culturally inappropriate tests and measurements for much of the twentieth centurry (Gould, 1981), could speak with authority on this matter. Much could be said of culturally insensitive psychotherapy over the same period. But now that the profession appears pro-active it could be said of the therapeutic setting:

> the knowledge base is still very restricted in understanding how language use affects the counseling process when a limited-English-proficient client is forced . . . to communicate deep-seated emotions and feelings in English.
> . . . [I]f a widespread English-only policy were adopted, it could be seen as justification to lessen concern for the needs of linguistic-minority clients. (p. 127)

The matter is not discussed solely in terms of psychological research findings and psychological practice. The authors hold that the English-only movement is disadvantageous and, as such, contradicts the ethical principles of the American Psychological Association (APA, 1981).

It may also be that the apparently pro-active efforts of the American Psychological Association to deal with matters related to race and racism are little more than a bureaucratised morality in which the printed page replaces determined action. Despite the clear documentation on the issue, it is also clear from what has gone before that American psychology shares many of the failings found elsewhere of not fully coming to terms with people not of European descent. For example, we have seen the exclusion of black people from research in mainstream American psychology journals.

The ultimate defence

too much ethics is a luxury psychological researchers and those *organisations set up to protect psychology* cannot afford. *Denial, which takes a number of elaborate forms in organisations, could be seen to be in operation.* One of the problems, which helps the process of denial, is that notions about what is decent behaviour in our relations with others, is not absolute or fixed in time; therefore, it *is always possible to put up a quasi-rational argument to defend the status quo and resist challenges* to current notions of research integrity. (Gale, 1993, p. 25, emphases added)

Gale should know what he is talking about. After all, he is a past president of the British Psychological Society and a long-serving member of the committee structure of that institution. That is to say, he is speaking from the inside. His major point is that psychology, and British psychology in particular, fails to engage students in a moral debate. Assuming that he includes all psychologists in the student category, then he ought to answer for the failure of the discipline as much as any. What he appears to be saying, based on his experience, is that his organisation deliberately fends off crucial moral debates in the interests of the expediency of psychological careers. In other words, moral concerns are not what they appear to be and statements about the appropriate morality for psychologists are something which should not be taken too seriously. Those who are seriously concerned about ethics in psychology clearly do not understand the game.

It is not in the nature of organisations that they normally leave themselves open to these charges. The process of 'closing ranks' ensures that criticism from the outside is neutralised or rejected. In this chapter we have seen a number of instances in which the moral, social, political and human issue of racism has demonstrably produced either corporate hostility towards those raising the issue or a resorting to a defensive posture of science. But these are really the signs of organisations unprepared and unwilling to change. They far from exhaust the processes involved in institutional racism. We have seen that the institutional racism of psychology does not entirely flow from its reluctance to change. It is partly built into the definitions of science that psychology seeks to work to – a sort of decontextualised universalism. Also, the reluctance to monitor and review policies and practices to find out whether there is a problem can be seen as part of the institutional inertia on race. Indeed, when we enquired about the ethnic composition of the British Psychological Society's workforce, particularly important as its headquarters are in an area with a high proportion of black people, mainly South Asian Indians, the answer came that the information was not available. This is a little surprising given the organisation's relatively small size and the fact that it occupies less than half of a small office complex. As one distinguished black biological scientist noted: 'Not playing a role in professional organizations is more significant than it sounds: it means fewer contacts in the various circles – the journals, the academic committees – that shape one's career' (Johnson, 1993, p. 132).

No one should be encouraged to explore racism in their profession without serious consideration of the problems they are likely to experience. Two medical doctors (Esmail and Everington, 1993) report a truncated study of discrimination in employment in the health service. They simply sent in applications for advertised medical posts including psychiatric ones varying systematically only in the name used on the application – it was either an Asian or an English one. Twice as many of the bogus applicants with English names were shortlisted as were equivalently qualified Asian-named ones. In no case was an Indian-named doctor shortlisted unless a bogus applicant with an English name also had been. Esmail and Everington (1993) explain: 'We originally planned a survey covering approximately 100 posts and all hospital specialties; unfortunately we were arrested by the fraud squad and charged with making fraudulent applications' (p. 692). Fortunately, they were not prosecuted (British Medical Journal, 1993), but the strength of hostility and the (ab)use of professional power which can be directed against anyone 'bucking the system' is apparent in their experience.

Chapter 8

Anti-racist psychology

There appears to be no limit to the variety of 'problems' which the white psychologist perceives as characteristic of black people. But the scientific methods employed are entrenched in institutionalized perspectives laced with cherished pathological notions regarding race. Research and services in psychology have enforced compliant behavior patterns among large numbers of black people. Voluminous clinical research on black people has yet to present us with a clear definition of the healthy black man. This is illustrated by the interchangeable use of the terms 'Negro' and 'black'. The distinction between learning how to live better in a pig pen and learning how to escape from a pig pen has not yet been mastered by most psychologists. (Thomas, 1973, p. 58)

Things have changed somewhat since Thomas wrote these words. Nevertheless there remains a pressing need for anti-racism strategies in psychology. This final chapter argues the case for an anti-racist psychology, partly by showing how some psychologists have responded to racism's new challenges. Society has changed, bringing different requirements for psychological practice, yet no substantial progress has been made as yet towards establishing anti-racism in psychology. It would be a deception to pretend otherwise despite certain aspects of anti-racism being on the agenda of some psychologists. A body of theory has developed alongside initiatives to curb Eurocentric psychology's worst abuses of black clients. Cross-cultural counselling is a crucial area which has recently been at the forefront of anti-racist work. This is not simply a question of black psychologists for black clients, Chinese psychologists for Chinese clients, or any such arrangements. Often such approaches merely create a sort of ghetto.

More than anything, the provision of psychologists from all ethnic groups signals acknowledgement of the importance of such groups to psychology. *Given appropriate training and attitudes within the profession*, much of the time, a psychologist of any ethnicity can deal appropriately with most clients. On the other hand, the profession will learn faster and better when it responds to the ideas and perspectives of a range of ethnic or cultural groups. Of course, there are situations in which a client's needs may be more effectively met by a psychologist of a similar socio-cultural background. Effective communication may be one reason for this. Sometimes a female client may prefer a same-sex therapist in order to avoid unwanted aspects of gender which can permeate psychotherapy. In much the same way, a black client who feels damaged by racism may work best with a black therapist who may be able to empathise with the client. Similar considerations apply to research; multi-cultural sensitivity is equally at a premium in these settings.

This chapter looks at: (1) the reasons why anti-racism should be a personal motive, (2) anti-racism as a professional responsibility of practitioners, and (3) anti-racism as an institutional responsibility in psychology.

The universal case for anti-racism in psychology

For some 500 years racism has been central to the activities of the European world. Characterised by policies and practices of racial discrimination, segregation, oppression and domination, racism is based on the supposed superiority of white people over 'impure' black peoples. Sometimes this assumption is conscious and clearly articulated, other times it may be unacknowledged but acted upon nevertheless. Either way, it motivates and justifies inequity in social arrangements between black and white people. Internationally and nationally, the benefits of these arrangements accrue to white people. In view of psychology's perennial complicity in this, the least today's psychology can do towards rectifying this legacy is to seek to be actively anti-racist; its theories, research and practice should arraign against racism.

Psychology's historical and contemporary guilt is not enough to make every psychologist feel personal responsibility. Morally and ethically, the case for anti-racism is as much to do with individual social responsibility as their discipline's institutional failings. In other words, anti-racism is both an individual and professional matter, but nevertheless ultimately indivisible. Clearly the special status of psychologists may allow them to revictimise racism's victims. Psychologists are employed in major social institutions, and also directly and indirectly advise and help them conduct their affairs. All psychologists should, therefore, understand the extent of racism's infestation of society and their workplace in order to tackle it effectively. There are objectives involved in this: to create empathy with racism's victims, to place one's personal anti-racism in an institutional context and to emphasise that racism is an in-depth and current issue. While similar pictures could be painted almost anywhere in the world, racism in Britain will be dealt with in some detail. Psychologists need awareness of racism locally but to dismiss events outside of one's immediate situation as irrelevant is to ignore the broad view essential to understanding racism's impact.

Racial discrimination

The following, then, represents a brief overview of racial discrimination and other manifestations of racism in Britain. It also highlights some of the settings in which psychologists have a particular interest: health services which employ substantial numbers of psychologists, especially clinical psychologists, and the criminal justice system which increasingly involves psychologists interested in the discipline's applications to the law, sometimes as expert witnesses on psychological matters.

In 1982, the Policy Studies Institute (PSI) undertook a comprehensive investigation of black people's circumstances in Britain (Brown, 1984). Sponsors of the project included major departments of the national government. It involved more than 5,000 black adults and over 2,000 white adults. Impressive response rates were achieved; they exceeded 70 per cent for all ethnic groups. The survey investigated the general situation of black people, including employment, housing, health status and education. The depressing conclusion was:

> As we systematically compared the jobs, the incomes, unemployment rates, private housing, local authority housing, local environments and other aspects of the lives of people with different ethnic origins . . . the circumstances of black people came to be and continue to be worse than those of white people. (Brown, 1984, pp. 315–16)

Acknowledging the findings of earlier related studies (e.g. Daniel, 1968; Smith, 1974; 1977), the report went on to describe how considerable declines in racial inequality had been expected. Instead it found a mixture of old and new inequalities centred around three different problems:

> First, it is clear that racialism and direct racial discrimination continue to have a powerful impact on the lives of black people. Second, the position of the black citizens of Britain largely remains, geographically and economically, that allocated to them as immigrant workers in the

1950s and 1960s. Third, it is still the case that the organisations and institutions of British society have policies and practices that additionally disadvantage black people because they frequently take no account of the cultural difference between groups with different ethnic origins. (Brown, 1984, p. 318)

A follow-up report, *Racial Discrimination: Seventeen Years after the Act* (Brown and Gray, 1985), presented an even gloomier picture of the economic circumstances of Britain's black population. (See Gary (1981) for a detailed review and discussion of the similarly depressing environment of black people in the USA.)

No studies on this scale have been published in Britain since these. So have black people's circumstances changed since? The answer is an emphatic 'no'. More recent evidence indicates that the situation might have even worsened for certain black groups (e.g. CRE, 1991; PSI, 1992). A number of studies into racism in Britain, in general, and in specific sectors of society, including the police, the health service and the legal system, have revealed the prevalence and pervasiveness of racism and discrimination.

Racial violence and harassment
Racial violence and harassment are not new phenomena to Britain (Gordon, 1986). Back in 1919, there was a series of attacks on black people in the dock areas including Glasgow, Manchester and London. And in the late 1940s there was further violence in Liverpool, Deptford and Birmingham. During the late 1950s, black people became a particular target for racist youths, including the first racially motivated killing in Britain of a black person. The 1960s and 1970s brought 'paki-bashing' of people of South Asian origins. The escalation of racial violence has been acknowledged by the central government. For example, in 1981 the Home Office published a report, *Racial Attacks*, which estimated that people of Indian origin were 50 times more likely than white people to be victims and African-Caribbeans 36 times more likely. As for most crimes, available statistics are very likely to be underestimates of the true incidence.

Not only does there seem to have been an increase in racial attacks and harassment in recent years, but these incidents have also acquired an uglier appearance. A survey by the Commission for Racial Equality (1987b) into racial violence and harassment in housing, *Living in Terror*, reported: 'While the number and severity of individual cases is particularly marked in London, racial harassment is common through-out the country' (p. 7). The report also emphasised the scale of unreported racial harassment. Similarly, London Metropolitan Police figures show that racial assaults in London rose by 16 per cent in

1991 to 3,373. For Britain as a whole, in 1992 there were 7,780 racial assaults, including nine known racially motivated murders. Worse still, it is believed that the true figures for racial violence exceed ten times those recorded by the police (Runnymede Trust, 1993).

In 1986, the Home Affairs Committee reported that one of the dispiriting aspects of race relations was 'the shameful incidence of racial attacks and harassment' (p. 22). But these attacks are not just 'shameful', they are 'hell' for the victims. There appears to be no sanctuary for them from racial harassment and violence ranging from verbal abuse and racist jokes to physical attacks and even murder:

> As a boy sleeps, a pig's head, its eyes, ears, nostrils and mouth stuffed with lighted cigarettes, is hurled through the window of his bedroom. . . . A family are held prisoner in their own flat by a security cage bolted to their front door by white neighbours. A family's home is burnt out and a pregnant woman and her three children killed. (Gordon, 1986, p. v)

Even young people are not safe at school or in college. A study by the CRE (1988a) found that:

> Racial harassment is widespread and persistent. . . . Young people in schools and colleges suffer no less than men and women on the streets and in their own homes in housing estates (p. 5). . . . The problem of racial harassment extends right through the educational system from nursery and infant schools to colleges and universities and affects pupils, students and staff. . . . Abuse, graffiti and violence as both threat and actuality serve as a constant reminder of the intolerance of white society and the vulnerability of ethnic minority people. (p. 16)

The report describes in detail eighteen cases to illustrate the above observations, including: 'At a primary school in the North-West a black child was forced by the teacher to stand up and spell out the word "golliwog" when the child refused to read it out in class because he found it offensive' (CRE, 1988a, p. 11).

It is convenient, although dangerous, to regard these extreme incidents as unfortunate but nevertheless atypical of the experience of many black people. Racial violence has a wider significance than its impact on the direct victim alone. Just as rape has a profound influence on how all women live their lives, and paedophilia profoundly affects how children are taught to relate to adults, racial violence makes all black people the indirect victims. Racial violence is:

> A particularly disturbing, very horrifying crime . . . which affects not only individual victims but minority ethnic group communities as a whole. It engenders fear and militates against the creation of a decent and civilised multi-racial society. (Home Affairs Select Committee, 1989, in Skellington and Morris, 1992, p. 62)

The health services
The National Health Service (NHS) in Britain is a cherished public
institution which symbolises the nation's humanitarian and egalitarian
values by providing health care according to need rather than ability
to pay. As such it might be expected to be an institution free from
discrimination on the grounds of race. Thus until 1988, the NHS
continued to deny vehemently and effectively racism in its midst. After
all, it had many black employees, including doctors and nurses. This was
argued to be proof that all was well, the service was racially healthy.

Black people, both staff and patients, knew better. They knew that
as far as race was concerned, the service was 'in a critical condition', to
borrow a phrase from the London Association of Community Relations
Councils (1985). To black employees racism was a palpable reality of
the workplace; they did not need research evidence to convince them
– collectively they were the evidence. Those who wished for research
evidence on racial discrimination in the service seemed unprepared to
look for it or believe it when they saw it. Such documentation already
existed in abundance (e.g. Brown, 1984; Cochrane, 1977; CRE, 1983,
1987d; Dean *et al.*, 1981; Doyal *et al.*, 1980; Hicks, 1982; Hughes, 1982;
Ineichen, 1986; Littlewood and Cross, 1980; London Association of
Community Relations Councils, 1985; McNaught, 1982, 1984, 1985;
Rack, 1982; Smith, 1980; Thomas and Williams, 1972; Townsend and
Davidson, 1982; Whitehead, 1987). The significant change came with
the 1988 report of the National Association of Health Authorities
(NAHA), *Action not Words*. This conceded the pervasiveness of racism
in the health services: 'Such discrimination can be seen in access to and
delivery of services as well as in employment practice. . . . In providing
health care, staff may apply racial stereotyping when making assessment
about black and minority ethnic individuals' (NAHA, 1988, p. 8).

Among areas particularly of concern, the report mentioned the following:

1. The standard of care: black patients generally receive substandard
   care.
2. Lack of response to health issues which particularly affect black
   people.
3. Inadequate mental health services: these were much the same as
   already documented in Chapter 4.
4. High infant mortality due to unequal access to health services for the
   black community.
5. Employment: black people in the service tend to be employed in
   low grade and low status jobs and not in management, on the least
   popular shifts and in less-favoured specialities.

In spite of the laudable suggestions and recommendations made by this report to rectify this disgraceful situation, in 1993, five years later, concern was still grave enough to motivate two doctors to attempt to expose the wide scale of racial discrimination in the NHS (Esmail and Everington, 1993).

Racism and the law

Freedom and justice for all are presumed to be enshrined in the 'British way'. Yet, black people's freedom is greatly curtailed relative to white people. Their freedom of abode and from terror at home, in the streets and on public transport is affected (CRE, 1987a; 1988a; Gordon, 1986). Racial injustice is rife despite legislation such as the Race Relations Act (1976) outlawing racial discrimination. In view of this catalogue of injustice, it might be expected that the legal system would compensate black people for injustice suffered elsewhere. Lamentably, numerous studies seem to suggest that black people cannot generally expect to be treated fairly even by this system. Evidence indicates that racial injustice is rampant at all levels of the justice system itself (Brogden, 1981; Cain, 1973; Coggan, 1981; Coggan and Walker, 1982; Crow, 1987; Gilroy, 1983, 1987; Gordon, 1983; Hall *et al.*, 1978; Home Office, 1986; Hudson, 1989; Jefferson, 1988; Lambert, 1970; Landau and Nathan, 1983; Mair, 1986; McConville and Baldwin, 1982; NACRO, 1986; Reiner, 1985, 1989, Sanders, 1985; Scarman, 1981; Smith and Gray, 1983; Southgate and Ekblom, 1984; Stevens and Willis, 1979; Waters, 1990; etc.).

The report into the Brixton confrontation between the police and the black community of 1981 in London brought to public attention the scale and extent of racism in the British criminal justice system (Scarman, 1981). Again, what has changed since then? Very little, if anything. Thus, in 1991, the Runnymede Trust submitted a research-based document to the Royal Commission on Criminal Justice. Its main points were:

1. 'The perception is that unequal treatment occurs at all stages of an individual's process through the system, from initial contact with the Police onwards.'
2. 'Black, Asian and ethnic minority people are treated worse by the criminal justice system when they are the victims of crime . . . [and] the criminal justice system is not sufficiently vigorous and strenuous in how it deals with such attacks.'
3. 'In employment, there is considerable racial discrimination which is not vigorously challenged or corrected by law.'
4. 'It is . . . of grave concern for everyone in the criminal justice system, if significant numbers of the population believe that the

Police and Courts cannot be trusted to behave fairly, and that on the contrary they are themselves infringing the spirit of the legislation in the Race Relations Act.' (Runnymede Trust, 1992, p. 11)

The law is the means through which authority implements its intentions; it appears that it enforces injustice against black people. As Hinds (1978) has observed in the context of North America, the legal system promises black people relief, but fails to deliver it; it denies them justice and then accuses them of criminality; this presumption of criminality is then used to justify more and greater injustice. (See, Townsey, 1981, for an overview of the American situation.) This vicious circle is also found in other sectors. For example, in housing black British people have been allocated the worst accommodation but then held responsible for inner-city decay; they are directly and indirectly denied adequate health care but then accused of being a burden on the service; their children attend the ill-equipped schools, are bullied, harassed or even murdered, then accused of lowering educational standards (Rack, 1982).

This is black people's life, their experience, their reality. It is something which psychologists, as individuals and professionals, should not tolerate.

Racism as a social not a psychological matter

Case Illustration . . . A 35–year old Black female goes to her White pastor's office, stating that she is having increasing problems with headaches. She describes herself as being under a great deal of stress because of her son, who is having problems at school. When asked to elaborate, she replied, 'Well, it's his teacher, she . . . well, she . . . never mind.' When asked to continue, she replied with hesitation, 'I think she's prejudiced but the principal thinks I'm crazy and doesn't believe me. I think that he's . . . well . . . you know. I've been real tired lately. Do you think I should go to a doctor?' The pastor agreed, suggested a particular specialist, and terminated the interview. (Wilson and Lyles, 1984, p. 134)

An important fact needs facing. Caution has to be exercised even when there appears to be an active stance against racism. Already we have seen some putative anti-racist positions to be little more than reactions against the crudest forms of biological and cultural racism. Sometimes rather sinister undertones are masked by superficially favourable treatments of black people. A case in point is Brantley's (1983) suggestions about appropriate ways of regarding racism in psychotherapy. One approach is to interpret a claim of racism as a manifestation of a symptom, clients might merely be using it to express their paranoia or as projected hostility. According to Brantley, early on in treatment:

> the therapist should help the patient explore his or her coping mechanisms and develop more productive ways of dealing with the anxiety triggered by racism. Negative self-perceptions often develop when blacks are subjected to racist behavior and concepts. (p. 1606)

However, for Brantley, the therapist should merely accept that these are the patient's feelings. It is inappropriate to explore whether the complaints of racism are soundly based. Non-judgementally, the therapist should explore the impact of the beliefs about racism on the individual's personality. Equally, for Brantley, ignoring the 'racism dimension' holds perils of its own. Important ramifications can be ignored if the therapist is not alert to racism as an issue. The therapist will miss important race-related messages – 'I am black and I am having difficulty coping with the racism I am destined to face' (p. 1607). But, curiously, the therapist should back off from involvement with an anti-racist stance:

> the therapist may try to adopt a racial stance and identify with the patient's aggression, thereby acting out his or her own hostility, racial or otherwise. At best this is countertherapeutic and ethically unsound. It is appropriate to help the patient develop positive coping styles that take into account the reality that racism does exist but indeed should not be the dominant force in a black person's life. The patient should be supported in developing a strong internal sense of self-worth that cannot be dissolved by narrow-sighted racist perceptions. (p. 1608)

It would appear that the role of the therapist is to act as the agent of the white racist society which is doing the damage. The job is to help the client cope with rather than fight the system. The problem is conceived of as being one of a weak victim who is affected by racism – the cure is to strengthen victims, or, indeed, to harden them up for more racism. This is training to live better in the pig pen, and would suit white racist society enormously. Gerrard (1991) writes of some aspects of racism and sexism in therapy as being 'systematic oppression by psychology'. Among the examples she cites is part of her interview with a black woman who describes the activities of a white male psychologist acting as her counsellor. She was expected to read certain black literature:

> He said, 'You've got to see the Black woman in your literature as you.' And I had to live through that. Oh God, help me. *The first time I cried . . . he said, 'Well, I'm so glad. You have proved now that you are a woman. Because you just face everything so head on and you never break down. And I was getting afraid that you are so much like the slave woman, I wanted to see the real woman in you.* I wanted that to come out.' And

for him, crying was healing. So I had to get to the place after facing it all, after living these experiments, then to cry. Then he said, 'You're getting there. You're ok.' (p. 563)

Gerrard explains that this counsellor was both racist and sexist. He appeared to follow a theoretical model that involves breaking down the client's defences so that 'pain' can be released. However, the pain that he appears to be tackling head-on was the woman's race and gender, which he sees as the overriding aspect of her situation.

Other implications underlie this sort of approach. Griffith and Griffith (1986) discuss how the attitude of the American legal system has changed on damages claims resulting from racial discrimination:

Until recently compensatory damages were rarely awarded in discrimination cases . . . little activity took place in this area of the law inasmuch as there was no public outrage against discrimination itself. Neither were blacks in the racial climate of yesteryear particularly enthusiastic about making claims for compensation. (p. 71)

According to Griffith and Griffith, the assessment of damage caused by racism has to involve consideration of the following. The expert witness has to believe that the racial humiliation led to 'severe mental distress' in order to warrant compensatory damages, for example, racial discrimination in regard to housing having caused 'stress response syndrome' with extreme psychological consequences: 'However, the psychiatrist must also realize that mental distress is not the automatic outcome of every racial slur; some blacks have become hardened to discriminatory conduct simply to survive' (p. 75). Fortunately, courts are apparently less concerned with such expert evidence and more bothered by the outrageous conduct of the defendant. Were the courts more dependent on the expert psychological witness, then the above comments would have obvious implications for black people – unless the black person showed psychological disintegration they could not have been damaged!

In stark contrast to Brantley, the South African psychologist, Dawes, proposes a radical view of the therapist's role. He starts with the observation that many practitioners see no relationship between clinical psychology and politics. Psychology's relationship with inherently political society of which it is a part is disregarded by them. Perhaps psychology's 'scientific' objectivity is threatened by the taint of politics. Dawes sees psychology's objectivity merely as 'collective subjectivity': 'When we operate with lack of awareness of the ideological influences in our work, we can believe passionately that we are dealing with truth' (p. 56). Built into the notion of 'cross-cultural' psychology are ideas which effectively disguise power differences across cultures. The spectre of culture as a major problem is raised to obfuscate the central issue of relative power. Apartheid's ideology relies on cultural differences to excuse power differences. For Dawes the 'cure' is diametrically opposite to that of Brantley: 'Band-aids are necessary in treating the casualties of the system, but the source of the illness needs attention if we are to move towards primary prevention' (p. 57). By ignoring politics, psychologists risk reproducing the ideology of the racist state. A nation at war with itself is the political reality which psychologists cannot afford to neglect.

Korchin (1980) summarises the positions which those wishing to provide better services for minorities demonstrate as follows:

> The first assumption is that the problems of minority people stem from the massive social stresses of a racist society and can only be rectified through social action aimed at revolutionary change. Mental health care, as developed by white middle-class professionals, is at best palliative; at worst, it distracts from recognition of the true source of the problem. . . . A second, less extreme assumption is that the concepts, institutions, and practices developed by the mental health establishment are ill-adapted to minority problems and needs. The ways of minority people are misunderstood and their behaviors mislabeled as pathological. (p. 265)

These are easily recognisable. While psychology ought always to be cognisant of the more radical views about racism, the anti-racist objectives available to most practitioners are rather more limited. The task of eliminating racism from the immediate work environment is much more manageable – difficult as it is in itself. Foolproof methods of eliminating racism from the work place do not exist. However, it is perfectly feasible to work to improve and monitor progress towards that end.

Psychology's multi-cultural clients

> suppose those who are familiar with mainstream American culture were asked by a foreign psychologist to explain how to conduct therapy with American clients. In a cultural sense, Americans are individualistic, competitive, and verbally direct. But how is the foreign psychologist to conduct therapy? . . . (a) we do not clearly know the relationship between such knowledge and skills development, (b) discussions of differences between ethnic groups ignore the richness of within group variability, and (c) knowledge lacking actual experience with the ethnic minority group in question is insufficient to adequately train therapists. . . . Knowing that Americans tend to be open, competitive, verbally direct, independent minded, or whatever, provides very few clues to the conduct of therapy with clients. (Sue, 1983, p. 589)

For Sue, a number of conflicts within psychology bear significantly on culturally sensitive work. These include the following:

Conflict 1: *Etic versus emic*: Etic is the search for 'human universals' whereas the emic has a culture-specific orientation. Few psychologists (including clinical psychologists) are trained in cultural diversity or ethnic minorities.

Conflict 2: *Mainstreaming versus pluralism*: This is the contrast between the assimilation of minorities into majority cultures as opposed to respecting the plurality of cultures.

Conflict 3: *Equal opportunity versus equality of outcome*: This is the failure to realise that equality of access to treatment is no guarantee that the outcomes will be equally successful.

Conflict 4: *Modal personality versus individual differences*: Often psychologists have resorted to the notion of the modal personality in order to deal with the diverse individuals who present from minorities. Others have tended to concentrate on the variety within a culture at the expense of dealing with the cultural diversity.

Some of these are the result of the deep-seated ways in which psychology has tackled its subject matter. Therapy across cultures has developed over the years and rather different underlying models have guided thinking in these various stages (Jackson, 1990). There are six major approaches:

1. *Differential or limited models*: These virtually ignore cultural factors – short-term psychotherapy and drug treatment are typical.
2. *Parallel treatment models*: Interpreters, for example, or client's own-race therapists are used in treatment; in all other respects traditional psychotherapy is used.
3. *Collaborative treatment models*: Traditional psychotherapists and health care providers from the minority group pool their skills co-operatively.
4. *Culture-free treatment models*: Here the emphasis is on those means of therapy which are held to be effective across socio-demographic boundaries; thus behavioural treatments would find favour in this approach.
5. *Culture-specific treatment models*: These involve identifiable cultural values in the process of treatment; thus, cultural norms have to be understood when giving consideration to whether behaviour is aberrant and in planning the goals of the treatment.
6. *Combined treatment models*: These incorporate both the traditional approaches and the cultural approaches; the assessment of the

client's culture is as important in this approach as it is for the culture-specific treatment models.

Which philosophy dominates in a given period is determined by factors unrelated to clients' therapeutic needs. The economic and political climate together with the level and type of racism in society help determine which approach is taken.

The delivery of psychological services across cultures requires a degree of cultural sensitivity generally atypical of the training and experience of psychologists. Service delivery needs considering on a broad front. It is not enough to rely solely on recruiting culturally sensitive psychologists to service ethnic groups. Culturally sensitive research needs to be carried out by the psychological community and the findings made generally available. Unless culturally sensitive research is to become a specialism within the discipline, all psychologists need to be made culturally aware. Cynics might suggest that psychologists *have* no choice but to respond to needs of a new clientele. There is evidence (Sue, 1991) that the ethnic groups in the USA will be the major contributors to welfare and pension services in the early part of the twenty-first century. The ethnic minority marketplace in the USA currently matches the gross national product of Canada. Psychologists as service providers cannot afford to ignore this. Perhaps this means that the pressures to change will be economically rather than ethically driven. After all, important advances in multi-cultural psychology have emerged out of therapy – the sharp edge of psychology's economy.

It is not the intention to provide a manual of cross-cultural service provision here. However, it is interesting to look at the experiences of one practitioner involved in therapy for African-American women. Boyd-Franklin (1991), herself African-American, discusses some of the main themes emerging in treatment groups for other African-American women:

1. Themes of racism and racial identification often had been dismissed when raised by the women in mixed-race groups. Black groups can supply a subtlety in appreciating the less blatant forms of racism which occur.
2. Sometimes black women see issues primarily as matters of racism rather than ones of gender and class.
3. Usually hidden feelings of shame concerning physical features can be helped in therapy groups.
4. The development of trust towards therapy and the therapist can be difficult. The therapist is part of a small black community in which information would easily spread if divulged by the therapist or other members of the group. Negative attitudes in the black community towards therapy do not help.

5. The religious side of the black community may be hostile to therapy. However, since the Church may be part of coping mechanisms, discussion of the spiritual side of a person ought to be part of therapy.

It is noticeable that virtually all of the discussion of racism in the context of therapeutic work deals with the individual client–therapist relationship. An exception to this is Dolan *et al.* (1991), who suggest that the therapeutic psychiatric hospital community might have some benefits in relation to anti-racist therapy on the more global level. One aspect of the therapeutic community which might be relevant to anti-racist practice is that it seeks to reduce or eliminate power relationships between the patients and medical/therapeutic staff. Amongst the advantages of the system is that black people may learn about how white patients have been marginalised by conventional psychiatric treatment and institutions. On the other hand, simple time-scheduling problems created by the five-day, nine-to-five working week makes for difficulties in religious observance on the part of some ethnic minority clients. Dolan *et al.* feel that the therapeutic community approach needs to address many issues such as the numbers of black people on the staff and the under-referral of black people to such therapeutic services.

The American Psychological Association's Board of Ethnic Minority Affairs (1993) published a set of guidelines for those who provide services to ethnically, linguistically and culturally diverse populations. They are presented as something to be aspired to. Included in the list are things like:

1. Psychologists seek consultation or make referrals when their training and knowledge is inadequate to deal with a particular client.
2. Psychologists seek education and training courses to enhance their understanding of culturally and other different groups.
3. Psychologists are well aware of their biases.
4. Psychologists help clients understand their own culture better.
5. Psychologists consult religious and spiritual practitioners and leaders from their clients' culture.
6. Psychologists work to eliminate prejudice and discrimination.
7. Psychologists develop sensitivity to oppression, sexism, elitism and racism.

Expressed in this form, it is difficult to imagine the psychologist who satisfies many of these standards. What is remarkable is that they are presented almost as rules for conduct, making them the responsibility of individual psychologists to meet rather than of the professional body to provide for. As such, it is a marginal statement relying on the good faith of individuals. If this is what psychologists should be like then whose responsibility must it be for ensuring that they are?

Tackling institutional racism in the workplace

> One credible explanation is the Marxist view that the privileged maintain their position by divisiveness among less privileged sectors of society. The analysis asserts that those with privilege control social institutions and that these institutions serve the interests of the controlling privileged group. (Pillay, 1984, p. 29)

Uba (1982) explains how white organizations can present 'hidden' barriers to minorities. The following all contribute to the exclusion of black people from predominantly white psychological organisations: (1) racial and cultural biases in the delivery of psychological services; (2) conflicts between Western understanding of the problems of clients in general and the specific values and expectations of clients from black cultures; (3) black cultures may be hostile to seeking psychological help; (4) language barriers including questionnaires and information materials; (5) lack of bilingual and culturally trained psychologists may result in inappropriate services and act as a deterrent to other members of that black community; and (6) information about the availability of mental health services may have not reached potential clients possibly due to biased communication and publicity networks. She considers three broad strategies for remedying this situation:

1. Trained personnel in mainstream facilities.
2. Special units in mainstream facilities.
3. Segregated facilities.

None of these alternatives finds particular support from available knowledge. Uba feels that to a large extent each of the alternatives can help overcome the barriers to the use of services. The choice would be largely dependent on other factors. So, for example, she suggests that the mainstream policy would be most appropriate for small organisations, areas where there is little need for bilingual services, and so forth. One of the difficulties with the assumption that psychologists can be leaders towards racially egalitarian organisations lies mainly in the source of their expertise. We have repeatedly seen how psychology has been far nearer to being at the root of the problem than the solution.

For some clinicians, institutional racism is responsible for some of the problems in therapy with ethnic minority group members. Hankins-McNary (1979) provides an extensive discussion of one point of view. She believes that institutional racism influences the relationship between therapists and black clients. Trust, essential to a therapeutic relationship, is wrecked if the organisation is itself racist. Furthermore, it does not matter that both the client and the therapist are black. It is suggested that the low status and low esteem accorded to work with black clients by the profession may frustrate the ambitions of black therapists. The therapists' resulting anger may well be directed towards their clients – almost as if to drive away such lowly individuals. The response of the therapist may edge towards regarding all of the client's problems as relating to broad social factors, or 'the therapist may go to the opposite extreme and deny identification with the black client by attributing all the problems to the client, rather than to the possible external effects of racial discrimination' (p. 28). No formal evidence is provided for any of this. Nevertheless, the author makes the interesting point that the church has been a major provider of mental health services for the black community since few professionals practise in black community psychiatric services in the USA.

Possibly considerations like these encouraged Lopez and Cheek (1977) to advocate the training of counselling psychologists as agents to prevent institutional racism. They proposed that since counselling psychologists have trained in individual and group techniques of intervention for change: 'The training provides the counselling psychologist with a sensitivity and understanding of the complexity of interpersonal relationships' (p. 65). Ignoring the arrogance of this claim in relation to racism, we can note that Lopez and Cheek see counselling skills as a means of helping organisational change towards the elimination of institutional racism. They suggest that racist behaviours and structures have to be tackled directly rather than concentrating on general human relationships within the organisation. A 'prevention and education' approach is suggested to replace the usual crisis management role of counselling psychologists. This would involve courses dealing with political, spiritual, economic and social needs. In psychological training, the emphasis on explanations of behaviour would diminish in favour of more work on psychological intervention towards change.

But to be fair to Lopez and Cheek (1977), it is only in recent years that the discipline has begun to take racism in psychological practice as a matter for systematic exploration and understanding. It is unlikely that the following would be seen as anything other than a naive rallying cry; given that it is hardly state-of-the-art, it takes on an air of quaintness which contrasts with more recent approaches:

> Too often, counselors engage in a game of hide-and-seek with bias using their complicated measuring devices, their expertise in the empirical, their concepts of validity and reliability, their jargon, and all the other sophisticated paraphernalia of the trade to rationalize and protect their own biases and overgeneralizations. Despite the difficulties, I am hopeful that all of us – assessors and assessed, victims and victimizers – will find a way to free ourselves from the shackles of bias by occasionally assuming the role of the stigmatized, of the 'most woebegotten'. (Schlossberg, 1977, p. 184)

Given the nature of much of the debate in psychology, it is perhaps inevitable that groups of practitioners seeking an anti-racist stance in their work dwell primarily upon mental testing. While there is good reason to be cautious about the use of psychological tests – that they are an issue in the black community is one reason – in many ways this represents only a limited view of what psychological practice in a multi-cultural society should be about. The psychological testing debate may deflect attention from the more important task of developing culturally sensitive psychological practice. But to make testing a starting point may be one of the more manageable options.

Some appear to want a fairly mechanical approach to anti-racism in psychology. Joyce (1988) lists a number of points which form the basis of an anti-racist code of practice for educational psychologists. A flavour of these is contained in the following excerpts:

> It may be theoretically possible to standardize a norm-referenced test separately for each ethnic group that it is to be used with but the problems involved in this – e.g. defining what constitutes an ethnic group – are legion. (p. 48)

> Norm-referenced tests . . . bias the results in favour of the majority group. The use of such measures in a multicultural setting is therefore racist. (p. 48)

> There needs to be a survey of all the tests currently in use by members of our service, with clarification of the purpose for which they are being used. (p. 48)

> Assessment of any 'behavioral' or 'emotional' problem must also take account of the cultural components of behaviour – e.g. body stance, eye contact. (p. 49)

Seemingly underlying these suggestions is the view that there are simple formulae sufficient to resolve these extremely complex problems. Questions need to be asked about this, however, such as, how does the assessment of a child begin to address the non-verbal aspects of communication? What should the educational psychologist make of a child who consistently avoids eye-contact by looking down? What should the educational psychologist make of a 'swaggering' style of movement? In what ways can adjustment be made to the assessment in the light of, say, the fact that a girl, for example, spent her first eight years in Morocco but the last three with native English foster-parents? Why are body stance and eye-contact being used as part of the assessment anyway? What do they tell us about the indigenous child? One is reminded of Thomas' (1973) comment:

> psychologists have confused knowledge *about* a people with knowledge *of* a people. The latter is a case of learning from within the group of people, sharing the conceptual framework or weltanschauung of that group. The former is a case of learning from without and imposing an alien conceptual framework on the observed behavior. (pp. 60–1)

Care should be taken not to be too dismissive when practising psychologists attempt to do something about racism. Evidence suggests that the basic training of educational psychologists does little to prepare them for their role in a multi-cultural society. For example, Carroll (1988) surveyed courses providing initial training in educational psychology in England and Wales, and found that none of them had any black tutors. A minority did use black field training supervisors and a small majority occasionally used black guest speakers. Nevertheless, the courses were overwhelmingly dominated by white staff. Only a quarter of the courses had as a training requirement experience of working with ethnic minority children and families. Similarly, Wolfendale (1988) surveyed educational psychological services in Britain and found that the vast majority had no in-service anti-racism training. Few had written policies on the assessment of children for whom English is a second language or on anti-racism and multi-cultural matters. A small majority had no contact with local black community groups.

Booker *et al.* (1989) promote an anti-racist stance; they suggest that psychologists have a responsibility at both the individual and collective levels to work to change racist attitudes. The starting point they recommend is one's own attitudes: 'At the same time we need to attend to those aspects of the environment and context which provide ideological and symbolic support for racism' (p. 123). The authors, all educational psychologists, attended a conference on racism which graphically brought home the extent to which members of an organisation can be insulated from the outside world; black parents were also invited. For the first time the nature of the wider situation hit home:

> The . . . Conference was an intense emotional experience. To receive such floods of anger and pain, to see the image of your profession through the eyes of people who saw you as the crucifiers of their youth, to sit

helpless and marginalised with no effective means of reply was physically and emotionally shattering. (p. 126)

Sometimes racism-awareness training workshops have inspired practising psychologists to review racism in their organisations. One group of educational psychologists publicly reported the outcome of a training exercise they applied to their own workplace (Desforges *et al.*, 1985). Among aspects of their organisation which could be examined or bettered they mentioned:

1. Would all types of client including those from ethnic minorities find the reception and waiting room hospitable and welcoming? Are reception staff approachable?
2. How representative of the community the organisation serves are the clerical and professional staff?
3. What efforts have been made towards improving the service for different minority groups? What has been considered? Are there ways in which the organisation involves ethnic minorities concerning improvements in service delivery?
4. Who sets the priorities for the organisation? Is there any unintended racism in these choices?
5. Are the psychological assessment methods used discriminatory?
6. Can non-fluent speakers of English read reports or discuss matters with you in their chosen language? Are interpreters and translators exploited?
7. Is racism seen as relevant to all those working in a multiracial society rather than being a matter solely for those working with ethnic minorities?

Such proposals, useful as they appear, are of little use unless there is some mechanism to ensure that the policy results in change. Burman (1988) suggests that anti-racism policies should include explicit objectives for change, a clear timescale, giving individuals responsibility for implementing certain decisions and a monitoring and review process. Corvin and Wiggins (1989) stress that it is vital to examine one's own racism though some training in cross-cultural psychology ignores this in favour of concentrating on aspects of the client. Failure to self-examine facilitates the self-serving excuse that individual psychologists are not responsible for racism – the problem lies elsewhere (i.e. the avoidance strategy). Rather than seeing connections between themselves and the racist society which oppresses black clients, the psychologist is allowed to stand apart from the client perhaps assuming that the client does not make the connection:

It is important to recognize that White racism is not the result of cultural differences, but the consequences of White ethnocentrism. Therefore, efforts to train White trainees to be effective cross-cultural counselors without addressing their own White racism are doomed to failure or at best only a modicum of pseudosuccess. (p. 106)

For this reason, following Hardiman (1979), the authors stress the stages by which white racial identity is developed. Quite clearly this reverses the conventional approach in psychology which seeks to explain the development of black identities, neglecting white identity because it does not need understanding – 'so natural is identity in Euro-Americans'. They characterise these stages as follows:

'*Stage 1: Acceptance.* In this stage, the White person denies that there is a race problem, tends to have a "people are people" view of the world, and operates under an unconscious assumption of Whiteness as "the norm"'(p. 108). In terms of psychology, the implication of this stage is that psychologists, believing themselves to be non-racist, feel that black people should change to white ways and values. This is described as a 'people are people' stage which dismisses the importance of cultural differences. However, it does not have the corollary that white psychologists would happily adopt black people's cultural values and practices.
'*Stage 2: Resistance.* The Resistance stage for White trainees is characterized by feelings of anger about being brainwashed by American myths' (p. 108). But this is entirely focused on other people, the anger is not turned to the question of one's own personal racism – it is a problem of white people in general instead.
'*Stage 3: Redefinition.* White trainees in the Redefinition stage redirect their energy toward the emergence of White identity and, consequently, a White culture without racism' (p. 108). At this stage, it is fully accepted that racism is an issue to be tackled by White people and that the onus of responsibility cannot be given over to the victims of racism.
'*Stage 4: Internalization.* Internalization represents the White person's integration of his or her race into his or her identity. The white person can now interact without being exploitative with those who are culturally different' (p. 108).

The earliest of these four stages are perfectly compatible with a self-definition as 'non-racist'. The later stages reflect an acceptance that individual non-racism is something of a contradiction within the context of racist society and the typical white view of the world. These fundamental shifts in identity perhaps bear as directly on the profession as on the individual consciousness. Recognition of the seat of the problem within white psychologists, rather than anti-racism being a service provided by *black* professionals, might also be a characteristic of the final stage of understanding one's white identity. It is not uncommon for well-meaning initiatives against racism or for multi-culturalism to be based on the black person as the 'expert' on white racism. Take, for instance, the following:

The . . . working party had many hours of discussion and debate on the question of the ethnic composition of the working group, because over a period of a year or more attempts to achieve an appropriate representation in terms of black educationalists and psychologists failed, so that the existing composition of the working group could have been deemed by some individuals as an example of tokenism. Those black educational psychologists who were approached to contribute to the working party either did not turn up to the meetings or refused to do so and in the end the largely white working group decided quite simply to go ahead and set task objectives even in the absence of what they felt was sufficient black representation. (Bryans, 1987, p. 16)

Or from a psychologist reporting on a meeting on multi-cultural communities for educational psychologists:

there was a view that a black E[ducational] P[sychologist] should have been used to introduce the day since this is where the expertise lies. Did the invitation to a white male reflect the inbuilt problem or state of the profession? (Lunt, 1988, p. 78)

Both of these excerpts imply that the problem does not lie with the white psychologists. The blame lies with the non-cooperation or absence of black people who are held to be responsible for solving the problem that white racism has created – just as though the victim of burglary would be a better informant in all regards than the burglar.

An anti-racist profession

A key aspect of anti-racist strategies is raising awareness of the nature, extent, prevalence and pervasiveness of racism in society. Equally important is highlighting the complexities and intricacies of the web of racism. Racism in one institution implicates other institutions or professions. Psychologists working in the health service or the criminal justice system may not contribute directly to racism but they inevitably do so indirectly. To allow, or fail to redress the wrong of, inequality of opportunity and service delivery between black and white employees and clients is racism by omission. On the other hand, tackling racism in one's workplace or profession is likely to have a significant knock-on effect on other parts of the organisation or other professions.

The all-important question is whether psychology, the craft of solutions to human problems, can help eliminate the legacy of racism. The answer ought to be 'yes' but only if the limiting parochial values of Eurocentric psychology change. Bluntly put, to achieve this, psychology has to broaden away from its emphasis on social control; to see a more moral, empowering and liberating role for itself than that of a cornerstone of the *status quo*. Usually this involves psychologists taking a long, hard look at their profession as their route to change.

Resistance to change within psychology

Any programme to challenge established ways will likely be resisted, tooth and nail, by some, especially those with a vested interest in present ways. Psychology's willingness to change is a vital consideration. Change, in the context of this book, requires a realistic understanding of racism, the ability to recognise it and an appreciation of its effects on the discipline. Individual and collective will is required for such a task.

Experience suggests that awareness of racism at the personal level is poor amongst psychologists. This is not to imply that they are unaware of racism as a social issue, but rather to point out that, generally, psychologists' training does not particularly encourage self-examination, especially when racism is concerned. This may be seen as paradoxical in a profession whose members require, in part, to be skilled in their sensitivity to the needs of their clients. But perhaps this failure helps keep the clients in their place, the provision of 'empowering psychotherapy' would rattle the system far too much. Otherwise what is it that stops psychology becoming humanistic and liberating? Schon (1971) has identified two pertinent barriers to institutional change: (a) psychology's alliance with social control; and (b) the 'dynamic conservatism' of the institution of psychology. Considering willingness to alter, Schon argues that the more radical are proposed changes to the *status quo* the more forcefully will they be resisted by social systems. In this vein, Fernando (1989) believes that peripheral change which does not disrupt the entire system would be relatively acceptable compared to something more drastic. Tokenistic gestures often made by institutions in the name of equal opportunities fit in well with this thesis.

Fernando also suggests that change is difficult since altering one part of a system affects the rest of it. In other words, the complex relationships between institutions mean that any planned changes in one are likely to be resisted by other professions who perceive such a change as a threat. Psychology is firmly rooted in universities which have strong conservative traditions, oblivious of the many subtle social changes which occur around them. Changes, initiated by psychology for example, in these institutions may well meet stronger resistance, therefore. This is evinced by Williams *et al.*'s (1989) report of a survey of equal opportunities policies (an important precursor to institutional change) in higher education:

A majority of universities (30 out of 42) and 14 out of 26 polytechnics had barely begun to think about the issues. . . . A tone of moral superiority and complacency plus ignorance on the issues and available evidence was pervasive. (p. 24)

The formulation of an outlook which allows change to take into account the priorities and frustrations of black people is an important precondition for an anti-racist psychology. To be anti-racist, psychologists need to shift their focus from aspects of the individual, and to take on institutions and social structures responsible for their clients' problems. Psychologists aware of and sensitive to black people's needs and circumstances are in no doubt that to provide an effective service they must work to change pathogenic social conditions as well as persons (Bulhan, 1985). This is essentially socio-cultural psychology. Such a perspective follows Ballard's (1979) suggestion that one should go beyond black clients' presenting needs to their social and cultural worlds, their social realities. Racism and racial discrimination constitute the core of the social reality of black people in white social structures. Any programme designed to benefit black people must, therefore, aim to change these structures.

Anti-racist strategies: planning for change

Psychology is a micro-political institution. Absorbing and mirroring the values and beliefs of wider society, it reproduces and influences reality from a European perspective. So comprehensive is allegiance to the European view that to combat racism within the discipline requires diverse strategies. Nevertheless, action for change in wisely chosen aspects of the discipline may well promote changes elsewhere. Fernando (1988) emphasised the following areas as needing attention in our efforts to combat racism within the discipline: research (methodology, conduct and interpretation of findings), editorial policies of journals and other publications, and student and personnel recruitment and training.

To enable psychology to undo the centuries of damage it has done to itself by harming, directly and indirectly, black people throughout the world, Owusu-Bempah and Howitt (1990) suggested a number of steps to be followed by the professional bodies of psychology to combat racism within those institutions and their memberships. With a little imagination, most of them could be used as a basis for an anti-racist strategy by any organisation involved with psychology:

1. Examine policies and practices with special reference to racism and its adverse consequences for its members and clients; the

prioritisation of resources is an important consideration; the publication of anti-racist materials, surveying practitioners and educators about race-related issues, and the like would also add to the information and knowledge base of the institution and its members.

2. Adopt and implement whole-heartedly an equal-opportunities policy – an effective antidote to institutional racism and other inequalities. While those charged with implementing such a policy may be only a small section of the members of an organisation, the process of implementation itself would keep the issue of racism much more in the forefront of all activities within the organisation.

3. Examine the curriculum of psychological education and training to make it more relevant to a multi-cultural society. Such reviews should address questions such as: just what is being taught to undergraduates about race through lectures, textbooks and other means? What anti-racist materials, if any, are being presented to those being trained as professional psychologists? How are they being prepared to meet the needs of their multi-cultural clientele?

4. Evaluate and monitor the professional practice of members; individual members ought to understand their personal role in the creation and maintenance of racism, and how they benefit from racism, in order for them to appreciate their professional and moral duty to combat it.

5. Psychological institutions should be clearly and genuinely committed to racial equality in all aspects of their activities. In part, this might be operationalised as a formal ethical requirement. It is essential that ethics cease to be regarded, for practical purposes, solely as matters of noticeable harm to individuals; the quality of service to clients (including students) warrants equal concern.

6. Join with other organisations to combat racism. This may well be narrowly defined as seeking the aid and assistance of other psychological organisations in a concerted effort against racism, but equally it might be the collaboration with a broader spectrum of organisations adopting an anti-racist stance.

7. Prepare and equip students and practitioners to provide anti-racist services to the multi-cultural/multi-racial society in which they operate. This might necessitate the commissioning of training materials concerned with multi-culturalism. Here collaboration with the medical, educational and other helping professions, in so far as they overlap with the needs of psychologists might prove beneficial.

8. Provide anti-racist resource materials for teachers and practitioners of psychology. This is different from professional training as it involves the general preparation of individuals for the multi-cultural world without being too concerned with the nature of professional

work. Perhaps this is to open a Pandora's box in that it raises the general issue of the level of self-awareness required of professional psychologists.

9. Journal editors need actively to monitor publications for unacceptable racist comments and interpretation of research findings; they should also draw up guidelines to deal with race-related issues. This may clash with the stance of value-free science ethos in psychology. Race is a moral issue transcending narrow scientific considerations. Papers on the adverse effects of racism on black people are uncommon in many mainstream psychological journals (e.g. Howitt and Owusu-Bempah, 1990b). This may be accounted for by the traditions of the journals, the dearth of black editors and reviewers, or that such papers are rarely submitted for publication. In marked contrast, in recent years a number of offensive, fundamentally racist papers have been published. Mainstream journals could benefit from actively soliciting materials on racism and its effects, together with ones generally promoting themes to do with race and culture. Referees should be recruited with a degree of sensitivity on racism and race-related issues.

10. Take the necessary steps to encourage the recruitment of black people to the profession through publicity and educational materials. There is even a case, given the negligible number of black psychologists in some countries, to consider means of helping black people more directly into the profession. While this may be problematic, the availability of bursaries for black people to enter psychological training (a form of positive action) might be the only practicable solution. The different experiences and perspectives brought to the discipline in this way would more than repay the effort required.

Research is an additional area which could benefit from a clearly anti-racist stance. Very often, research on black people is carried out and its findings interpreted in ways which reinforce racist concepts and stereotypes about black people. Thus, to rectify the situation, Fernando (1989) has suggested that it is important that ethical committees which vet proposals for psychological research should have a policy on racial and cultural matters. Obviously having help from professionals or lay individuals with knowledge, experience and sensitivity on racial and cultural issues would be a core strategy. Research projects involving black research participants ought to take into account the effects of racism, overt and covert, on the thinking and activities of the researchers. Care also needs to be taken over the possible social and emotional stress caused the community by the research. Especially in

Europe, there is a lack of research orientated to the major concerns of black people. Fernando (1989) claims that ethical committees tend to stand in the way of such research; researchers who conduct such investigations are frequently misrepresented as being politically motivated.

To implement many of these changes would require recruiting the help of outside consultants or established organisations dealing with racial equality. The process of self-examination is never easy, and unlikely to be smooth in a discipline so historically bedded with racism. Nevertheless we have a moral and professional duty to move in these directions with the ultimate aim of teaching and/or practising a racism-free psychology. Ballard (1979) summarised the obligation thus:

> For the practitioner the question of whether ethnic minorities ought, or ought not, to remain ethnically distinct should be irrelevant. The fact is that they are. Insofar as his specialism, whatever it is, demands that he should take into account the social and cultural worlds in which his clients live, he needs to make a response to ethnic diversity. If he does not, his practice is inadequate in purely professional terms. (p. 164)

This means that although individual psychologists may be unwilling to participate in public campaigns against racism, they have a moral and professional duty at least to ensure that their own actions do not aggravate the inequalities and disadvantages that black people suffer (Rack, 1982).

References

Adorno, T., Frenkel-Brunswik, E., Levinson, D.J., and Sanford, R.N. (1950). *The Authoritarian Personality*. New York: Harper and Row.

Alhibai, Y. (1987). The racist child. *New Society*, 4 December, 13–15.

Allport, G. (1954). *The Nature of Prejudice*. Reading, Mass.: Addison Wesley.

Allport, G. W. (1958). *The Nature Of Prejudice*. New York: Doubleday.

American Psyschological Association (1981). Ethical principles for psychologists. *American psychologist*, 36, 633–8.

American Psychological Association (1992). Ethical principles of psychologists and code of conduct. *American Psychologist*, 47 (12), 1597–611.

American Psychological Association Office of Ethnic Minority Affairs (1993). Guidelines for providers of psychological services to ethnic, linguistic, and culturally diverse populations. *American Psychologist*, 48 (1), 45–8.

Anderson, J. L. (1991). Rushton's racial comprisons: an ecological critique of theory and method. *Canadian Psychology*, 32 (1), 51–60.

Andreasen, N. C., Flaum, M., Swayze, V., O'Leary, Alliger, R., Cohen, G., Ehrhardt, J., and Yuh, W. T. C. (1993). Intelligence and brain structure in normal individuals. *American Journal of Psychiatry*, 150 (1), 130–4.

Ankney, C.D. (1992). Sex differences in relative brain size: the mismeasure of woman, too? *Intelligence*, 16, 329–36.

Antaki, C., Levy, P., Hay, D., Smyth, M., Condor, S., Flude, B. M., Gilmour, J., Bremner, G., Lewis, C., Archer, J., Gathercole, S., Conway, M. A., and Ridgeway, J. (1990). Rushton and race differences. *The Psychologist: Bulletin of the British Psychological Society*, 3 (7), 316.

Apple, M. W., and Christian-Smith, L. K. (1991). 'The politics of the textbook', in M. W. Apple and L. K. Christian-Smith (eds) *The Politics of the Textbook*. New York: Routledge, pp. 1–21.

Asante, M. (1980). *Afrocentricity: Theory of Social Change*. New York: Amulefi Publishing.

Asante, M. (1987). *The Africentric Idea*. Philadelphia: Temple University Press.

Astley, M. (1991). Personalities behind the Gulf opponents. *Leicester Mercury*, 11 January, 38–9.

Atkinson, R. L., Atkinson, R. C., Smith, E. E., Bem, D. J., and Hilgard, E. R. (1990). *Introduction to Psychology* (10th Edn.). San Diego: Harcourt Brace Jovanovich.

Azibo, D. A. (1992). Understanding the proper and improper usage of the comparative research framework, in A.K.H. Burlew, W.C. Banks, H.T. McAdoo and D.A. Azibo (eds), *African American Psychology: Theory, Research and Practice*. California: Sage, pp. 18–27.

Bache, R. (1895). Reaction time with reference to race. *The Psychological Review*, 2, 475–986.

Bagley, C. (1971). Mental illness in immigrants in London. *Journal of Biosocial Science*, 3, 449–59.

Baldwin, J. A. (1979). Theory and research concerning the notion of black self-hatred: a review and reinterpretation. *Journal of Black Psychology*, 5, 51–77.

Baldwin, J. A. (1992). The role of black psychologists in black liberation', in A. K. H. Burlew, W. C. Banks, H. T. McAdoo and D. A. Azibo (eds), *African American Psychology: Theory, Research and Practice*. California: Sage, pp. 48–61.

Ballard, R. (1979). Ethnic minorities and the social services: What type of service?, in V. Khan (ed.) *Minority Families In Britain: Support and Stress*. London: Macmillan, pp. 147–68.

Banks, J. A., and Gramb, J. B. (eds) (1972). *Black Self-Concept: Implications for Education and Social Science*. New York: McGraw Hill.

Banks, W. C., Stitt, K. R., Curtis, H. A., and McQuater, G. V. (1977). Perceived objectivity and the effects of evaluative reinforcement upon compliance and self-evaluation in Blacks. *Journal of Experimental Social Psychology*, 13, 452–63.

Bannister, R.C. (1979). *Social Darwinism: Science and Myth in Anglo-American Social Thought*. Philadelphia: Temple University Press.

Banton, M. (1986). Epistemological assumptions in the study of racial differentiation, in J. Rex and D. Mason (eds), *Theories of Race and Ethnic Relations*. Cambridge: Cambridge University Press, pp. 42–63.

Barker, M. (1981). *The New Racism: Conservatives and the Ideology of the Tribe*. London: Junction Books.

BBC TV. (1983). *Black*. Tuesday Documentary. London: BBC.

Bean, R. B. (1906). Some racial peculiarities of the negro brain. *American Journal of Anatomy*, 5, 353–415.

Beckham, A. S. (1929). Is the negro happy? A psychological analysis. *Journal of Abnormal and Social Psychology*, 24, 186–90.

Beckham, A. S. (1934). A study of race attitude in negro children of adolescent age. *Journal of Abnormal and Social Psychology*, 29, 18–29.

Ben-Tovim, G., Gabriel, J., Law, I., and Stredder, K. (1986). A political analysis of local political equality, in J. Rex and D. Mason (eds), *Theories of Race and Ethnic Relations*. Cambridge: Cambridge University Press, pp. 131–56.

Bender, M. P. (1990). The ethnic composition of clinical psychology in Britain. *The Psychologist: Bulletin of the British Psychological Society*, 3 (6), 250–2.

Berkowitz, L., and Geen, R. G. (1966). Film violence and the cue properties of available targets. *Journal of Personality and Social Psychology*, 3, 525–30.

Berkowitz, L., and Rawlings, E. (1963). Effects of film violence on inhibitions against subsequent aggression. *Journal of Abnormal and Social Psychology*, 66, 405–12.

Bernard, J. (1966). *Marriage and Family Among Negroes*. Englewood Cliffs, N.J.: Prentice Hall.

Berne, E. (1964). *Games People Play*. New York: Grove.

Berne, E. (1972). *What Do You Say After You Say Hello?* New York: Grove Press.

Berry, B. (1958). *Race and Ethnic Relations*. Cambridge: Riverside Press.

Berry, J. W. (1983). The sociogenesis of social sciences: an analysis of the cultural relativity of social psychology, in B. Brain (ed.), *The Sociogenesis of Language and Human Conduct*. New York: Plenum, pp. 449–58.

Bethleim, B. (1943). Individual and mass behavior in extreme situations. *Journal of Abnormal and Social Psychology*, 38, 417–52.

Biesheuvel, S. (1943). *African Intelligence*. Johannesburg: Institute of Race Relations.

Biesheuvel, S. (1958). Objectives and methods of African psychological research. *The Journal of Social Psychology*, 47, 161–8.

Biesheuvel, S. (1987). Psychology: science and politics. Theoretical developments and applications in a plural society. *South African Journal of Psychology*, 17 (1), 1–8.

Billig, M. (1976). *Social Psychology and Intergroup Relations*. London: Academic Press.

Billig, M. (1978). *Fascists: A Social Psychological View of the National Front*. Academic Press: London.

Billig, M. (1979). *Psychology, Racism and Fascism*. Birmingham: A.F. and R. Publications.

Billig, M. (1981). *L'Internationale raciste*. Paris: Masperon.

Billig, M. (1982). *Ideology and Social Psychology*. Oxford: Blackwell.

Bishop, L. K. (1946). Democracy demands cooperative living. *Education*, LXVIII, 12–18.

Black, D. (Chairman) (1980). *Inequalities in Health: Report of A Research Working Group*. London: Department of Health and Social Security.

Bogardus, E. S. (1928). *Immigration and Race Attitudes*. Boston: Heath.

Bolton, P. (1984). Management of compulsorily admitted patients to a high security unit. *International Journal of Social Psychiatry*, 30 (1–2), 77–84.

Booker, R., Hart, M., Moreland, D., and Powell, J. (1989). Struggling towards better practice: a psychological service team and anti-racism. *Educational Psychology in Practice*, October, 123–9.

Boring, E. G. (1950). *A History of Experimental Psychology*. New York: Appleton-Century-Crofts.

Boyd-Franklin, N. (1991). Recurrent themes in the treatment of African-American women in group psychotherapy. *Women and Therapy*, 11 (2), 25–40.

Bracken, H. (1973). Essence, accident and race. *Hermathena*, CXVI, 88–95.

Bramel, D., and Friend, R. (1981). Hawthorne, the myth of the docile worker, and class bias in psychology. *American Psychologist*, 36 (8), 867–78.

Brantley, T. (1983). Racism and its impact on psychotherapy. *American Journal of Psychiatry*, 140 (12), 1605–8.

Brazziel, W. F. (1973). White research in black communities: when solutions become a part of the problem. *Journal of Social Issues*, 29 (1), 41–4.

Breakwell, G. M. (1989). *Facing Physical Violence*. Leicester: British Psychological Society.

Breakwell, G., and Davy, G. (1990). Rushton and race differences. *The Psychologist: Bulletin of the British Psychological Society*, 3 (7), 318.

Brehm, S. S., and Kassin, S. M. (1990). *Social Psychology*. Boston: Houghton Mifflin.

British Medical Journal (1993). Deception in research and racial discrimination in medicine. *British Medical Journal*, 365, 668–9.

British Psychological Society (1988a). A resolution on apartheid. *The Psychologist: Bulletin of the British Psychological Society*, 2 (8), 328.

British Psychological Society (1988b). Guidelines for the use of non-sexist language. *The Psychologist: Bulletin of the British Psychological Society*, 1 (2) 53–4.

British Psychological Society (1989). *How About Psychology?: A Guide to Courses and Careers*. Leicester: British Psychological Society.

Brittan, A., and Maynard, M. (1984). *Sexism, Racism and Oppression*. Oxford: Blackwell

Brogden, A. (1981). 'SUS' is dead: but what about 'SAS'? *New Community*, 9, 44–52.

Broome, R. (1982). *Aboriginal Australians: Black Response to White Dominance 1788–1980*. Sydney: George Allen and Unwin.

Brown, A., Goodwin, B. J., Hall, B. A., and Jackson-Lowman, H. (1985). A review of psychology of women textbooks: focus on the Afro-American woman. *Psychology of Women Quarterly*, 9 (1), 29–38.

Brown, C. (1984). *Black and White Britain: the Third Policy Studies Institute Survey*. London: PSI/Heinemann.

Brown, C., and Gray, P. (1985). *Racial Discrimination: Seventeen Years after the Act*. London: PSI.

Brown, G. A. (1973). An exploratory study of interaction amongst British and immigrant children. *British Journal of Social and Clinical Psychology*, 12, 159–62.

Brown, K. (1985). Turning a blind eye: racial oppression and the unintended consequence of white 'non-racism'. *Sociological Review*, 33, 670–90.

Brown, K. M. (1986). Keeping their distance: the cultural production and reproduction of 'racist non-racism'. *Australian and New Zealand Journal of Sociology*, 22 (3), 387–98.

Brown, L. S. (1991). Antiracism as an ethical imperative: an example from feminist therapy. *Ethics and Behavior*, 1 (2), 113–27.

Bryans, T. (1987). Educational psychologists working in multicultural communities: an analysis. *Educational and Child Psychology*, 5 (2), 8–18.

Bulhan, H. A. (1981). Psychological research in Africa: genesis and function. *Race and Class*, XXIII (1), 25–41.

Bulhan, H. A. (1985). *Frantz Fanon and the Psychology of Oppression*. Boston: Boston University Press.

Burman, L. H. (1988). Anti-racist policy development in Manchester School Psychological and Child Guidance Service (SPCGS). *Educational and Child Psychology*, 5 (2), 38–43.

Burns, A. (1948). *Colour Prejudice: With Particular Reference to the Relationship Between Whites and Negroes*. London: Allen and Unwin.

Burstein, P., and Pitchford, S. (1990). Social-scientific and legal challenges to education and test requirements in employment. *Social Problems*, 37 (2), 243–57.

Burt, C. (1937). *The Backward Child*. London: University of London Press.

Cain, D. P., and Vanderwolf, C. H. (1990). A critique of Rushton on race, brain size and intelligence. *Personality and Individual Differences*, 11 (8), 777–84.

Cain, M. (1973). *Society and the Policeman's Role*. London, Routledge.

Carothers, J. C. (1951). Frontal lobe function and the African. *Journal of Mental Science*, 97, 12–48.

Carothers, J. C. (1953). *The African Mind in Health and Disease: A Study in Ethnopsychiatry*. World Health Organization monograph no. 17. Geneva: World Health Organisation.

Carothers, J. C. (1972). *The mind of man in Africa*. London: Stacey.

Carpenter, L., and Brockington, I. F. (1980). A study of mental illness in Asians, West Indians and Africans living in Manchester. *British Journal of Psychiatry*, 137, 201–5.

Carroll, H. C. M. (1988). Training educational psychologists for working in multicultural communities: what are training courses in England and Wales doing? *Educational and Child Psychology*, 5 (2), 57–61.

Cashmore, E. (1979). *Rastaman: The Rastafarian Movement in England*. London: Allen and Unwin.

Cashmore, E. E. (1987). *The Logic of Racism*. London: Allen and Unwin.

Chase, A. (1977). *The Legacy of Malthus: The Social Costs of the New Scientific Racism*. New York: Alfred A. Knopf.

Chase, A. (1980). *The Legacy of Malthus: The Social Costs of the New Scientific Racism*. Urbana: University of Illinois Press.

Chomsky, N. (1976). *Reflections on Language*. London: Temple Smith.

Chomsky, N, (1979). *Language and Responsibility*. Hemel Hempstead: Harvester Wheatsheaf.

Clark, J. (1986). *For Richer for Poorer: Western Connections with World Hunger*. Oxford: Oxfam.

Clark, K. B. (1965). *Dark Ghetto: Dilemmas of Social Power*. New York: Harper and Row.

Clark, K. B., and Clark, M. (1939). The development of the consciousness of self and emergence of racial identity in Negro pre-school children. *Journal of Social Psychology*, 10, 591–9.

Clark, K. B., and Clark, M. (1947). Racial identification and preference in Negro children, in T. M. Newcomb and E. L. Hartley (eds), *Readings in Social Psychology*; New York: Holt, Rinehart and Winston, pp. 602–11.

Coard, B. (1971). *How the West Indian Child is Made Educationally Sub-Normal in the British School System*. London: New Beacon Books/The Caribbean Education and Community Coworkers Association.

Cochrane, R. (1977). Mental illness in immigrants in England and Wales: an analysis of mental hospital admissions, 1971. *Social Psychiatry*, 12, 25–35.

Cochrane, R. (1990). Rushton and race differences. *The Psychologist: Bulletin of the British Psychological Society*, 3 (7), 316.

Coggan, G. (1981). Prison staff wear union jack badges. *Searchlight*, November.

Coggan, G, and Walker, M. (1982). *Frightened For My Life: An Account of Deaths in British Prisons*. Fontana.

Commission for Racial Equality (1983). *Ethnic Minority Hospital Staff*. London: Commission for Racial Equality.

Commission for Racial Equality (1984). *Code of Practice in Employment*. London: Commission for Racial Equality.

Commission for Racial Equality (1987a). *Racial Attacks: A Survey in Eight Areas in Britain*. London: Commission for Racial Equality.

Commission for Racial Equality (1987b). *Living in Terror: A Report on Racial Violence and Harassment in Housing*. London: Commission for Racial Equality.

Commission for Racial Equality (1987c). *Employment of Graduates from Ethnic Minorities: A Research Report*. London: Commission for Racial Equality.

Commission for Racial Equality (1987d). *Overseas Doctors: Experience and Expectations: A Research Study*. London: Commission for Racial Equality.

Commission for Racial Equality (1988a). *Learning in Terror: A Survey of Racial Harassment in Schools and Colleges*. London: Commission for Racial Equality.

Commission for Racial Equality (1988b). *Medical School Admission: A Report of a Formal Investigation into St. George's Hospital Medical School*. London: Commission for Racial Equality.

Commission for Racial Equality (1988c). *Ethnic Minority Shool Teachers: A Survey in Eight Local Education Authorities*. London: Commission for Racial Equality.

Commission for Racial Equality (1991). *CRE Annual Report 1991*. London: Commission for Racial Equality.

Condor, S. (1986). 'sex role beliefs and 'traditional' women: feminist and intergroup perspectives, in S. Wilkinson (ed.) *Feminist Social Psychology: Developing Theory and Practice*. Milton Keynes: Open University Press, pp. 97–118.

Condor, S. (1988). 'Race stereotypes' and racist discourse. *Text*, 8, 69–90.

Connolly, K. (1985). Can there be a psychology for the Third World? *Bulletin of the British Psychological Society*, 38, 249–57.

Cook, N., and Kono, S. (1977). Black psychology: the third great generation. *The Journal of Black Psychology*, 3, 18–28.

Cooley, C. H. (1902) *Human Nature and Social Order*. New York: Scribner.

Cooper, R. (1986). Race, disease and health, in T. Rathwell and D. Philips (eds), *Health, Race and Ethnicity*. London: Croom Helm, pp. 21–79.

Cooper, S. (1973). A look at racism in clinical work. *Social Casework*, 54, 76–84.

Cope, R. (1989). The compulsory detention of Afro-Caribbeans under the Mental Health Act. *New Community*, 15, 343–56.

Corvin, S. A., and Wiggins, F. (1989). An antiracism training model for white professionals. *Journal of Multicultural Counseling and Development*, 17, 105–14.

Cowlishaw, G. (1986). Race for exclusion. *Australian and New Zealand Journal of Sociology*, 22 (1), 3–24.

Cox, O. C. (1948). *Caste, Class and Race*. New York: Monthly Review Press.

Crawford, C., Smith, M., and Krebs, D. (eds) (1987). *Sociobiology: Ideas, Issues, and Applications*. Hillsdale, New Jersey: Lawrence Erlbaum Associaties.

Crosby, F., Bromley, S., and Saxe, L. (1980). Recent unobtrusive studies of black and white discrimination and prejudice: a literature review. *Psychological Bulletin*, 87 (3), 546–63.

Crow, I. (1987). Black people and criminal justice in the UK. *Howard Journal Criminal Justice*, 26, 303–14.

Cunningham, M. R., and Barbee, A. P. (1991). Differential K-selection versus ecological determinants of race differences in sexual behavior. *Journal of Research in Personality*, 25 (2), 205–17.

Currer, C. (1984). Pathan women in Bradford – Factors affecting mental health with particular reference to the effects of racism. *International Journal of Social Psychiatry*, 30 (1–2), 73–6.

Curtin, P. D. (1965). *The Image of Africa*. London: Macmillan.

Curvier, G. (1927). *The Animal Kingdom*. Quoted in P. D. Curtin, (1965). *The Image of Africa*. London: Macmillan, p. 231.

Da-Cocodia, L. (1984). The probable effects of racism in nursing and related disciplines. *International Journal of Social Psychiatry*, 30 (1–2), 17–21.

Dalal, F. (1988). Jung: a racist. *British Journal of Psychotherapy*, 4 (3), 263–79.

Dana, R. H. (1987). Training for professional psychology: science, practice, and identity. *Professional Psychology: Research and Practice*, 18 (1), 9–16.

D'Andrea, M., Daniels, J., and Heck, R. (1991). Evaluating the impact of mulicultural counseling training. *Journal of Counseling and Development*, 70, 143–50.

Daniel, W. W. (1968). *Racial Discrimination in England*. Harmondsworth: Penguin.

Datcher, E., Savage, J. E., and Checkosky, S. F. (1973). School type, grade, sex, and race of experimenter as determinants of the racial preference and awareness in black and white children. *Proceedings of the 81st Annual Conference of the American Psychological Association*, 8, 223–4.

Davey, A. (1983). *Learning to be Prejudiced*. London: Edward Arnold.

Davidson, B. (1984). *The Story of Africa*. London: Mitchell Beazley.

Davis, A. (1981). *Women, Race and Class*. New York: Random House.

Dawes, A. (1985). Politics and mental health: the position of clinical psychology in South Africa. *South African Journal of Psychology*, 15 (2), 55–61.

Dawes, A. (1992). Psychotherapy with political activists: reflections on some South African experiences. *Changes*, 10 (2), 82–9.

Dawson, J. L. M. (1969). Exchange theory and comparison level changes among Australian aborigines. *British Journal of Social and Clinical Psychology*, 8, 133–40.

Dean, G., Walsh, D., Downing, H., and Shelley, E. (1981). First admissions of native born and immigrants to psychiatric hospital in south-east England, 1976. *British Journal of Psychiatry*, 30, 41–9.

Dean, G., Walsh, D., Downing, H., and Shelley, E. (1981). First admissions of native-born and immigrants to psychiatric hospitals in south-east England, 1970. *British Journal of Psychiatry*, 139, 506–12.

Degler, C. (1991). *In Search of Human Nature: The Decline and Revival of Darwinism in American Social Thought*. New York: Oxford University Press.

Desforges, M. F., Goodwin, C., and Kerr, A. (1985). Do you work in a subtly racist psychological service? *Educational Psychology in Practice*, 1 (1), April, 10–13.

Devine, P. G. (1989). Stereotypes and prejudice: their automatic and controlled components. *Journal of Personality and Social Psychology*, 56 (1), 5–18.

Dobbins, J. E., and Skillings, J. H. (1991). The utility of race labeling in understanding cultural identity: a conceptual tool for the social science practitioners. *Journal of Counseling and Development*, 70, 37–44.

Dolan, B., Polley, K., Allen, R., and Norton, K. (1991). Addressing racism in psychiatry: is the therapeutic model applicable? *International Journal of Social Psychiatry*, 37 (2), 71–91.

Dollard, J. (1937). *Caste and Class in a Southern Town*. New York: Doubleday Anchor.

Dominelli, L. (1989). An uncaring profession? an examination of racism in social work. *New Community*, 15, 391–401.

Doob, L. (1960). *Becoming More Civilised: A Psychological Exploration*. New Haven: Yale University Press.

Dovidio, J. F., and Gaertner, S. L. (1983). Race, normative structure and help-seeking, in B. M. DePaulo, A. Nadler and J. D. Fisher (eds) (1983). *New directions in helping*, 2, 285–302.

Doyal, L., Gee, F., and Hunt, G. (1980). *Migrant Workers in the NHS: A Report to the SSRC*. London: Polytechnic of North London.

du Preez, P. (1980). *Social Psychology of Politics: Ideology and the Human Image*. Oxford: Blackwell.

Dummett, A. (1984). *A Portrait of English Racism*. London: Caraf.

Duncan, B. L. (1976). Differential social perceptions and attributions of intergroup violence testing the lower limits of stereotyping blacks. *Journal of Personality and Social Psychology*, 34, 590–8.

Eckhardt, W. (1988). *Political Psychology*, 9 (4), 681–91.

Eckholm, E. (1982). Human wants and misused lands. *Natural History*, 9 (1), 33–48.

Eiser, J. R., and Roiser, M. J. (1972). The sampling of social attitudes: comments on Eysencks' 'social attitudes and social class'. *British Journal of Social and Clinical Psychology*, 11, 397–401.

Esmail, A. and Everington, S. (1993). Racial discrimination against doctors from ethnic minorities. *British Medical Journal*, 306, 691–2.

Essed, P. (1987). *Academic Racism: Common Sense in the Social Sciences*. Centre for Race and Ethnic Studies, University of Amsterdam, Working Paper no. 5.

Etzioni, A. (1968). A model of significant research. *British Journal of Psychiatry*, 6, 279–80.

Eysenck, H. J. (1953). *Uses and Abuses of Psychology*. Harmondsworth: Penguin.

Eysenck, H. J. (1964). *Crime and Personality*. London: Routledge and Kegan Paul.

Eysenck, H. J. (1965). *Fact and Fiction in Psychology*. Harmondsworth: Penguin.

Eysenck, H. J. (1971). *Race, Intelligence and Education*. London: Temple Smith.

Eysenck, H. J. (1973; 1975a, second edition). *The Inequality of Man*. Glasgow: Fontana/Collins.

Eysenck, H. J. (1975b). Social attitudes and social class. *British Journal of Social and Clinical Psychology*, 14, 323–31.

Eysenck, H. J. (1976). After Burt. *New Scientist*, 72, 488.

Eysenck, H. J. (1977). The case of Sir Cyril Burt. *Encounter*, 48, 19–24.

Eysenck, H. J. (1991). Introduction: science and racism, in R. Pearson (ed.), *Race, Intelligence and Bias in Academe*. Washington D.C.: Scott-Townsend, pp. 16–55.

Fairchild, H. H. (1991). Scientific racism: the cloak of objectivity. *Journal of Social Issues*, 47 (3), 101–15.

Fanon, F. (1967). *Black Skin, White Masks*. London: Pluto Press.

Faranda, J. A., and Gaertner, S. L. (1979). The effects of inadmissible evidence introduced by the prosecution and the defense, and the defendant's race on the verdicts of high and low authoritarians. Paper presented at the annual meeting of the Eastern Psychological Association, New York.

Quoted by S. L. Gaertner and J. F. Dovidio in J. F. Dovidio and S. L. Gaertner (eds) (1986). *Prejudice, Discrimination and Racism*. New York: Academic Press, 61–89.

Fatkmilehin, I., Ricard, W., Flintoff, R., Diamond, B., Fatimilehin, I., Jones, H., Swartz, A., and Bostock, J. (1990). Rushton and race differences. *The Psychologist: Bulletin of the British Psychological Society*, 3 (10), 451–2.

Fernando, S. (1988). *Race and Culture in Psychiatry*. London: Croom Helm.

Fernando, S. (1989). *Race, Culture and Psychiatry*. London: Routledge.

Fernando, S. (1991). Racial stereotypes. *British Journal of Psychiatry*, 158, 289–90.

Figes, E. (1970). *Patriarchal Attitudes*. London: Faber.

Finison, L. J. (1986). The psychological insurgency: 1936–1945. *Journal of Social Issues*, 42 (1), 21–33.

Fletcher, R. (1991). *Science, Ideology and the Media: The Cyril Burt Scandal*. London: Transaction.

Flynn, J. R. (1980). *Race, IQ and Jensen*. London: Routledge and Kegan Paul.

Flynn, J. R. (1989). Rushton, evolution, and race: an essay on intelligence and virtue. *The Psychologist: Bulletin of the British Psychological Society*, 9, 963–6.

Flynn, J. R. (1990). Rushton and race differences. *The Psychologist: Bulletin of the British Psychological Society*, 3 (10), 450.

Foster, D., Nicholas, L., and Dawes, A. (1993). Psychology in South Africa: a reply to Raubenheimer. *The Psychologist: Bulletin of the British Psychological Society*, 6 (4), 172–4.

Foster-Carter, O. (1986). Insiders, outsiders and anomalies: a review of studies of identity. *New Community*, 13, 224–34.

Fox, D. and Jordan, V. B. (1973). Racial preference and identification of black American Chinese and white children. *Genetic Psychological Monographs*, 88, 229–86.

Franklin, V. P. (1980). Black social scientists and the mental testing movement, 1920–1940, in R. L. Jones (ed.), *Black Psychology* (2nd edn). New York: Harper and Row, pp. 201–15.

Frazier, E.F. (1947). *The Negro Family in the United States*. Chicago: University of Chicago Press.

Freire, P. (1972). *Pedagogy of the Oppressed*. Harmondsworth: Penguin.

Freud, S. (1905). *Jokes and their Relation to the Unconscious*. New York: Moffatt.

Freud, S. (1950, first published 1913). *Totem and Taboo: Some Points of Agreement between the Mental Lives of Savages and Neurotics*. London: Routledge and Kegan Paul.

Frosh, S. (1993). The seeds of masculine sexuality, in J. M. Ussher and C. D. Baker (eds), *Psychological Perspectives on Sexual Problems: New Directions in Theory and Practice*. London: Routledge, pp. 41–55.

Gaertner, S. L. (1976). Non-reactive measures in racial attitude research: a focus on 'liberals', in P. A. Katz (ed.) (1976). *Towards the elimination of racism*. New York: Pergamon Press, 183–211.

Gaertner, S. L., and Dovidio, J. F. (1986). The aversive form of racism, in J. Dovidio and S. Gaertner (eds), *Prejudice, Discrimination, and Racism*. London: Academic Press, pp. 61–89.

Gale, A. (1993). Do we need to think a bit more about ethical issues?

The British Psychological Society: Social Psychology Section Newsletter, 29 (Summer), 23–8.

Galton, F. (1869). *The Hereditary Genius: An Inquiry Into Its Laws and Consequences*. London: MacMillan.

Gary, L. E. (1981). Health status, in L.E. Gary (ed.), *Black Men*. Beverly Hills: Sage, pp. 47–71.

Gary, L. E. (ed.) (1981). *Black Men*. Beverly Hills: Sage.

Gelles, R. J., and Straus, M. E. (1979). Determinants of violence in the family: towards a theoretical investigation', in W. R. Burr (ed.), *Contemporary Theories about the Family*. New York: Free Press, pp. 549–81.

Gerber, M. (1958). The psycho-motor development of African children in the first year, and the influence of maternal behavior. *The Journal of Social Psychology*, 47, 185–95.

Gergen, K. (1985). The social constructionist movement in modrn psychology. *American Psychologist*, 40 (3), 266–75.

Gerrard, N. (1991). Racism and sexism, together, in counselling: three women of colour tell their stories. *Canadian Journal of Counselling*, 24 (4), 555–66.

Geuter, U. (1987). German psychology during the Nazi period, in M. G. Ash and W. R. Woodward (eds), *Psychology in Twentieth-Century Thought and Society*. Cambridge: Cambridge University Press.

Gilbert, D. T., and Hixon, J. G. (1991). The trouble with thinking: activation and application of stereotypic beliefs. *Journal of Personality and Social Psychology*, 60 (4), 509–17.

Gilroy, P. (1983). *White Law*. London: Pluto Press.

Gilroy, P. (1987). *There ain't no Black in the Union Jack*. London: Hutchinson.

Gilroy, P. (1990). One nation under a groove: the cultural politics of 'race' and racism in Britain, in D. T. Goldberg (ed.), *Anatomy of Racism*. Minneapolis: Minnesota University Press; pp. 263–82.

Goldberg, D., and Hodes, M. (1992). The poison of racism and the self-poisoning of adolescents. *Journal of Family Therapy*, 14, 51–67.

Goldstein, B. L., and Patterson, P. O. (1988). Turning back the title VII clock: the resegregation of the American work force through validity generalization. *Journal of Vocational Behavior*, 33, 452–62.

Gordon, P. (1983). *White Law: Racism in the Police, Courts and Prisons*. London: Pluto Press.

Gordon, P. (1986). *Racial Violence and Harassment*. Runnymede research report. London: The Runnymede Trust.

Gordon, P. (1989). *Citizenship For Some? Race and Government Policy 1979–1989*. London: The Runnymede Trust.

Gordon, P., and Klug, F. (1986). *New Right New Racism*. London: Searchlight.

Gould, S. J. (1981). *The Mismeasure of Man*. New York: W.W. Norton.

Graham, S. (1992). 'Most of the subjects were white and middle class': trends in published research on African Americans in selected APA journals, 1970–1989. *American Psychologist*, 47 (5), 629–39.

Greenspan, M. (1983). *A New Approach to Women and Therapy*. New York: McGraw-Hill.

Greenwald, H. J., and Oppenheim, D. B. (1968). Reported magnitude of self-misidentification among negro children: artefact? *Journal of Personality and Social Psychology*, 8, 49–52.

Griffith, E. E. H., and Griffith, E. J. (1986). Racism, psychological injury, and compensatory damages. *Hospital and Community Psychiatry*, 37 (1), 71–8.

Guthrie, R. (1976). *Even the Rat was White: A Historical View of Psychology.* New York: Harper and Row.

Hale, J. (1982). *Black Children: Their Root, Culture and Learning Styles.* Provo, Utah: Brigham Young University Press.

Hall, S., Crilcher, C., Jefferson, T., Clarke, J., and Roberts, B. (1978). *Policing the Crisis: Mugging, the State and Law and Order.* London: Macmillan.

Halstead, B. (1990). Rushton and race differences. *The Psychologist: Bulletin of the British Psychological Society,* 3 (10), 451.

Halstead, M. (1988). *Education, Justice and Cultural Diversity: An Examination of the Honeyford Affair, 1984–85.* London: The Falmer Press.

Hanauske-Abel, H. M. (1986). From Nazi holocaust to nuclear holocaust: a lesson to learn. *The Lancet,* 2 August, 2271–3.

Hankins-McNary, L. D. (1979). The effect of institutional racism on the therapeutic relationship. *Perspectives in Psychiatric Care,* 17 (1), 25–30.

Hardiman, R. (1979). *White identity development theory.* Unpublished manuscript.

Harris, B. (1986). Reviewing 50 years of the psychology of social issues. *Journal of Social Issues,* 42 (1), 1–20.

Harrison, G., Ineichen, B., Smith, J., and Morgan, H. G. (1984). Psychiatric hospital admissions in Bristol: 2. social and clinical aspects of compulsory admission. *British Journal of Psychiatry,* 145, 605–11.

Harrison, G., Owens, D., Holton, A., Neilson, D., and Boot, D. (1988). A prospective study of severe mental disorder in Afro-Caribbean patients. *Psychological Medicine,* 18, 643–57.

Hartmann, P., and Husband, C. (1972). The mass media and racial conflict, in D. McQuail (ed.), *Sociology of Mass Communication.* Harmondsworth: Penguin, pp. 435–55.

Hartmann, P., and Husband, C. (1974). *Racism and the Mass Media: A Study of the Role of the Mass Media in the Formation of White Beliefs and Attitudes in Britain.* London: Davies-Poynter.

Haskell, R. E. (1986). Social cognition, language, and the non-conscious expression of racial ideology. *Imagination, Cognition and Personality,* 6 (1), 75–97.

Haskins, E. W. (1984). Black: defiance, sensationalism and disaster. *ETC,* 41 (4), 398–401.

Haward, L. R. C., and Roland, W. A. (1954). Some inter-cultural differences in the Draw-a-Person test: part I, Goodenough Scores. *Man,* 54, 86–8.

Haward, L. R. C., and Roland, W. A. (1955). Some inter-cultural difference on the Draw-a-Person test: part II. *Man,* 55, 27–9.

Hayes, P. (1980). The contribution of British intellectuals to fascism, in K. Lunn and R. C. Thurlow (eds), *British Fascism,* London: Croom Helm, pp. 168–86.

Hayes, W. A. (1980). Radical black behaviorism, in R.L. Jones (ed.), *Black Psychology* (2nd edn). New York: Harper and Row, pp. 37–47.

Hearnshaw, L. S. (1979). *Cyril Burt, Psychologist.* London: Hodder and Stoughton.

Hearnshaw, L. S. (1990). The Burt affair – a rejoinder. *The Psychologist: Bulletin of the British Psychological Society,* 3 (2), 61–4.

Hegel, G. W. F. (1894). *Philosophy of Mind.* Oxford: Clarendon Press

Heiss, J., and Owen, S. (1972). Self-evaluation of blacks and whites. *American Journal of Sociology,* 78, 360–9.

Hewstone, M., and Giles, H. (1984). Intergroup conflict, in A. Gale, and A. J. Chapman (eds), *Psychology and Social Problems*. Chichester: Wiley, pp. 275–95.

Hicks, C. (1982). Racism in nursing. *Nursing Times*, 5 May, 743–8.

Hill, R. B. (1972). *The Strength of Black Families*. New York: Emerson Hall.

Hinds, L. (1978). Illusions of justice: human rights in the United States. Cited by R. D. Townsey (1981). The incarceration of black men, in L. E. Gary (ed.). *Black Men*. Beverly Hills: Sage, pp. 229–56.

Hodge, J. L. (1990). Equality: beyond dualism and oppression, in D. T. Goldberg (ed.), *Anatomy of Racism*. Minneapolis: Minnesota University Press, pp. 89–107.

Home Affairs Committee (1986). *Racial Attacks and Harassment*. London: HMSO.

Home Affairs Select Committee (1989). *Racial Attacks and Harassment*. London: HMSO.

Home Office. (1981). *Racial Attacks: Report of the Home Office Study*. London: HMSO.

Home Office (1986). The ethnic origin of prisoners: the prison population on 30th June 1985 and persons received July 1984 – March 1985. *Statistical Bulletin* 17/86. London: HMSO.

Honeyford, R. (1983a). Multi-ethnic intolerance. *The Salisbury Review*, 4, Summer, 12–13.

Honeyford, R. (1983b). When east is west. *Times Educational Supplement*, 2 September, 19b.

Honeyford, R. (1984) Education and race – an alternative view. *The Salisbury Review*, 6 (winter), 30–2.

Honeyford, R. (1986). Anti-racist rhetoric, in F. Palmer (ed.), *Anti-Racism – an Assault on Education and Value*. London: Sherwood Press, pp. 43–56.

Howard, G. S. (1985). The role of values in the science of psychology. *American Psychologist*, 40 (3), 255–65.

Howitt, D. (1991). *Concerning Psychology: Psychology Applied to Social Issues*. Milton Keynes: Open University Press.

Howitt, D. (1993). Racist psychology where? *The Psychologist: Bulletin of the British Psychological Society*, 6 (5), 202–3.

Howitt, D., and Owusu-Bempah, J. (1990a). Emergent racism in psychologists' texts: a test of the reflexivity hypothesis. Unpublished manuscript, Department of Social Sciences, Loughborough University.

Howitt, D., and Owusu-Bempah, J. (1990b). Racism in a British journal? *The Psychologist: Bulletin of the British Psychological Society*, 3 (9), 396–400.

Howitt, D., and Owusu-Bempah, J. (1990c). The pragmatics of institutional racism: Beyond words. *Human Relations*, 43, 885–9.

Hraba, J., and Grant, J. (1970). Black is beautiful: a reexamination of racial preference and identification. *Journal of Personality and Social Psychology*, 16, 398–402.

Hudson, B. (1989). Discrimination and disparity: the influence of race on sentencing. *New Community*, 16, 23–34.

Hughes, J. (1982). *Ethnic Minorities and Health Care in London*. London: King's Fund.

Husband, C. (1982). *'Race' in Britain*. London: Hutchinson.

Ineichen, B. (1986). Compulsory admission to psychiatric hospital under the 1959 Mental Health Act: the experience of ethnic minorities. *New Community*, 13, 86–93.

Jackson, A. M. (1990). Evolution of ethnocultural psychotherapy. *Psychotherapy*, 27 (3), 428–35.

James, G. (1954). *Stolen Legacy*. New York: Philosophical Library.

Jefferson, T. (1988). Race, crime and policing: empirical, theoretical and methodological issues. *International Journal of the Sociology of Law*, 16, 521–39.

Jenkins, A. H. (1989). The liberating value of constructionism for minorities. *Humanistic Psychology*, 17 (2), 161–8.

Jensen, A. R. (1969). How much can we boost IQ and scholastic achievement? *Harvard Educational Review*, 39, 1–123.

Jensen, A. R. (1985). Methodological and statistical techniques for the chronometric study of mental abilities, in C. R. Reynolds and V. L. Willson (eds), *Methodological and Statistical Advances in the Study of Individual Differences*. New York: Plenum, pp. 51–116.

Jensen, A. R. (1992). Scientific fraud or false accusations? the case of Cyril Burt, in D. J. Miller and M. Hersen (eds), *Research Fraud in the Behavioral and Biomedical Sciences*. New York: Wiley, pp. 97–124.

Johnson, H. M. (1993). The life of a black scientist. *Scientific American*, 268 (1), 132.

Jones, H. (1981). *Bad Blood: The Tuskegee Syphilis Experiment*. New York: Free Press.

Jones, J. M. (1972). *Prejudice and Racism*. Reading, Mass.: Addison Wesley.

Jones, J. M. (1983). The concept of race in social psychology: from color to culture, in L. Wheeler, and P. Shaver (eds), *Review of Personality and Social Psychology: 4*. Beverly Hills: Sage, pp. 117–50.

Joseph, G. G., Reddy, V., and Searle-Chatterjee, M. (1990) Eurocentrism in the social sciences. *Race and Class*, 31 (4), 1–26.

Joyce, J. (1988). The development of an anti-racist policy in Leeds. *Educational and Child Psychology*, 5 (2), 44–50.

Joynson, R. B. (1989). *The Burt Affair*. London: Routledge.

Joynson, R. B. (1990). The Burt affair – a reply. *The Psychologist: Bulletin of the British Psychological Society*, 3 (2), 65–8.

Jung, C. G. (1920). *Collected Works of C.G. Jung*, vol. 10: *Civilization in Transition*. Princeton University Press.

Jung, C. G. (1921). *Collected Works of C.G. Jung*. Princeton University Press.

Jung, C. G. (1930). Your Negroid and Indian behavior. *Forum*, 83, 193–199.

Jung, C. G. (1963). *Memories, Dreams and Reflections*. London: Collins and Sons.

Kadushin, L. (1972). The racial factor in the interview. *Social Work*, 17, 82–7.

Kamin, L. (1981). *Intelligence: The Battle For the Mind, H. J. Eysenck versus Leon Kamin*. London: MacMillan.

Kamin, L. J. (1974). *The Science and Politics of IQ*. New York: Wiley.

Kamin, L. J. (1977). *The Science and Politics of IQ*. Harmondsworth: Penguin.

Kamin, L. J., and Grant-Henry, S. (1987). Reaction time, race, and racism. *Intelligence*, 11, 299–304.

Kardiner, A., and Ovesey, L. (1951). *The Mark of Oppression: Explorations in the Personality of the American Negro*. New York: Norton.

Katz, I. (1991). Gordon Allport's *The Nature of Prejudice*. *Political Psychology*, 12 (1), 125–57.

Katz, J. (1978). *White Awareness: Handbook for Anti-Racism Training*. Norman: University of Oklahoma.

Kimble, G. A. (1984). Psychology's two cultures. *American Psychologist*, 39 (8), 833–9.

Kinder, D. R. (1986). The continuing American dilemma: white resistance to racial change 40 years after Myrdal. *Journal of Social Issues*, 42 (2), 151–71.

Kinder, D. R., and Sears, D. O. (1981). Prejudice and politics: symbolic racism versus racial threats to the good life. *Journal of Pesonality and Social Psychology*, 40, 414–31.

King, J.E. (1991). Dysconscious racism: ideology, identity, and the mis-education of teachers. *Journal of Negro Education*, 60 (2), 133–46.

Klinberg, O. (1975). Race and psychology: the problem of genetic difference, in L. Kuper (ed.), *Race, Science and Society*. London: Allen and Unwin, pp. 173–207.

Kline, P. (1967), The use of the Cattell 16 P.F. test and Eysenck's E.P.I. with a literate population in Ghana. *British Journal of Social and Clinical Psychology*, 6, 97–107.

Kline, P. (1969). The anal character: a cross-cultural study in Ghana. *British Journal of Social and Clinical Psychology*, 8, 201–10.

Klineberg, O. (1986). SPSSI and race relations, in the 1950s and after. *Journal of Social Issues*, 42 (4), 53–9.

Kloss, R. J. (1979). Psychodynamic speculations on derogatory names for Blacks. *The Journal of Black Psychology*, 5 (2), 85–97.

Knowles, L., and Prewitt, K. (1969). *Institutional Racism in America*. Englewood Cliffs, N.J.: Prentice Hall.

Korchin, S. J. (1980). Clinical psychology and minority problems. *American Psychologist*, 35 (3), 262–9.

Kovel, J. (1970/88). *White Racism: A Psychohistory*. London: Free Association Books.

Krech, D., and Crutchfield, R. S. (1948). *Theory and Problems of Social Psychology*. New York: Mcgraw-Hill.

Kumar, S. (1988). A survey of assessment of ethnic minority pupils. *Educational and Child Psychology*, 5 (2), 51–6.

Kuper, A. (1988). *The Invention of Primitive Society*. London: Routledge.

Lambert, J. (1970). *Crime, Police and Relations*. Oxford: Oxford University Press.

Lambert, J. (1990). *Crime, Police and Relations*. Oxford: Oxford University Press.

Lampley, P. (1980). *The Psychology of Apartheid*. London: Secker and Warburg.

Landau, S., and Nathan, G. (1983). Selecting delinquents for cautioning in the London metropolitan area. *British Journal of Criminology*, 28, 128–49.

Landau, S. F., and Nathan, G. (1983). Discrimination in the criminal justice system. *British Journal of Criminology*, 23, 186–93.

LaPiere, R. T. (1934). Attitudes vs. action. *Social Forces*, 13, 230–7.

Lawrence, D. (1987). Racial violence in Britain: trends and a perspective. *New Community*, 14, 151–60.

Lawrence, E. (1982). In the abundance of water the fool is thirsty: sociology and black 'pathology', in Centre For Cultural Studies (eds), *The Empire Strikes Back*. London: Hutchinson, pp. 95–142.

Lea, M., Wagner, H. L., O'Boyle, D. J., Ward, V. J., Lloyd, P., Gregory, A. H., Davies, C., Christensen, I. P., Lieven, E. V. M., Pollock, J. A., Liggett, T. D., Hutcheson, G. D., Leudar, I., Long, K. M., Valentine, T., Paller, K. A., Pycock, J., Kamara, I. K., Andrade, J. C., Connolly, S. A., Hitch, G., Arnold, P., Lee, S., and Keleman, D. (1990). Rushton and race differences. *The Psychologist: Bulletin of the British Psychological Society*, 3 (7), 316–17.

Leiser, B. (1989). Racism in 'The Psychologist'. *The Psychologist: Bulletin of the British Psychological Society*, 2 (10), 445.

Levi-strauss, C. (1975). Race and history, in L. Kuper (ed.), *Race, Science and Culture*. London: Allen and Unwin, pp. 95–134.

Lewis, G., Croft-Jeffreys, C., and David, A. (1990). Are British psychiatrists racist? *British Journal of Psychiatry*, 157, 410–15.

Lewis, D. K. (1977). A response to inequality: black women, racism and sexism. *Journal of Women in Culture and Society*, 3, 339–61.

Lewis, D. O, Balla, D. A., and Shanok, S. S.(1979). Some evidence of race bias in the diagnosis and treatment of the juvenile offender. *American Journal of Orthopsychiatry*, 49 (1), 53–61.

Lindsay, R. O., and Paton-Saltzberg, R. (1990). Rushton and race differences. *The Psychologist: Bulletin of the British Psychological Society*, 3 (7), 317–18.

Littlewood, R., and Cross, S. (1980). Ethnic minorities and psychiatric services. *Sociology of Health and Illness*, 2, 194–201.

Littlewood, R., and Lipsedge, M. (1989). *Aliens and Alienists: Ethnic Minorities and Psychiatry* (2nd edn). London: Unwin Hyman.

Lobo, E. (1978). *Children of Immigrants to Britain: Their Health and Social Problems*. London: Allen and Unwin.

Loehlin, J. C., Lindzey, G., and Spuhler, J. N. (1975). *Race Differences in Intelligence*. San Francisco: Freeman.

London Association of Community Relations Council (1985). *In a Critical Condition: A Survey of Equal Opportunities in Employment in London's Health Authorities*. London: LACRC.

Lopez, R. E., and Cheek, D. (1977). The prevention of institutional racism: training counseling psychologists as agents for change. *The Counseling Psychologist*, 7 (2), 64–9.

Lorde, A. (1984). *Sister Outsider*. New York: Crossing Press.

Lorenz, K. (1966). *On Aggression*. New York: Harcourt Brace Janovich.

Lorenz, K. (1981). *The Foundations of Ethology*. New York: Springer.

Loring, M., and Powell, B. (1988). Gender, race and DMS-iii: a study of the objectivity of psychiatric diagnostic behaviour. *Journal of Health and Social Behaviour*, 29, 1–22.

Louw, J. (1987). From separation to division: the origins of two psychological associations in South Africa. *Journal of the History of the Behavioral Sciences*, 23, 341–52.

Louw-Potgieter, J. (1989). Covert racism: an application of Essed's analysis in a South African Context. *Journal of Language and Social Psychology*, 8 (5), 307–19.

Lunt, I. (1988). Educational psychologists in multicultural communities: report from the study day held on 16 December 1987. *Educational and Child Psychology*, 5 (2), 75–84.

Lyles, M. R., and Carter, J. H. (1982). Myths and strengths of the black family. A historical and sociological contribution to family therapy. *Journal of the National Medical Association*, 74 (11), 1119–23.

Lynn, M. (1989a). Criticisms of an evolutionary hypothesis about race differences: a rebuttal to Rushton's reply. *Journal of Research in Personality*, 23 (1), 21–34.

Lynn, M. (1989b). Race differences in sexual behavior: a critique of Rushton and Bogaert's evolutionary hypothesis. *Journal of Research in Personality*, 23 (1), 1–6.

MacCann, D., and Woodward, G. (1977). *Cultural Conformity in Books for Children: Further Readings in Racism*. Metuchen, N.J.: Scarecrow Press.

Mackenzie, B. (1984). Explaining race differences in IQ: the logic, the methodology, and the evidence. *American Psychologist*, 39 (11), 1214–33.

MacLeod, M., and Saraga, E. (1988). Challenging the orthodoxy: towards a feminist theory and practice. *Feminist Review*, 28, 16–55.

Mahoney, M. J. (1987). Scientific publications and knowledge politics. *Journal of Social Behavior and Personality*, 2 (1), 165–76.

Mair, G. (1986). Ethnic minorities and the magistrates' courts. *British Journal of Criminology*, 26, 147–55.

Mapstone, E. (1991). Unpublished.

Masson, J. (1989). *Against Therapy: Psychotherapy may be Hazardous to your Mental Health*. London: Collins.

Mattoon, M. A. (1981). *Jungian Psychology in Perspective*. New York: The Free Press.

McAdoo, J. (1981a). Black father and child interactions, in L. E. Gary (ed.), *Black Men*. Beverly Hills: Sage, pp. 115–30.

McAdoo, J. (1981b). Involvement of fathers in the socialization of black children, in H. P. McAdoo (ed.). *Black Families*, Beverly Hills: Sage, pp. 225–37.

McCleod-Bryant, A. (1993). Racism and psychotherapy. *American Journal of Psychiatry*, 150 (7), 1128–9.

McConville, M., and Baldwin, J. (1982). The influence of race on sentencing in England. *Criminal Law Review*, 26, 652–8.

McDougall, W. (1908). *An Introduction to Social Psychology*. London: Methuen.

McDougall, W. (1921). *Is America Ready for Democracy?* New York: Charles Scribner's Sons.

McGovern, D., and Cope, R. (1987). First psychiatric admission rates of first and second generation Afro-Caribbeans. *Social Psychiatry*, 122, 139–49.

McLaren, A. (1989). Secret racism. *The Psychologist: Bulletin of the British Psychological Society*, 2 (2), 72.

McNaught, A. (1982). Race relations in the NHS. *Hospital and Health Service Review*, 78, 86–8.

McNaught, A. (1984). *Race and Employment in the NHS*. London: King's Fund.

McNaught, A. (1985). *Race and Health Care in the United Kingdom: Occasional Paper No. 2*. London: Health Education Council.

Mead, G. H. (1934). *Mind, Self and Society*. Chicago: University of Chicago Press.

Mealey, L. (1990). Differential use of reproductive strategies by human groups? *Psychological Science*, 1 (6), 385–7.

Mercer, K. (1984). Black communities' experience of psychiatric services. *International Journal of Social Psychiatry*, 30 (1–2), 22–7.

Messick, D. M., and Mackie, D. M. (1989). Intergroup relations. *Annual Review of Psychology*, 40, 45–81.

Miles, R. (1989). *Racism*. London: Routledge.

Milgram, S. (1963). Behavioral study of obedience. *Journal of Abnormal and Social Psychology*, 67, 371–8.

Milgram, S. (1964). Group pressure and action against a person. *Journal of Abnormal and Social Psychology*, 69, 137–43.

Milgram, S. (1974). *Obedience to Authority*. London: Tavistock.

Milner, D. (1973). Racial identification and preference in black British children. *European Journal of Social Psychology*, 3, 281–95.

Milner, D. (1975). *Children and Race*. Harmondsworth: Penguin.

Milner, D. (1983). *Children and Race: Ten Years On*. London: Ward Lock Educational.

Milner, D. (1991). *Innocence, Ignorance and Belief*. The Polytechnic of Central London, Inaugural Professorial Lecture, 5 December.

MIND (1993). *MIND's Policy on Black and Minority Ethnic People and Mental Health*. MIND: London.

Mitchell, J. (1974). *Psychoanalysis and Feminism*. London: Allen Lane.

Mixon, D. (1972). Instead of deception. *Journal for the Theory of Social Behaviour*, 2, 145–78.

Montagu, A. (1974). *Man's Most Dangerous Myth: The Fallacy of Race*. New York: Oxford University Press.

Moore, R. (1979). 'Foreword', in M. Billig, *Psychology, Racism and Fascism*, Birmingham: A.F. and R. Publications.

Morawski, J. G. (1986). Psychologists for society and societies for psychologists: SPSSI's place among professional organizations. *Journal of Social Issues*, 42 (1), 111–26.

Morris, P. (1990a), '*The Psychologist May 1990 Issue – J. Philippe Rushton*'. Letter of 27 April from the British Psychological Society's Director of Information.

Morris, P. (1990b), '*The Psychologist May 1990 Issue – J. Philippe Rushton*'. Letter of 1 May from the British Psychological Society's Director of Information.

Moynihan, D. (1965). *The Negro Family in the United States: The Case for Action*. Washington: US Government Printing Press.

Muller-Hill, B. (1988). *Murderous Science: Elimination by Scientific Selection of Jews, Gypsies, and Others, Germany 1933–1945*. Oxford: Oxford University (trans. G. R. Fraser).

Mydral, G. (1944). *An American Dilemma: The Negro Problem and Democracy*. New York: Harper.

Naik, D. (1988). Racism in education. *Educational and Child Psychology*, 5 (2), 62–9.

Nash, M. (1962). Race and the ideology of race. *Current Anthropology*, 3, 285–8.

National Association for the Care and Resettlement of Offenders (1986). *Black People and the Criminal Justice System*. London: NACRO.

National Association of Health Authorities (1988). *Action not Words: A Strategy to Improve Health Services For Black and Minority Ethnic Groups*. Birmingham: NAHA.

Newman, G. (1979). *Understanding Violence*. New York: Lippincot.

Nobles, W. (1978). African root and American fruit: the black family. *Journal of Social and Behavioral Sciences*, 20, 1–18.

Nobles, W. (1980). African philosophy: foundations for black psychology, in R. Jones (ed.) *Black Psychology*. New York: Harper and Row, pp. 23–36.

Nobles, W. W. (1973). Psychological research and the black self-concept: a critical review. *Journal of Social Issues*, 29 (1), 11–27.

Nobles, W. W. (1986). *African Psychology: Toward Its Reclamation*. Oakland, Calif.: Black Family Institute Publications.

Notman, M. T., and Nadelson, C. C. (1978). *The Woman Patient*. New York: Plenum Press.

O'Brien, C. (1990). Family therapy with black families. *Journal of Family Therapy*, 12, 3–16.

O'Neil, W. M. (1968). *The Beginnings of Modern Psychology*. Harmondsworth: Penguin.

Orne, M. T., and Holland, C. C. (1968). On the ecological validity of laboratory deceptions. *British Journal of Psychiatry*, 6, 282–93.

Owusu-Bempah, J. (1985). Racism: a white problem? *Community Librarian*, 3, 21–23.

Owusu-Bempah, J. (1989). The new institutional racism. *Community Care*, 14 September, 23–5.

Owusu-Bempah, J. (1990). Toeing the white line. *Community Care*, 1 November, 16–17.

Owusu-Bempah, J. (1994). Race, self-identity and social work. *British Journal of Social Work*, 24(2), 123–36.

Owusu-Bempah, J., and Howitt, D. (1990). Racism and the British Psychological Society: asking the impossible? Unpublished (banned) manuscript.

Padilla, A. M., Lindholm, K. J., Chen, A., Duran, R., Hakuta, K., Lambert, W., and Tucker, G. R. (1991). The English-only movement. *American Psychologist*, 46 (2), 120–30.

Parekh, B. (ed.) (1974). *Colour, Culture and Consciousness*. London: Allen and Unwin.

Parin, P., and Morgenthaler, F. (1969). Character analysis based on the behaviour patterns of 'primitive' Africans, in W. Micensterberger (ed.), *Man and his Culture: Psychoanalytic Anthropology after 'Totem and Taboo'*. London: Rapp and Whiting, pp. 187–208.

Pearn, M. A. (1976). Race relations legislation and the role of the occupational psychologist. *Bulletin of the British Psychological Society*, 29, 300–2.

Pearson, K., and Moul, M. (1925). The problem of alien immigration into Britain illustrated by an examination of Russian and Polish Jewish children. *Annals of Eugenics*, 1, 5–127.

Pearson, R. (1991). *Race, Intelligence and Bias in Academe*. Washington D.C.: Scott-Townsend.

Pearson, V. (1973). Telegony: a study of this belief and its continued existence. Unpublished MSc. thesis, University of Bristol.

Pettigrew, T. F. (1964). *A Profile of the Negro American*. Princeton, New Jersey: Van Nostrand.

Pillay, H. M. (1984). The concepts, 'causation', 'racism' and 'mental illness'. *International Journal of Social Psychiatry*, 30 (1–2), 29–39.

Plutchik, R. (1974). *Foundations of Experimental Research*. New York: Harper and Row.

Policy Studies Institute. (1992). *Britain's Ethnic Minorities*. London: Policy Studies Institute.

Ponterotto, J. G., and Casas, J. M. (1991). *Handbook of Racial/Ethnic Minority Counseling Research*. Springfield, Ill.: Charles C. Thomas.

Pope, K. S., and Vetter, V. A. (1992). Ethical dilemmas encountered by members of the American Psychological Association. *American Psychologist*, 47 (3), 397–411.

Prilleltensky, I. (1989). Psychology and the status quo. *American Psychologist*, 44 (5), 795–802.

Proshansky, H., and Newton, P. (1968). The nature and meaning of Negro self-identity, in M. Deutsch, I. Katz and A. R. Jensen (eds), *Social Class, Race, and Psychological Development*. New York: Rinehart and Winston, pp. 178–218.

Pryce, K. (1979). *Endless Pressure*. Harmondsworth: Penguin.

Pushkin, I. (1973). The development of racial awareness and prejudice in young children, in P. Watson (ed.), *Psychology and Race*. Harmondsworth: Penguin, pp. 23–42.

Rack, P. (1982). *Race, Culture and Mental Disorder*. London: Tavistock.

Ralston, S. M. (1988). The effect of applicant race upon personnel selection decisions: a review with recommendations. *Employee Responsibilities and Rights Journal*, 1 (3), 215–26.

Raubenheimer, I. v. W. (1993). Psychology in South Africa. *The Psychologist: Bulletin of the British Psychological Society*, 6 (4), 169–71.

Ray, J. J. (1974). *Conservatism as Heresy: An Australian Reader*. Sydney: Australian and New Zealand Book Company.

Ray, J. J. (1988a). Cognitive style as a predictor of authoritarianism, conservatism and racism: a fantasy in many movements. *Political Psychology*, 9 (2), 303–8.

Ray, J. J. (1988b). Why the F scale predicts racism: a critical review. *Political Psychology*, 9, 671–9.

Reich, W. (1933/trans. 1946). *The Mass Psychology of Fascism*. New York: Orgone Institute Press.

Reid, P. T. (1988). Racism and sexism: comparisons and conflicts, in P. A. Katz, and D. A. Taylor (eds), *Eliminating Racism: Profiles in Controversy*. New York: Plenum Press, pp. 203–21.

Reiner, R. (1985). *The Politics of the Police*. Hemel Hempstead: Harvester Wheatsheaf.

Reiner, R. (1989). Race and criminal justice. *New Community*, 16, 5–21.

Reuning, H., and Wortly, W. (1973). Psychological studies of the Bushmen. *Psychologica Africana*, Monography Supplement No. 7.

Rex, J. (1983). *Race Relations in Sociological Theory*. London: Routledge and Kegan Paul.

Rex, J., and Mason, D. (eds) (1986). *Theories of Race and Ethnic Relations*. Cambridge: Cambridge University Press.

Rex, J., and Tomlinson, S. (1979). *Colonial Immigrants in a British City: A Class Analysis*. London: Routledge and Kegan Paul.

Rich, J. M., and DeVitis, J. L. (1985). *Theories of Moral Development*. Springfield, Ill.: C. C. Thomas.

Richardson, J., and Lambert, J. (1985). *The Sociology of Race*. Ormskirk: Causeway Press.

Richardson, K. R., and Spears, D. (1972). *Race, Culture and Intelligence*. Harmondsworth: Penguin.

Riegel, K. F. (1978). *Psychology Mon Amour*. Boston: Houghton Mifflin.

Rist, R. C. (1974). Race, policy and schooling. *Society*, 2, 161–85.

Ritchie, J. F. (1943). *The African as Suckling and as Adult*. Livingstone: Rhodes Livingstone.

Roberts, J. V., and Gabor, T. M. (1990). Lombrosian wine in a new bottle: research on crime and race. *Canadian Journal of Criminology*, 32 (2), 291–313.

Robbertse, P. M. (1967). Rasserverskille en die sielkunde. *South African Psychologist*, Monograph No. 72.

Robbertse, P. M. (1971). Sielkundige navorsing en Bantoetuisland – ontwikkeling. *South African Psychologist*, 1 (1), 1–9.

Rodney, W. (1972). *How Europe Underdeveloped Africa*. London: Bogle-L'Ouverture.

Rogers, A., and Faulkner, A. (1987). *A Place of Safety*. London: MIND/RAP.

Rogers, R. W., and Prentice-Dunn, S. (1981). Deindividuation and anger-mediated interracial aggression: unmasking regressive racism. *Journal of Personality and Social Psychology*, 41 (1), 63–73.

Rokeach, M. (1960). *The Open and Closed Mind*. New York: Basic Books.

Rokeach, M. (1980). Milton Rokeach, in R. L. Evans (ed.), *The Making of Social Psychology*. New York: Gardner Press, pp. 112–24.

Ross, E. (1908). *Social Psychology: An Outline and Sourcebook*. New York: MacMillan.

Runnymede Trust (1992). *The Runnymede Trust Annual Report from 1991–1992*. London: The Runnymede Trust.

Runnymede Trust (1993). Policing and racial violence. *The Runnymede Bulletin* 267, July/August, 3.

Ruse, M. (1979). *The Darwinian Revolution: Science Red in Tooth and Claw*. Chicago, Ill.: University of Chicago Press.

Rushton, J. P. (1990). Race differences, r/K theory, and a reply to Flynn. *The Psychologist: Bulletin of the British Psychological Society*, 5, 195–8.

Rushton, J. P. (1991). Racial differences: a reply to Zuckerman. *American Psychologist*, 46 (9), 983–4.

Rushton, J. P. (1992). Cranial capacity related to sex, rank, and race in a stratified random sample of 6,325 U.S. military personnel. *Intelligence*, 16, 401–13.

Sabini, J. (1991). *Social Psychology*. New York: Norton.

Sagar, H. A., and Schofield, J. W. (1980). Racial and behavioural cues in black and white children's perceptions of ambiguously aggressive acts. *Journal of Personality and Social Psychology*, 39, 590–8.

Samelson, F. (1974). History, origin myth and ideology: 'discovery' of social psychology. *Journal for the Theory of Social Behavior*, 4, 217–31.

Sampson, E. E. (1981). Cognitive psychology as ideology. *American Psychologist*, 36 (7), 730–43.

Sanders, A. (1985). Class bias in prosecutions. *Howard Journal of Criminal Justice*, 24, 176–99.

Sanford, N. (1986). A personal account of the study of authoritarianism. *Journal of Social Issues*, 42 (1), 209–14.

Sarason, S. B. (1981). *Psychology Misdirected*. New York: The Free Press.

Sawyer, J., and Senn, D. J. (1973). Institutional racism and the American Psychological Association, *Journal of Social Issues*, 29 (1), 67–79.

Scarf, M. (1980). *Unfinished Business: Pressure Points in the Lives of Women*. New York: Ballantine.

Scarman, Lord. (1981). *The Brixton Disorders: Report of an Inquiry*. London: HMSO.

Scarr, S. (1988). Race and gender as psychological variables: social and ethical issues. *American Psychologist*, 39 (7), 725–38.

Schlossberg, N. K. (1977). Hide and seek with bias. *Personnel and Guidance Journal*, 55 (8), 181–4.

Schoenfeld, C. G. (1988). Blacks and violent crime: a psychoanalytically oriented analysis. *The Journal of Psychiatry and Law*, Summer, 269–301.

Schon, D. A. (1971). *Beyond the Stable State: Public and Private Learning in Changing Society*. London: Temple Smith.

Searle, C. (1989). *Your Daily Dose: Racism and the Sun*. London: Campaign for Press and Broadcasting Freedom.

Sears, D. O. (1988). Symbolic racism, in P. A. Katz and D. A. Taylor (eds), *Eliminating Racism: Profiles in Controversy*. New York: Plenum Press, pp. 53–84.

Secord, P. F., and Backman, C. W. (1964). *Social Psychology*. London: Mcgraw-Hill.

Senn, D. J., and Sawyer, J. (1971). Institutional racism: a problem for psychology? *American Psychologist*, 26, 671–4.

Shaikh, A. (1985). Cross-cultural comparison: psychiatric admission of Asian and indigenous patients in Leicester. *International Journal of Social Psychiatry*, 31, 3–11.

Sherif, M. (1953). *Groups in Harmony and Tension*. New York: Harper and Row.

Sherif, M. (1967). *Group Conflict and Cooperation: Their Social Psychology*. London: Routledge and Kegan Paul.

Sidanius, J. (1988). Intolerance of ambiguity, conservatism, and racism – whose fantasy, whose reality? A reply to Ray. *Political Psychology*, 9 (2), 309–16.

Sik, G. (1989). Famous, but unheard of. *The Psychologist: Bulletin of the British Psychological Society*, 2 (5), 224.

Silverman, I. (1987). Race, race differences, and race relations: perspectives from psychology and sociobiology, in C. Crawford, M. Smith and D. Krebs (eds), *Sociobiology and Psychology: Ideas, Issues and Applications*, Hillsdale, N.J.: Lawrence Erlbaum Associates, pp. 205–21.

Simon, R. J. (1974). *Public Opinion in America: 1936–1970*. Chicago: Rand McNally.

Simpson, G. E., and Yinger, J. M. (1958). *Racial and Cultural Minorities*. New York: Harper and Row.

Simpson, G. E., and Yinger, J. M. (1985). *Racial and Cultural Minorities: An Analysis of Prejudice and Discrimination* (5th edn). New York: Plenum.

Skellington, R., and Morris, P. (1992). *Race in Britain Today*. London: Sage.

Smith, D. (1974). *Racial Disadvantage in Employment*. London: Political and Economic Planning.

Smith, D. (1977). *Racial Disadvantage in Britain*. Harmondsworth: Penguin.

Smith, D. (1980). *Overseas Doctors in the NHS*. London: Heinemann/PSI.

Smith, D., and Gray, J. (1983). *Police and People in London*. London: Heinemann/PSI.

Sniderman, P. M., and Tetlock, P. E. (1986a). Reflections on American racism. *Journal of Social Issues*, 42 (2), 173–87.

Sniderman, P. M., and Tetlock, P. E. (1986b). Symbolic racism: problems of motive attribution in political analysis. *Journal of Social Issues*, 42 (2), 129–50.

Southgate, P., and Ekblom, P. (1984). *Contacts Between Police and Public: Findings from the British Crime Survey*. Home Office Research Study 77, London: HMSO.

Spencer, H. (1870). *Principles of Psychology*. London: Williams and Norgate.

Squadrito, K. (1979). Racism and empiricism. *Behaviorism*, 7 (1), 105–15.

Stagner, R. (1986). Reminiscences about the founding of SPSSI. *Journal of Social Issues*, 42 (1), 35–42.

Stein, G. J. (1987). The biological bases of ethnocentrism, racism and nationalism in National Socialism, in V. Reynolds, V. Falger and I. Vine (eds), *The Sociobiology of Ethnocentrism*. London: Croom Helm, pp. 251–67.

Stephenson, W. (1980). Professor Kamin, Sir Cyril Burt, and Hyperbole. *American Psychologist*, 35 (12), 1144–6.

Stern, E. (1987). The race script of the counsellor: concepts from transactional analysis. *International Journal for the Advancement of Counselling*, 19, 35–43.

Stevens, P., and Willis, C. (1979). *Race, Crime and Arrests*. Home Office Research Study 58, London: HMSO.

Sue, D. W. (1991). Foreword, in J. G. Ponterotto and J. M. Casas (eds), *Handbook of Racial/Ethnic Minority Counseling Research*. Springfield, Ill.: Charles C. Thomas, pp. vii–ix.

Sue, S. (1983). Ethnic minority issues in psychology: a reexamination. *American Psychologist*, 38, May, 583–92.

Swartz, L. (1991). The politics of black patients' identity: ward-rounds on the 'black side' of a South African psychiatric hospital. *Culture, Medicine and Psychiatry*, 15, 217–24.

Tajfel, H. (1969). Cognitive aspects of prejudice. *Journal of Social Issues*, 25, 79–97.

Tajfel, H. (1978a). *Differentiation between Social Groups: Studies in the Social Psychology of Intergroup Relations*. London: Academic Press.

Tajfel, H. (1978b). Social psychology of intergroup relations. *Annual Review of Psychology*, 32, 1–30.

Tajfel, H. (1982). Social psychology of intergroup relations. *Annual Review of Psychology*, 33, 1–39.

Tajfel, H., Flament, C., Billig, M., and Brundy, R. (1971). Social categorisation and intergroup behaviour. *European Journal of Social Psychology*, 1, 149–78.

Taylor, D. A., and Katz P. A. (1989). The resurgent and cyclical nature of racism. *Revue Internationale de Psychologie Sociale*, 2 (3), 257–89.

Terman, L. (1916). *The Measurement of Intelligence*. Boston: Houghton.

Terman, L., and Oden, M. H. (1947). *The Gifted Child Grows Up*. Stanford University Press.

Thielman, S. B. (1985). Psychiatry and social values: the American Psychiatric Association and Immigration Restriction, 1880–1930. *Psychiatry*, 48, 299–310.

Thomas, C. W. (1973). The system-maintenance role of the white psychologist. *Journal of Social Issues*, 29 (1), 57–65.

Thomas, M., and Williams, S. (1972). *Overseas Nurses in Britain: A PEP Study for the UK Council for Overseas Student Affairs*. London: Political and Economic Planning.

Thomas, W. (1904). The psychology of race prejudice. *American Journal of Sociology*, 9, 593–611.

Thorndike, E. L. (1940). *Human Nature and the Social Order*. London: MacMillan.

Thurstone, L. L. (1928). Attitudes can be measured. *American Journal of Sociology*, 33, 529–54.

Thurstone, L. L., and Chave, E. J. (1929). *The Measurement of Attitude.* Chicago: University of Chicago Press.

Townsend, P., and Davidson, N. (eds) (1982). *Inequalities in Health: The Black Report.* Harmondsworth: Penguin.

Townsey, R. D. (1981). The incarceration of black men, in L. E. Gary (ed.), *Black Men.* Beverly Hills: Sage, pp. 229–56.

Trimble, J. E. (1988). Stereotypical images, American Indians, and prejudice, in P. A. Katz and D. A. Taylor (eds), *Eliminating Racism: Profiles in Controversy.* New York: Plenum Press, pp. 181–202.

Tumin, M. M. (1958). Readiness and resistance to desegregation: a social portrait of the hard core. *Social Forces,* 36, 256–63.

Turner, C., and Sevinc, M. (1974). Interaction amongst British and immigrant children: a methodological note. *British Journal of Social and Clinical Psychology,* 13, 215–16.

Uba, L. (1982). Meeting the mental health needs of Asian Americans: mainstream or segregated services. *Professional Psychology,* 13 (2), 215–21.

UNESCO. (1950). *Statement on Race.* Paris: UNESCO.

UNESCO. (1951). *Statement on the Nature of Race and Race Differences.* Paris: UNESCO.

UNESCO. (1964). *Proposals on the Biological Aspects of Race.* Moscow and Paris: UNESCO.

UNESCO. (1967). *Statement on Race and Racial Prejudice.* Paris: UNESCO.

Van den Berghe, P. L. (1981). *The Ethnic Phenomenon.* New York: Elsevier.

Van den Berghe, P. L. (1986). Ethnicity and the sociobiology debate, in J. Rex and D. Mason (eds), *Theories of Race and Ethnic Relations.* Cambridge: Cambridge University Press, pp. 246–63.

Van Dijk, T. A. (1987). *Communicating Racism: Ethnic Prejudice in Thought and Talk.* Newbury Park: Sage.

Van Dijk, T. A. (1991). *Racism and the Press.* London: Routledge.

Van Dijk, T. A. (1992). Discourse and the denial of racism. *Discourse and Society,* 3 (1), 87–118.

Vanderwolf, C. H., and Cain, D. P. (1991). The neurobiology of race and Kipling's cat. *Personality and Individual Differences,* 12 (1), 97–8.

Vaughan, G. (1963). The effect of the ethnic grouping of the experimenter upon children's responses to tests of an ethnic nature. *British Journal of Social and Clinical Psychology,* 3, 66–70.

Ward, I. (1988). Introduction, in J. Kovel, *White Racism: A Psychohistory.* London: Free Association Books, pp. vii–lxi.

Ward, S., and Braun, J. (1972). Self-esteem and racial preference in Black children. *American Journal of Orthopsychiatry,* 42, 644–7.

Waters, R. (1990). *Ethnic Minorities and the Criminal Justice System.* Aldershot: Avebury.

Weigel, R. H., and Howes, P. W. (1985). Conceptions of racial prejudice: symbolic racism reconsidered. *Journal of Social Issues,* 41 (3), 117–38.

Weinreich, P. (1979). Cross-ethnic identification and self-rejection in black adolescents, in G. Verma and C. Bagley (eds), *Race, Education and Identity.* London: MacMillan, pp. 157–75.

Weizmann, F., Wiener, N. I., Wiesenthal, D. L., and Ziegler, M. (1990). Differential K theory and racial hierarchies. *Canadian Psychology,* 31 (1), 1–13.

Weizman, F., Wiener, N. I., Wiesenthal, D. L., and Ziegler, M. (1991). Eggs, eggplants and eggheads: a rejoinder to Rushton. *Canadian Psychology*, 32 (1), 45–50.

Wellman, D. (1977). *Portraits of White Racism*. Cambridge: Cambridge University Press.

Wetherell, M., and Potter, J. (1992). *Mapping the Language of Racism*. London: Harvester Wheatsheaf.

Whitbourne, S. K., and Hulicka, I. M. (1990). Ageism in undergraduate psychology texts. *American Psychologist*, 454 (10), 1127–36.

Whitehead, M. (1987). *The Health Divide: Inequalities in Health in the 1980s*. London: Health Education Council.

Wicker, A. W. (1969). Attitudes versus actions: the relationship between verbal and overt behavioral responses to attitude objects. *Journal of Social Issues*, 25 (4), 41–78.

Wilkinson, S. (ed.) (1986). *Feminist Social Psychology: Developing Theory and Practice*. Milton Keynes: Open University Press.

Williams, C. (1976). *The Destruction of Black Civilization*. London: Third World Press.

Williams, J., Cocking, J., and Davies, L. (1989). *Words or Deeds? A Review of Equal Opportunity Policies in Higher Education*. London: CRE.

Williams, R. M. (1947). *The Reduction of Intergroup Tensions*. New York: SSRC.

Williams, S. (1988). *Psychology on the Couch*. Hemel Hempstead: Harvester Wheatsheaf.

Wilson, E. O. (1975). *Sociobiology: The New Synthesis*. Cambridge, Mass.: Belknap Press of Harvard University Press.

Wilson, G. D., and Patterson, J. R. (1968). A new measure of conservatism. *British Journal of Social and Clinical Psychology*, 7, 264–9.

Wilson, L., and Rogers, R. W. (1975). The fire this time: Effects of race of target, insult, and potential retaliation on black regression. *Journal of Personality and Social Psychology*, 32, 857–64.

Wilson, L. L., and Stith, S. M. (1991). Culturally sensitive therapy with black clients. *Journal of Multicultural Counseling and Development*, 19, January, 32–43.

Wilson, M. H., and Lyles, M. R. (1984). Interracial pastoral counseling with black clients. *The Journal of Pastoral Care*, 38 (2), 133–41.

Wilson, M. N. (1992). Perceived parental activity of mothers, fathers and grandmothers in three-generational black families, in A. K. H. Burlew, W. C. Banks, H. T. McAdoo and D. A. Azibo (eds), *African American Psychology: Theory, Research and Practice*. London: Sage, pp. 87–104.

Wober, M. (1971). Race and intelligence. *Transition*, 40, (8), 17–26.

Wober, M. (1990). Racism and prejudice. *The Psychologist: Bulletin of the British Psychological Society*, 3 (11), 504.

Wolfendale, S. (1988). Current professional practice for working in a multi-cultural society: findings from a national survey of local authority educational psychologists. *Educational and Child Psychology*, 5 (2), 19–37.

Working Party on the Training of Psychologists to the Standing Committee on Equal Opportunities (1988). Key equal opportunities issues that should be covered in the British Psychological Society criteria for evaluating training courses in applied psychology. *Educational and Child Psychology*, 5 (2), 92–4.

Wrench, J. (1990). New vocationalism, old racism and the careers service. *New Community*, 16 (3), 425–40.

Yeboah, S. K. (1988). *The Ideology of Racism*. London: Hansib.

Young, V. H. (1970). Family and childhood in a Southern Negro Community. *American Anthropologist*, 72, 269–88.

Young-Eisendrath, P. (1987). The absence of black Americans as Jungian Analysts. *Quadrant*, 20 (2), 41–53.

Zimet, S. G. (1976). *Print and Prejudice*. London: Hodder and Stoughton.

Zuckerman, M. (1990). Some dubious premises in research and theory on racial differences. *American Psychologist*, 45 (12), 1297–1303.

Zuckerman, M. (1991). Truth and consequences: responses to Rushton and Kendler. *American Psychologist*, 46 (9), 984–6.

Zuckerman, M., and Brody, N. (1988). Oysters, rabbits and people: a critique of 'Race differences in behavior' by J. P. Rushton. *Personality and Individual Differences*, 9 (6), 1025–33.

Zuniga, M. E. (1988). Assessment issues with Chicanas: practice implications. *Psychotherapy*, 25 (2), 288–93.

Name index

Adorno, T., 56, 90
Alhibai, Y., 123
Allport, G., 88, 89
American Psychological Association, 62, 157
American Psychological Association's Board of
    Ethnic Minority Affairs, 173
Anderson, J. L., 31, 186
Andreasen, N. C., 156
Ankney, C. D., 156
Antaki, C., 155
Apple, M. W., 69
Asante, M., 137
Astley, M., 83
Atkinson, R. L., 72–5
Azibo, D. A., 135, 137

Bache, R., 33
Bagley, C., 67, 74
Baldwin, J. A., 120–3, 138, 166
Ballard, R., 185
Banks, J. A., 120
Banks, W. C., 121
Bannister, R. C., 22
Barbee, A. P., 31
Barker, M., 2, 10, 141
Beckham, A. S., 122
Ben-Tovim, G., 12
Bender, M. P., 150
Berkowitz, L., 101
Bernard, J., 45
Berne, E., 83
Berry, B., 106
Berry, J. W., 126
Biesheuvel, S., 144, 146
Billig, M., 18, 25, 28, 35
Bogardus, E. S., 86–7
Bolton, P., 63
Booker, R., 109, 177
Boring, E. G., 2, 6
Boyd-Franklin, N., 53, 171, 188
BPS, 76, 132, 152
Bramel, D., 69, 85
Brantley, T., 168
Braun, J., 122

Brazziel, W. F., 110
Breakwell, G., 35, 155
Brehm, S. S., 21, 75
British Medical Journal, 159
British Psychological Society, 76, 132,
    152
Brittan, A., 11
Brody, N., 31
Brogden, A., 166
Broome, R., 114
Brown, A., 56
Brown, C., 142, 163
Brown, G. A., 78
Brown, K., 105–6
Bryans, T., 180, 189
Bulhan, H. A., 5, 37, 72, 111–12, 120, 139,
    145, 182
Burman, L. H., 178
Burns, A., 72
Burnstein, P., 29
Burt, C., 24, 27–8

Cain, D. P., 31
Cain, M., 166
Carothers, J. C., 8, 111
Carpenter, L., 74
Carroll, H. C. M., 177
Casas, J. M., 128, 157
Cashmore, E., 45, 79, 104
Chase, A., 4, 5, 7, 22, 24, 25, 26,
    33
Chave, E. J., 87
Cheek, D., 175
Chomsky, N., 115
Clark, K. B., 3, 5, 120–2
Clark, M., 3, 5, 121–2
Coard, B., 28–9
Cochrane, R., 67, 74, 155, 164
Coggan, G., 166
Commission for Racial Equality, 16, 142–3,
    149, 163–4, 166
Condor, S., 56, 104
Connolly, C., 1
Cook, N., 71

211

Subject index

215